*SharePoint 2007*
*Developer's Guide*
*to Business Data Catalog*

# SharePoint 2007

## Developer's Guide to Business Data Catalog

BRETT LONSDALE
NICK SWAN

MANNING

Greenwich
(74° w. long.)

For online information and ordering of this and other Manning books, please visit
www.manning.com. The publisher offers discounts on this book when ordered in quantity.
For more information, please contact

> Special Sales Department
> Manning Publications Co.
> Sound View Court 3B    fax: (609) 877-8256
> Greenwich, CT 06830    email: orders@manning.com

Manning Publications Co.
Sound View Court 3B
Greenwich, CT 06830

Development editor:  Tom Cirtin
Copyeditor:  Benjamin Berg
Proofreaders:  Anna Welles, Deepak Vohra
Typesetter:  Dottie Marsico
Cover designer:  Marija Tudor


ISBN 978-1-933988-81-8
Printed in the United States of America

1 2 3 4 5 6 7 8 9 10 – MAL – 14 13 12 11 10 09

*To my daughter, Rio Enna Lonsdale,*
*and to my wife, Vicki Lonsdale*
*—B.L.*


*To all the people still creating silos of data*
*who need a solution like SharePoint and the BDC!*
*—N.S.*

# *brief contents*

# contents

# *preface*

Both Nick Swan and I have been deeply involved on a day-to-day basis with SharePoint for some time now. I've been teaching SharePoint development for many years, while Nick has been developing solutions in SharePoint on a consultancy basis.

Nick Swan formed the SharePoint User Group in the UK (http://www.suguk.org), which led to the two of us being introduced in early 2006. We shared an interest in the Business Data Catalog feature of MOSS 2007 Enterprise Edition, and we were both impressed by how powerful this feature could be within an organization. BDC Meta Man is a tool that makes life easier for people developing projects using the Business Data Catalog. Off the back of this tool, Nick and I decided to join forces and establish a company, Lightning Tools Ltd, that specializes in SharePoint and, more specifically, in the Business Data Catalog. Since then, we've created a collection of web parts and tools that help make BDC developing easier, and extend the functionality of the BDC.

Because we've been programming, supporting customers, and writing about the BDC every day for the last two years, we decided to author this book together. This book provides you with our in-depth knowledge on the subject, as well as ways around everyday issues that we have encountered or that our customers have faced. We hope you will find it valuable and useful in your daily work.

BRETT LONSDALE

# *acknowledgments*

Both Nick and I have contributed to SharePoint books in the past, but even with the experience of doing that, we completely underestimated the time and the dedication that a book like this requires. We couldn't have completed the book without support from our families, colleagues, and friends.

I'd specifically like to thank Vicki Lonsdale and Rio Lonsdale (wife and daughter) for their patience during the writing of this book. Nick and I would also like to thank Vicki and Sophie Calienda (Nick's fiancée) for their continued support for Lightning Tools. Todd Bleeker of Mindsharp provided us with the opportunity of writing this book for Manning, and I want to thank him for that and also for his advice on some of the content.

There were two areas of this book that couldn't be written without help from other experts. Joseph Fultz from Microsoft provided appendix A, which explains how the Business Data Catalog could be used to connect to an SAP data source. Phill Duffy from Lightning Tools Ltd provided an excellent example of using the Business Data Catalog API with Windows Workflow Foundations (WF) in chapter 9.

Hrayr Diloyan, Rob Foster, Paul Culmsee, Steve Smith, Spence Harbar, Bob Fox, and Andrew Connell also reviewed the book and offered some good hints and tips on how to improve some of the content. Christina Wheeler (CM Portal Solutions) helped out by providing the technical review of the book, and thankfully didn't find too many code changes that were required.

These reviewers took time out of their busy schedules to read the manuscript at different times during development, and we are grateful for their feedback: Kanwal Khipple, Nikander Bruggeman, Margriet Bruggeman, Prajwal Khanal, Darren Neimke, Monty Grusendorf, Peter Lee, Ed Richard, Dave Corun, and Hasan Shahid.

Finally, a big thank you to Marjan Bace, Tom Cirtin, Steven Hong, Karen Tegtmeyer, and Michael Stephens at Manning for believing in the book and helping to get it published.

# *about this book*

This book is designed to provide a detailed developer's guide to the SharePoint 2007 Business Data Catalog. Its primary focus is to explore all five services that the Business Data Catalog provides out of the box, before taking a leap to the next level, where we'll begin to develop solutions using the Business Data Catalog and its object model. Having read this book, you'll be armed with all of the information required to tackle any Business Data Catalog project.

## How this book is organized

This book has 11 chapters and three appendixes. The first three chapters will get you started with the Business Data Catalog, beginning with a gentle introduction, through to understanding the application definition file in depth. We then take a look at security and how that should be configured for us to connect to our line-of-business data.

Chapter 1 provides an introduction to the Business Data Catalog. In this chapter, we discuss the architecture of the Business Data Catalog, and briefly describe the services that are offered by the BDC.

Chapter 2 provides a detailed understanding of the application definition file. We explore the methods, entities, associations, actions, and so on that make up the ADF. We do this keeping in mind that today you wouldn't write an ADF by hand, but still require an understanding so that you can support it.

Chapter 3 enables us to fully understand the implications of using each authentication method within the BDC. We explore each authentication type, as well as how to overcome authentication issues by using Single Sign-On or Kerberos. We then explore the security trimming provided by the BDC.

The next four chapters explore the out-of-the-box functionality of the Business Data Catalog. Each chapter looks at how to use our development skills to customize or extend the functionality of a different service.

Chapter 4 explores the out-of-the-box web parts for displaying line-of-business data. We look to customize the out-of-the-box web parts with Microsoft Office SharePoint Designer providing web part connections, conditional formatting, and aggregate functions.

Chapter 5 gives us insight into the Business Data field type. After exploring the out-of-the-box functionality, we look at customizing the Document Information panel using Microsoft Office InfoPath, before creating our own Business Data field type using Visual Studio.NET to overcome some of the limitations.

Chapter 6 provides an understanding of how to configure Business Data Search, both using the Shared Services Provider and the application definition file. After exploring the configuration, we look to customize the search results using custom search pages, XSL, and the Search API.

Chapter 7 ensures that we understand MOSS user profiles and how the Business Data Catalog can be used to provide line-of-business data to them. We look at the advantages, such as audience targeting using line-of-business data.

The last part of this book is development-focused. Now that we have a handle on the out-of-the-box functionality, we begin to explore how to use the BDC object model and our Visual Studio.NET development skills to create custom solutions.

Chapter 8 gives us insight into the ApplicationRegistry namespace, which provides an object model to manipulate the Business Data Catalog and obtain line-of-business data programmatically. In this chapter, we create a Windows Communication Foundation (WCF) web service that returns line-of-business data for use in remote applications. We then use the BDC object model with Windows Workflow Foundation (WF) to create a Visual Studio workflow that can update or be triggered by changes in the line-of-business system.

Chapter 9 provides a detailed walkthrough of creating a custom web part that displays line-of-business data from the BDC object model. The result is a Business Data List-style web part that refreshes data automatically using a JavaScript callback method.

Chapter 10 explores how to get the most out of your Microsoft Office applications by using Office Business Applications (OBA) that utilize the Business Data Catalog. We explore using LOB data in Word, Excel, and Outlook applications.

Chapter 11 provides two methods of writing back to the line-of-business system. The BDC is marketed as a read-only view of data. We can provide two techniques that give us the ability to update or insert data as well.

The appendixes provide specific information on data sources other than Microsoft SQL:

- Appendix A provides information about how to connect to SAP.

- Appendix B provides information about how to connect to Oracle.

- Appendix C provides information about how to connect to data sources via web services.

## Who should read this book

*SharePoint 2007 Developer's Guide to Business Data Catalog* is for Microsoft SharePoint 2007 information workers and developers who need to learn how to use, customize, and create solutions using the Business Data Catalog. Information workers will appreciate the introduction to the Business Data Catalog, as well as the coverage of how to create the application definition file using tools and how to use or customize the out-of-the-box services such as web parts and the Business Data field type. .NET Developers will appreciate the same, but can extend the Business Data Catalog solutions by using the BDC object model, authoring WCF web services, and creating Office-based applications with Visual Studio Tools for Microsoft Office (VSTO).

## How to use this book

If you're new to the Business Data Catalog, you should first read chapters 1 and 2. Chapter 1 provides background information and a brief description of what the Business Data Catalog consists of. Chapter 2 provides in-depth coverage of the application definition file. Even if your ADF is already created, chapter 2 will ensure that you've grasped many terms that will be used throughout the book.

It's common for people using the Business Data Catalog to hit a brick wall fairly early on with security issues. Chapter 3 provides insight into likely problems and how to overcome them. We explore some best practices when it comes to authentication and authorization, so reading chapter 3 should be useful for any stakeholder in the Business Data Catalog project.

Chapters 4-7 describe each service provided by the Business Data Catalog. Not all of these services will be used by your company. For example, maybe you've decided not to use the MOSS user profiles or My Sites. Therefore, each of these chapters has been written so that they can be read and understood without any prerequisites.

Chapters 8–11 should be read by Visual Studio.NET developers who already have a good grasp of SharePoint and the BDC, and wish to extend the functionality or create solutions using the BDC to manipulate or present line-of-business data in a custom format.

Finally, the appendixes are useful to anybody requiring information about a specific data source. Everything in this book is applicable to each data source, but most of the examples are provided for Microsoft SQL only. Therefore, any differences that you need to be aware of can be found in the appendixes.

### *Source code conventions and downloads*

This book contains source code examples written in XML, XSL, and C#.NET. All source code in listings or in text is in a `fixed-width font like this` to separate it from ordinary text. Code annotations accompany many of the listings, highlighting important concepts.

The source code can be downloaded from http://www.manning.com/lonsdale or http://www.manning.com/SharePoint2007DevelopersGuidetoBusinessDataCatalog.

The source code should be used in conjunction with the instructions provided, so that any references to DLLs or used namespaces aren't missed within your Visual Studio Projects.

# online resources

Manning's Author Online forum provides a location where questions related to this book or the Business Data Catalog can be posted for the authors: http://www.manning.com/SharePoint2007DevelopersGuidetoBusinessDataCatalog

BDC Meta Man, which has been referenced in this book as a useful tool to create your application definition file, can be downloaded from http://www.lightningtools.com.

The SharePoint Server 2007 Software Development Kit, which contains some code samples used within this book along with a tool to help create your application definition file, can be downloaded from http://www.microsoft.com/downloads/details.aspx?FamilyId=6D94E307-67D9-41AC-B2D6-0074D6286FA9&displaylang=en.

The Northwind database was used as a sample database in SQL 2005 for this book. Northwind can be downloaded from http://www.microsoft.com/Downloads/details.aspx?FamilyID=06616212-0356-46a0-8da2-eebc53a68034&displaylang=en.

Episode 12 of the SharePoint Pod Show is a podcast recording of Brett Lonsdale, Nick Swan, and Rob Foster introducing the Business Data Catalog, and is a useful accompaniment to this book. You can download episode 12 from http://www.sharepointpodshow.com.

The author's personal blog sites are http://www.brettlonsdale.com and http://www.sharepointnick.com.

# *about the cover illustration*

The illustration on the cover of *SharePoint 2007 Developer's Guide to Business Data Catalog* is taken from a French book of dress customs, *Encyclopédie des Voyages* by J. G. St. Saveur, published in 1796. Travel for pleasure was a relatively new phenomenon at the time and illustrated guides such as this one were popular, introducing both the tourist as well as the armchair traveler to the inhabitants of other far-off regions of the world, as well as to the more familiar regional costumes of France and Europe.

The diversity of the drawings in the Encyclopédie des Voyages speaks vividly of the uniqueness and individuality of the world's countries and peoples just 200 years ago. This was a time when the dress codes of two regions separated by a few dozen miles identified people uniquely as belonging to one or the other, and when members of a social class or a trade or a tribe could be easily distinguished by what they were wearing. This was also a time when people were fascinated by foreign lands and faraway places, even though they could not travel to these exotic destinations themselves.

Dress codes have changed since then and the diversity by region, so rich at the time, has faded away. It is now often hard to tell the inhabitant of one continent from another. Perhaps, trying to view it optimistically, we have traded a world of cultural and visual diversity for a more varied personal life. Or a more varied and interesting intellectual and technical life.

We at Manning celebrate the inventiveness, the initiative, and the fun of the computer business with book covers based on native and tribal costumes from two centuries ago brought back to life by the pictures from this travel guide.

# Introducing the Business Data Catalog

One problem that organizations face today is that they're surrounded by islands of data. By this, we mean that organizations have many different applications, databases, and spreadsheets, perhaps on different servers and within different departments. These applications are often isolated from one another and quite often duplicate data. Having all of these islands of data makes it difficult and time-consuming to see the big picture on how the organization is progressing. And even in a small- to medium-sized company, it means that obtaining the information in a report format is time-consuming, and that information is usually out of date by the time it reaches management. This problem arises with the natural growth of a company, and no matter how much effort you put into planning the systems and communicating with other departments, one application often will just not work for the entire organization.

Each of these systems may also have a different interface that users must learn to interact with, plus separate login and password credentials. All of these things are barriers in front of your users that were supposed to be solved by system x. What we really need is a single portal for displaying and interacting with our business data—even if that data resides in separate fit-for-purpose silos.

Within this chapter, we'll discuss the issues that businesses face and how the Business Data Catalog can help resolve those issues. We'll then broadly explore the services that the Business Data Catalog provides, allowing us to elaborate on each service during the rest of the book. First, let's find out what life was like before the Business Data Catalog.

## 1.1   *Life before the Business Data Catalog*

The existence of islands of data within an organization isn't a new problem. In fact, that problem has been around ever since information has been stored in an electronic format, even before SharePoint was around! But as we're SharePoint-focused, we'll concentrate on how this problem could be tackled in the SharePoint 2003 environment. A tool that's widely used in SharePoint to display data is the Data View Web Part.

### 1.1.1   *Data View Web Part*

If you've used Microsoft FrontPage 2003 with SharePoint 2003, or Microsoft Office SharePoint Designer 2007 with Microsoft SharePoint 2007, you'll probably be familiar with the Data View Web Part (now known as the *Data Form Web Part*). Using a wizard, and being armed with the correct database information and credentials, you could display data within minutes to your users. With a little help from Microsoft SharePoint Designer, you can manipulate the data in the grid; modify the display; use conditional formatting, formulas, and functions; and choose from several predefined styles. You could also connect multiple Data Form Web Parts to display master/detail information, or connect the data to other web parts such as third-party charting web parts.

With the Business Data Catalog, you can achieve the same results as with the Data Form Web Part, with or without the use of Microsoft SharePoint Designer. One of the many advantages of both BDC and the Data Form Web Part is the fact that you can connect web parts together. You can also create your own custom web part to display line-of-business (LOB) data.

### 1.1.2 *Custom web part*

Developers are born to write code! And if you needed a way to display a SQL table of data, your developers would claim to be able to write some C# or VB.NET code in a web part to accomplish this in a matter of minutes. Of course, we all know that any custom development will take a lot longer, and with a business-critical application such as SharePoint and your line-of-business system, it should go through a lifecycle of development, testing, staging, and deployment. Any changes—no matter how small—should also go through the same steps. A quick two-minute web part could turn into weeks and months of work.

Many companies provide third-party web parts for you. If you aren't a developer, or don't have the time to develop your own custom web part, purchasing a third-party tool may be an option.

### 1.1.3 *Third-party components*

There are a number of third-party components that would help you integrate your system with SharePoint similar to how the Business Data Catalog does now. You have to be careful when choosing a third-party integration component that isn't from Microsoft, whether it's open source or costs. Consider the following:

- Will your IT team want to learn a new integration suite that may not be relevant elsewhere?
- Will you get support from the third-party company or Microsoft?
- What is the total cost of ownership?

The three preceding solutions only address the simple display of data in Share-Point. What if you want to tag your documents with metadata values that exist in a database, or search a set of customers from a web service? Microsoft understood the concerns and shortcomings associated with these solutions and those available in SharePoint 2003. For SharePoint 2007, they have built a new component called the Business Data Catalog.

## 1.2 What's the Business Data Catalog?

The Business Data Catalog (BDC) is a component of Microsoft Office SharePoint Server (MOSS) 2007 Enterprise Edition.

**NOTE**    If you're using the standard edition of MOSS or WSS (Windows Share-Point Services) 3.0, you'll need to upgrade to get the BDC functionality we're going to be talking about in this book.

The BDC is a way of defining your data sources so that SharePoint is aware of them. SharePoint can then execute methods and stored procedures to display and use your data within SharePoint. Pretty much all data sources are covered, as the following options are available to you:

- Microsoft SQL Server
- Oracle
- ODBC (Open Database Connectivity)
- Web services

Once you've defined your data source to SharePoint, it's available in a catalog-type fashion so that your information workers can build dashboards and displays from predefined sources. Your line-of-business data can be used in five main ways once it has been defined within the BDC:

- Business Data Web Parts
- Business Data column
- Search
- User profile import
- Custom solutions

We'll touch on each of these now briefly and delve into them in depth in further chapters of the book. The first service we'll look at is the Business Data Web Parts.

## 1.2.1  *Business Data Web Parts*

The Business Data Catalog comes with five web parts out of the box that users can add to web part pages and get data displayed with a few clicks. Also there's our old friend the Data View Web Part, which can choose the BDC as a data source. We'll concentrate on the main five for now. In figure 1.1, you can see the All Web Parts dialog box with the BDC Web Parts highlighted.

### BUSINESS DATA LIST WEB PART

The Business Data List Web Part is much like a data grid. It displays all of the data you've defined to be available within the BDC in a column and row format. Using the Edit View Properties page, you can add or remove columns. The web part can

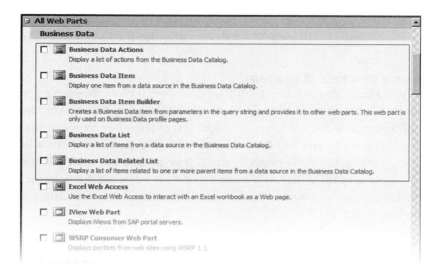

**Figure 1.1  The five available BDC Web Parts**

also provide connections to other web parts and consume connections from other web parts. This is the most commonly used web part out of the five, as it's the main component for building dashboards and driving content for the other five web parts when connected together.

### BUSINESS DATA RELATED LIST WEB PART

Among the data sources you define within the BDC, some will have relationships. For example, a customer can have many orders. By using the Data List Web Part and the Related List Web Part together, you can easily display this related data and enable your users to select a customer to display the relevant orders. All of these relationships need to be defined within the BDC. We'll cover that shortly.

### BUSINESS DATA ACTIONS WEB PART

When you're using your BDC data within SharePoint, you can perform actions on it. This can include such things as taking a product name and conducting an internet search on it, or looking up a customer's address on geo-mapping web services. The Business Data Actions Web Part provides links to these various actions when set up as a dashboard.

### BUSINESS DATA ITEM WEB PART

The Business Data List Web Part is used to return many rows of data from your data source, whereas the Business Data Item Web Part displays only a single item.

This can be done by either explicitly selecting the row of data to display, linking web parts together to build a dashboard, or using the Business Data Item Builder Web Part.

**BUSINESS DATA ITEM BUILDER WEB PART**
The Business Data Item Builder Web Part is a special case, as it isn't actually displayed on the web part page (unless you're in Edit mode). But it's very important, as it enables you to build solutions and link pages together to make up complex dashboards. This web part will grab any query string parameters that have been added to the URL of the current page, and if it links together with BDC data, it will pass the values on to the other web parts listed to determine the data they display.

Figure 1.2 provides a master/detail view of your business data using two of the out-of-the-box web parts.

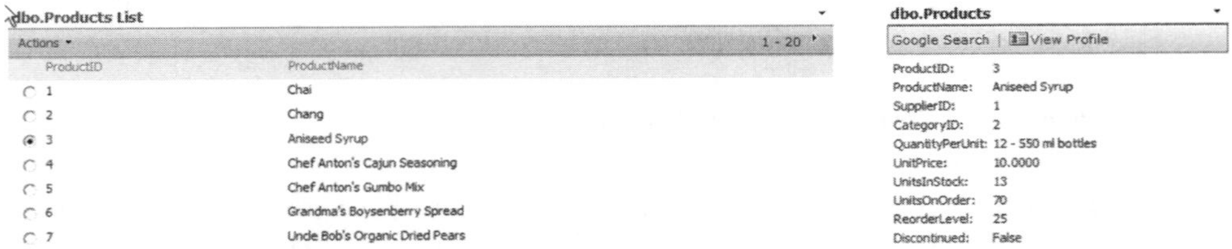

**Figure 1.2**   **The Business Data List Web Part connected to the Business Data Item Web Part**

So we have a number of great web parts with which to display our business data, but that's not all. We're just getting started here! The Business Data column is useful throughout SharePoint lists and libraries when looking up data from your line-of-business system.

### 1.2.2 *Business Data column*

Tagging documents with metadata in SharePoint is central to how the many pieces of the pie (such as search, workflow, records management, and so on) work better. You can tag documents with free text fields and predefined numerical values, and you can even look up a list of values from another SharePoint list. If you were using a database and ASP.NET application to manage customers and orders, you would want to tag them by using a lookup field to live business data, and not have to duplicate that business data in a source such as a SharePoint list. Thankfully, this is where the Business Data column comes to the rescue. Figure 1.3 is a snapshot from Word 2007 that displays the Document Information panel (DIP) with a Business Data column in use.

**Figure 1.3  The Document Information panel in Word 2007**

When using the Business Data column, the field will also be displayed in the Document Information panel in Microsoft Office when you create a document within the library where the Business Data column is used. The Document Information panel can be modified and have logic added to it using Microsoft InfoPath. This is something we'll be doing later on in the book.

Another major benefit of BDC is the search. Although you could previously search documents and list items using SharePoint, Business Data has been added as a content source to crawl, so you can also configure SharePoint to search the underlying data itself, even if it's stored in Oracle, SQL, or SAP.

### 1.2.3  *Business Data Search*

BDC data sources can be indexed, allowing your information workers to search the data via SharePoint. (See figure 1.9.) You can configure the data source to be indexed and set up an index schedule; you can even create your own custom search pages so that only the results from that data source are shown.

We'll learn later in this book how we can create new search scopes that will search a single table, multiple tables, or an entire database. We can then create our own tabs in the Search Center, similar to the People tab. You can see the Search results displaying line-of-business data in figure 1.4.

Another useful service offered by the Business Data Catalog is the user profile import. User profile information is stored in lots of applications nowadays. The BDC can be used to aggregate that information into your SharePoint user profile.

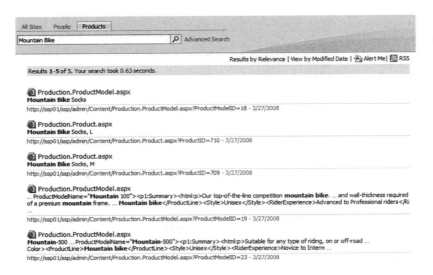

**Figure 1.4   The Search Center displays results from a line-of-business system**

### 1.2.4   *User profile import*

SharePoint integrates nicely with Active Directory to populate SharePoint profiles and websites with information such as email address, phone number, and so on. But many organizations don't use Active Directory to store this information and have deployed a specialist HR application—a great example of an island of data!

Rather than having to copy this information over from the HR application to Active Directory and keep it maintained in two places, you can define the HR application as a BDC data source, and then marry the Active Directory and BDC-HR information together, as shown in figure 1.5.

All of this out-of-the-box functionality with the Business Data Catalog is great if it's exactly what you need—and 99% of the time it will be—but sometimes your requirements mean you have to crack open Visual Studio and start typing some code. For this scenario, we'd like to introduce the Business Data Catalog object model.

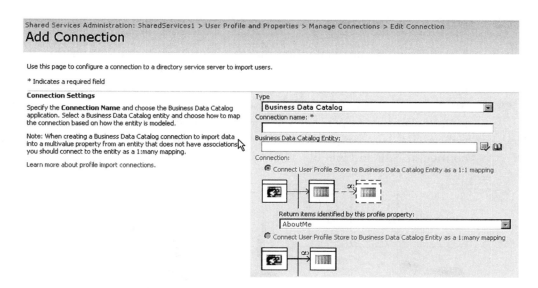

**Figure 1.5   The Add Connection page for the user profile information**

### 1.2.5  *Custom solutions*

If your requirements aren't met by the out-of-the-box uses described previously, you may think that you'll end up using ADO.NET to access your data source, but the Business Data Catalog object model is also an attractive alternative. Imagine the scenario: you have customer data in SQL Server and order data in Oracle. If your developers were to try marrying this data together, they'd need to learn and understand how to connect to and access both SQL Server and Oracle—and figure out all the nuisances and tricks of each. But if you define both data sources as a Business Data Catalog data source, your developers would only need to learn a single method of getting to data—the BDC way! The great thing about this is, no matter what type of data source you're using (SAP, MySQL, Informix, and so forth), you can use exactly the same code and things you've learned, without having to learn the ins and outs of SAP BAPIs (Phew!).

If you want to delve straight into some code, make sure you check out chapter 8, which demonstrates two good examples of a custom application using the Business Data Catalog object model.

Before we tell you how to set up your Business Data Catalog connections, we'll dig into the underlying architecture of how the BDC works and where it sits within SharePoint.

## 1.3 BDC architecture

The Business Data Catalog architecture can be described using the diagram in figure 1.6. Several data sources are listed, but theoretically we should be able to connect to any data source by using either ODBC or a custom web service. ADO.NET or web services can be used as a provider to the data sources. ADO.NET includes most providers such as the SQLOLEDB, Jet, and Oracle providers. Via a web service, you can pretty much expose any data you like, and that's how we can connect to SAP and Siebel.

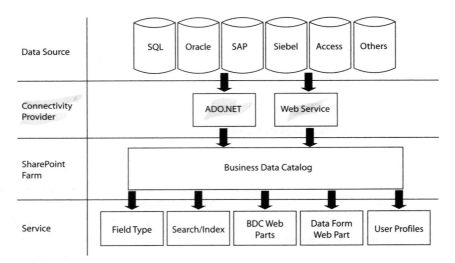

**Figure 1.6   The services that BDC provides and how they relate to one another**

The Business Data Catalog enables you to connect to live line-of-business data. The data is linked to as opposed to fetched and stored within SharePoint, as is sometimes assumed. The application definition file (ADF), described later in this chapter, is written specifically for each database or web service that you wish to connect to. The purpose of the ADF is to describe the database and tables using metadata. This metadata is then stored and used by the BDC Metabase to provide the connection to the database. The BDC Metabase consists of a few tables that are in turn stored in the Shared Services database. You may have more than one Shared Services database, depending on how many Shared Services Providers (SSPs) you have within your farm.

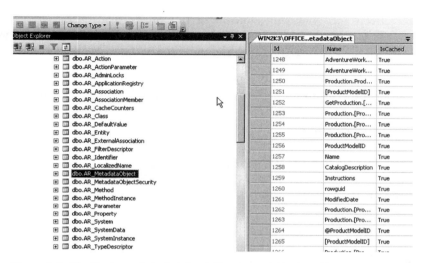

**Figure 1.7   The Business Data Catalog tables from within the SQL Shared Services database**

In figure 1.7, you can see all of the tables in the Shared Services database that store BDC metadata. All of the BDC tables are prefixed with *AR*, which stands for *Application Registry*. Application Registry was the original term for the Business Data Catalog. Selected is the `MetadataObject` table, which displays a series of metadata items for the Adventure Works database and `Production.Product` table.

> **NOTE**    As with all Microsoft SharePoint databases, manipulating the database directly in SQL isn't supported. Instead, make your changes to this database using the application definition file or the object model using .NET code.

The Business Data Catalog is a component of Shared Services. This enables you to define your BDC data source once, and then make use of it across the many web applications associated with the Shared Services Provider. By creating multiple Shared Services Providers, you can also separate out your BDC data sources. The most common scenario is a single SSP per farm.

A schema file called `BDCMetaData.xsd` found in the bin of the 12 hive (c:\program files\common files\microsoft shared\web server extensions\12) can be used to create the application definition file. Alternatively, tools are available that help you to author the file:

- The Microsoft tool, which is part of the MOSS 2007 SDK
- BDC Meta Man—available from www.lightningtools.com

> **NOTE**    Brett and Nick—the authors of this book—are the developers behind BDC Meta Man, and their experiences of writing the tool and working together with customers has gone into this text.

So we now know how we can use our BDC data in SharePoint, how the BDC is structured architecturally, and how it sits as a shared service. The final thing we need to do is see how we define our application definition file that describes our data source to SharePoint.

## 1.4    Data sources and how we connect to them

The Business Data Catalog supports many different data sources. From our experience, the vast majority of BDC users are connecting to Microsoft SQL Server, Oracle, or web services.

### 1.4.1    Oracle and SQL

There are many different Microsoft applications that require or use a SQL database, including Microsoft Dynamics CRM, NAV, and GP. Of course, custom applications are also commonly written in-house that require and store business data in SQL. Oracle is also popular with BDC users who want to connect and use their data in Microsoft SharePoint. Throughout this book, we'll refer to some of the issues that BDC metadata authors face when connecting to either of these data sources.

### 1.4.2    Web services

Many business applications provide you with web services for connecting to data remotely. SAP provides web services for you to consume, and so do the Microsoft Dynamics applications. You may have also written web services that return data yourself for your own custom applications.

When working with web services, the Business Data Catalog is quite picky about how it wants the data to be returned. We cover this in full detail in the web service appendix, and also cover why some third-party web services won't work nicely with the BDC.

### 1.4.3    Other data sources

Other data sources include DB2, Microsoft Access, Fox Pro and most other databases we can think of. Because BDC is capable of connecting over ODBC, that even opens it up to applications such as Lotus Notes.

In the next section, we'll describe the application definition file, and how we connect to a data source in general. Keep in mind that chapter 2 goes into detail on the application definition file and how to connect to various data sources.

### 1.4.4 *Application definition file*

After deciding which data source to connect to and which authentication mechanism to use, the next task is to author an XML file known as the application definition file. This file is covered in depth in the next chapter. The application definition file is typically written by a developer. You can either write the ADF by hand using the provided `BDCMetaData.xsd` schema, or you can use a tool such as the Microsoft Application Definition Editor or the Lightning Tools BDC Meta Man. Both of these tools have free versions that can be downloaded to get you started. The Microsoft Application Definition Editor is available using the Microsoft Office SharePoint Server Software Development Kit (MOSS SDK). BDC Meta Man is available from http://www.lightningtools.com and comes in two editions: BDC Meta Man Developer and BDC Meta Man Professional.

It's important to understand what the application definition file comprises so that you can enhance, change, or maintain the file manually. Through the use of the tools available, you won't need to write the file by hand. The only time you'd write it by hand is if you were a consultant with a very high daily rate!

Within the ADF, you'll provide the following information that will be uploaded to the farm using the Shared Services Provider Administration page:

- *LobSystem*—The LobSystem is the container for all of the other objects in the Metadata object model, and the root node in the application definition file. Usually the name provided to the LobSystem contains the database name, for example, AdventureWorksLobSystem.

- *LobSystemInstance*—The LobSystemInstance contains properties that handle the authentication of the connection and the provider used to connect to the data source.

- *Entity*—Each LobSystemInstance contains one or more entities. An entity represents the data returned, for example, customers or overdue orders. Each row in the entity is known as an *entity instance*. Each entity also contains methods, actions, and identifiers.

- *Identifier*—An identifier is required for each entity so that data can be uniquely identified. Usually the primary key for the data source or some form of unique column is used.

- *Method*—A method is something you can do with the entity, such as return all rows or return a specific row. To return all rows, you'd create a *finder method*; to find a specific row from the entity you'd use a *specific finder method*.

- *Method instance*—A method instance can be executed, whereas a method can't.

- *Parameter/filter*—A parameter can be used to pass a value or values to the back-end database, such as through a stored procedure. A return value can also be sent via the stored procedure and displayed using BDC.

- *Type descriptor*—A type descriptor describes the data type for each column name or value returned in a parameter or entity. For example, CustomerID would be an Integer data type. It's also used to assign a default value.

- *Actions*—An action is something that can be performed with the data. For example, it might be that you want to look up a product name on a product comparison site on the internet, or do a people search on a person entity. It usually involves going to a specific URL and passing through a parameter such as a product name.

- *Association*—An association is the link between two entities. It's similar in concept to a relational database diagram. You associate the connection between two entities—for example, `Customers.CustomerID` to `Orders.CustomerID`. This enables you to use the connected web parts to display the related items in a one-to-many scenario.

Figure 1.8 illustrates the population of the Shared Services BDC Metabase. This occurs during the import of the ADF and can also be populated via the BDC Object Model.

**NOTE**     The next chapter covers the application definition file in depth. My suggestion is to read the chapter to gain background knowledge, but don't feel that at this point you need to understand how to write the XML by hand. You can get away without writing any XML, but an understanding of XML would be valuable for tweaks or alterations that you may want to make that are beyond the tools.

Once the application definition file has been authored, it's uploaded to the Shared Services database via the Shared Services Provider page available from SharePoint Central Administration. The metadata is then stored there until it's updated, either with another ADF, or via the object model. Figure 1.9 displays the Shared Services Provider page that's used to upload the ADF, and also configure security trimming on the business data.

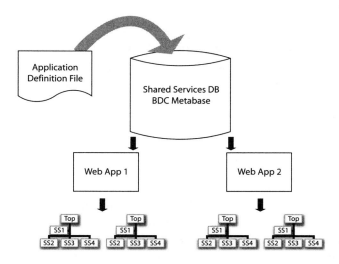

**Figure 1.8   The application definition metadata being loaded into the Shared Services database. The data is then available throughout the farrm.**

Once the application definition file is complete, and has been uploaded without any problems, it's recommended that you test whether you can see the data using the Business Data List Web Part. We'll explore exactly how to configure these web parts in chapter 4.

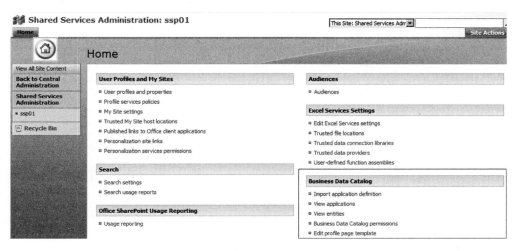

**Figure 1.9   The Shared Services Provider page where the application definition file is uploaded**

## *1.5* *Summary*

This chapter explained the benefits of BDC, and what BDC has to offer. We explored how islands of data can be viewed and searched via one application.

There are many ways of getting data into SharePoint, so those of us considering other options had the benefit of comparing BDC with custom web parts and the Data Form Web Part.

This led us on to the major benefits of BDC. BDC isn't just about displaying data. If it were, we'd certainly use the easier-to-configure Data Form Web Part. BDC provides field types that allow back-end data to be used and stored against documents and list items in SharePoint. This brings our documents and other SharePoint content closer to other business data, even allowing us to link document libraries to BDC Web Parts for filtering purposes.

We explored how search can be configured in SharePoint to index and allow the searching of business data. This means you don't have to know which table to query, or which stored procedure to execute. Many users love MSN Search, Google, or Yahoo! What do they use mainly? One text box! We can search business data in the same way with BDC.

Finally, we explored the architecture, listed the services, and examined a sample application definition file. In the next chapter, you'll explore the application definition file in a lot more depth, studying each and every option.

# *Understanding the application definition file*

Our first chapter was an introduction into the business problems the Business Data Catalog is trying to solve, and how you can use your line-of-business (LOB) data within SharePoint. We briefly mentioned that, before you can use your LOB data within SharePoint, you need to create an XML application definition file that lets SharePoint know how to connect to your LOB system and get the data from it. This chapter will focus on that application definition file in detail. Although there are tools now available for creating the application definition file, it's still important to understand what these files are doing in case you need to edit or troubleshoot an error. Initially we'll discuss how to connect to the line-of-business system using the file.

## 2.1   *Introducing the application definition file*

Initially when going through our application definition file, we'll concentrate on a database system. Do we really need to write all this XML? When the BDC was first marketed by Microsoft, it was touted as being a no-code solution for data integration with SharePoint that administrators could set up. Many people consider writing a long XML application definition file by hand to be writing code, and who can really blame them? We decided that creating a tool to assist with the development of these application definition files would be a good idea and something people would love, and so BDC Meta Man was born! Microsoft recently also brought out its own tool, which is part of the MOSS 2007 SDK. Although these tools alleviate a lot of the manual XML crafting, it's still crucial that you understand the structure of the application definition files to assist you with troubleshooting and manual edits.

> **NOTE**    In appendix C, you'll learn how to go about using web services—creating both BDC-friendly web services and the changes required to the application definition file.

Rather than listing a whole application definition file and expecting you to page through reams of XML, we're going to break it down into smaller manageable chunks. The application definition file is made up of the sections shown in figure 2.1.

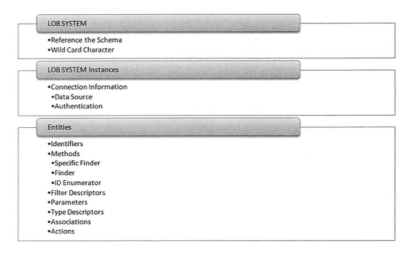

**Figure 2.1   The sections of the application definition file**

Now that we've listed what we're going to configure, we'll begin by configuring the LOB system.

### 2.1.1   *LOBSystem section*

*LOB* stands for line-of-business system, and as we'll see, this acronym is reused in a number of other places in our application definition files. There are a few standard attributes here, such as the XML schema definition, but `Type`, `Version`, and `Name` are very important.

Listing 2.1 is an example of how to configure the LOB system. The `LOBSystem` section allows us to specify the schema and also the wildcard character for the LOB system that we're connecting to.

**Listing 2.1   How to create a LOB system in your application definition file**

```
<?xml version="1.0" encoding="utf-8" standalone="yes" ?>
<LobSystem xmlns:xsi="http://www.w3.org/2001/XMLSchema-instance"      ◁─┐
xsi:schemaLocation="http://schemas.microsoft.com/office/2006/03/        Database
 ⇒ BusinessDataCatalog BDCMetadata.xsd" Type="Database"                   schema
Version="1.0.0.0" Name="Northwind"                                     information
xmlns="http://schemas.microsoft.com/office/2006/03/BusinessDataCatalog">
  <Properties>
    <Property Name="WildcardCharacter" Type="System.String">%
 ⇒  </Property>              ◁─┐ Wildcard character
  </Properties>                 for database
</LobSystem>
```

The LOB system has the following properties:

- *Type*—The LOB system type can be either database or web service.
- *Version*—The version here is important, especially if you're already using the BDC in a live system and want to make changes to it. Functionality such as the BDC Web Parts and the Business Data column will always utilize the latest application definition version, so if you want to make changes to a LOB system that's already being used, simply increase the version number and reimport. If you do this, ensure your latest version has all of the entities you'd originally defined; otherwise you may find that web parts that were already consuming BDC data could stop working.
- *Name*—This name must be unique, but isn't actually displayed within the SharePoint UI.

For our `LobSystem` element, you can also see that we can have properties defined. From experience, the only property ever used here is the `WildcardCharacter`. This describes which character you'd like to use for wildcard searches. We'll dig

deeper into this when we discuss entities and filters. The next section to configure
is the LOBSystemInstances section.

### 2.1.2   *LOBSystemInstances section*

So we have the beginnings of our application definition file; now we need to
describe how SharePoint can connect to this LOB system. Within our LobSystem
XML elements, we have the code example in listing 2.2.

**Listing 2.2   How to create a LOB system instance within your ADF**

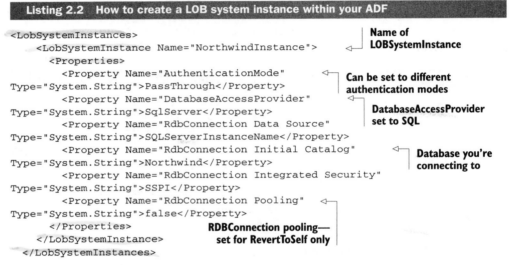

```
<LobSystemInstances>
    <LobSystemInstance Name="NorthwindInstance">          Name of
        <Properties>                                      LOBSystemInstance
            <Property Name="AuthenticationMode"
Type="System.String">PassThrough</Property>              Can be set to different
            <Property Name="DatabaseAccessProvider"       authentication modes
Type="System.String">SqlServer</Property>
            <Property Name="RdbConnection Data Source"    DatabaseAccessProvider
Type="System.String">SQLServerInstanceName</Property>     set to SQL
            <Property Name="RdbConnection Initial Catalog"
Type="System.String">Northwind</Property>                Database you're
            <Property Name="RdbConnection Integrated Security"  connecting to
Type="System.String">SSPI</Property>
            <Property Name="RdbConnection Pooling"
Type="System.String">false</Property>
        </Properties>                     RDBConnection pooling—
    </LobSystemInstance>                  set for RevertToSelf only
</LobSystemInstances>
```

It seems here, with the opening element being LobSystemInstances, that you can
actually define many line-of-business systems within a single ADF. With MOSS 2007,
this isn't the case, and if you try to do that, you'll receive an error when trying to
import the file to SharePoint. So within our LobSystemInstances element, we
can define how we're going to connect to a single line-of-business system. We've
already indicated that this is going to be a database connection; therefore Share-
Point will expect a number of things to appear here. As you can see, our connection is actually made up of a number of properties. SharePoint will use a number
of these properties to build a connection string when it comes to getting data.

**AUTHENTICATION MODE PROPERTY**
Which authentication mode SharePoint is going to use is a biggie! Lots of issues
can arise when trying to configure the BDC if you don't understand how each
authentication mode works and what it means to your setup:

- `PassThrough`—Pass-through authentication attempts to execute queries against your LOB system as the person who's logged in to SharePoint. Typically this will be a user's Active Directory account.

- `RevertToSelf`—RevertToSelf authentication takes no notice of which user is logged in to SharePoint. Instead it uses the Active Directory account that the SharePoint application pool is running under to try to access the LOB system. RevertToSelf has a number of advantages:

  It can use connection pooling if the LOB system implements it, as only one account (the application pool) is ever used to connect to the LOB system. The "double hop" issue never occurs, because only a single hop ever takes place: from the IIS (Internet Information Services) app pool to the LOB system.

  Although you may think that using `RevertToSelf` removes the ability to restrict individual users to access the LOB resource, remember that these permissions can actually also be set per-user for each BDC application via the Shared Services Administration pages.

- `Credentials`—Only ever used for SSO (Single Sign-On).

- `WindowsCredentials`—Same as above.

- *Database credentials*—A word of warning: database credentials isn't actually a value that can be used for the authentication mode, but is more commonly used to describe when your SQL Server is set up to use SQL User Accounts. You may want to connect to SQL Server or Oracle by directly specifying the username and password the BDC should use. To do this, the actual authentication mode should be set to PassThrough, but the BDC will ignore this and then utilize the username and password set in the Rdb Connection properties (details following shortly). Having to set the authentication mode to PassThrough to allow you to supply a database user account is counterintuitive, but trust us, it does work! Utilizing a database user account is another method of bypassing the double hop issue.

### DATABASEACCESSPROVIDER PROPERTY

The `DatabaseAccessProvider` is a property that you'll only use when connecting to a database LOB system. The name supplied here indicates the ADO.NET client that you'll use to connect to the system. SQL Server, OleDB, Oracle, and ODBC are the options available. We've always had issues getting OleDB to work, though. So when integrating with these types of data sources, we've proceeded with an ODBC connection, which is usually also available.

There are a number of `LOBSystemInstance` properties that are prefixed with `RdbConnection`. These properties are pieced together by the BDC to build the connection string of how to connect. The various properties are:

- `RdbConnection Data Source`—This is the data source that you want to connect to. If you're using SQL Server, this would be the server name and instance—for example, `databaseserver\sqlinstance1`.

- `RdbConnection Initial Catalog`—If you're connecting to SQL Server, this will be the actual database that you want to pull data from.

- `RdbConnection Integrated Security`—If you're using pass-through authentication, setting this property to SSPI indicates that you'll pass through the credentials using the Security Support Provider interface.

- `RdbConnection Pooling`—Set this to true if you wish to use connection pooling.

The previous parameters are the minimum required to enable a connection to SQL Server using pass-through authentication. There are two additional parameters you may also want to use.

- `RdbConnection User Id`—If you want to connect using a database user account, you can specify the username with this property. If you're using these values, SSPI should be set to a value of false. This should be used in conjunction with the next property.

- `RdbConnection Password`—As previously, this is required if you want to connect with a database account.

If you're using the Single-Sign-On service as an authentication vehicle, there are a few other properties that are required to describe how to connect to the SSO application:

- `SsoProviderImplementation`—This is the fully qualified type name of the ISsoProvider implementation that stores credentials used to log in to the database. It's used if authentication mode is set to `Credentials` or `WindowsCredentials`.

- `SsoApplicationId`—This is the ID of the SSO Enterprise Application Definition that stores credentials used to connect to the database.

Phew! That's about it. Those are the general settings you'll use to connect to your line-of-business database system. Now let's move on to how you can actually get at the data via things called *entities*.

### 2.1.3   *Entities*

Now we need to describe the data from your LOB system in SharePoint. We do this via entities. An entity should be thought of as a real-world object—for example, a customer, product, or order. To programmers who are familiar with object-oriented programming, this concept is the same as describing objects as classes.

A LOB system can contain many entities, so we need to be able to define many entities within our application definition file. We also want to be able to give entities useful names, such as Customer or Product. Because the user will be selecting from a list of entities within SharePoint, a meaningful name makes it a lot easier for people to select the right entity.

Listing 2.3 shows an outline of how three entities can be described within our `LOBSystem` element.

> **Listing 2.3   How to create an entity within your application definition file**

```
<Entities>
    <Entity EstimatedInstanceCount="10000" Name="Product">
    </Entity>
    <Entity EstimatedInstanceCount="10000" Name="Customer">
    </Entity>
    <Entity EstimatedInstanceCount="10000" Name="Order">
    </Entity>
</Entities>
```

Giving our entity a nice name will help our users select the correct data in SharePoint. Each entity also has an `EstimatedInstanceCount`. This property can be used by client-based applications to change how it displays or pages through your entity data. You don't actually get any problems with your entities if you supply an estimated count of 0, although it's a required field and therefore must exist and contain some number.

Within each entity, you need to define a number of properties and settings for various bits of BDC functionality to work correctly. First, your entity can have a `Title` property, as we see in listing 2.4.

> **Listing 2.4   Property descriptors in the application definition file**

```
<Properties>
      <Property Name="Title" Type="System.String">Name</Property>
</Properties>
```

This `Title` property is the column that will have the drop-down actions menu set against it. This column must be returned by our finder method and, when set in our application definition file, must also be of type `System.String`. You can change this to a field of any type through editing the BDC Data List Web Part once it is displayed on your SharePoint page. Your entity can have many identifiers, as shown in listing 2.5.

**Listing 2.5    How to create an identifier in your application definition file**

```
<Identifiers>
      <Identifier Name="ProductID" TypeName="System.Int32" />
</Identifiers>
```

As with SQL Server database tables, you should think of an identifier as being the primary key field. The field that's marked as an identifier can be used to uniquely identify each row of data. Note that, in the `Identifiers` element, all we do is define the name of our identifier and its type. The name doesn't relate to a column; we need to explicitly tie an identifier to a column later in our XML.

Now we need each entity to be able to pull some data back. We do this by defining methods within our entity. Which method types we create in our entity will have an impact on how our business data can be used within SharePoint. Table 2.1 breaks this down into a simple table.

| Method type | Where used |
| --- | --- |
| Finder | BDC Data List Web Part<br>Business Data column |
| SpecificFinder | BDC Profile page<br>Business Data column<br>Search |
| IdEnumerator | Search |

**Table 2.1    The application definition file method types**

The `Finder` method is the one to return your general BDC data. In terms of databases, it'll do a `select` within your database and return the information to either the BDC Data List Web Part or the Business Data column entity picker. The finder method can have SQL `where` clauses to allow users to filter what data is bought back.

The `SpecificFinder` method returns just a single row of data. This means you must pass in the necessary parameters to uniquely identify a row of data from your chosen table or stored procedure. If your `SpecificFinder` method is configured incorrectly and returns multiple rows of data for a given parameter, you'll get errors when you try to crawl your line-of-business system with MOSS Search.

The `IdEnumerator` method is only ever used for the crawling process of MOSS Search. When you set a crawl, MOSS will first execute the `IdEnumerator` method. It's a simple method that returns a list of identifier values that MOSS should crawl. The crawler will then call the `SpecificFinder` method for each identifier value returned, passing this identifier in as the necessary parameter to uniquely identify the record. As the `SpecificFinder` is used in this manner, any field that you want your users to be able to search should be returned in the `Specific-Finder` method.

We'll initially study the `Finder` method, as this is generally the most complex of the three. Currently within our entity, we have the code shown in listing 2.6.

**Listing 2.6   Code to create an entity with a number of methods**

```
<Entity EstimatedInstanceCount="10000" Name="Product">
// properties
// identifiers
<Methods>
<Method Name="GetProducts">          Unique Finder
                                      method name

    // Properties
    // FilterDescriptors
    // Parameters
    // MethodInstances

</Method>
</ Methods>
</Entity>
```

First, our method needs a unique name. A meaningful name that explains the functionality is always a good idea. Within our method, we've labeled the different elements that can make up our method: properties, filter descriptors, parameters, and method instances. Listing 2.7 deals with properties.

**Listing 2.7   How to create properties in your application definition file**

```
<Properties>
        <Property Name="RdbCommandText" Type="System.String">
        SELECT ProductID, Name, ProductNumber, ListPrice FROM Product
WHERE (ProductID = @ProductId) AND (Name LIKE @Name) AND
      (ProductNumber LIKE @ProductNumber)
        </Property>
        <Property Name="RdbCommandType"            For databases, can be
   Type="System.Data.CommandType">Text</Property>  Text, StoredProcedure,
</Properties>                                       or TableDirect
```

As we've seen already within our application definition file, properties are used to add values to particular objects within our file. A method for a database needs two properties: `RdbCommandText` and `RdbCommandType`. `RdbCommandType` can have the possible values of `Text`, `StoredProcedure`, or `TableDirect`. `RdbCommandText` will have the value associated with the `RdbCommandType`—for example, a stored procedure name, some SQL `select` statement, or the name of the table. You'll notice that, in our example, our SQL `select` statement has a number of parameters added in the `where` clause. These parameters need to be defined in the `Parameters` section, but if you want your users to have use of these parameters as filters, they also need to be described as filter descriptors.

### 2.1.4   *Filter descriptors*

The BDC Data List Web Part and the entity data picker used with the Business Data column will execute whatever SQL statement or stored procedure is defined in the finder method's `Properties` section. This `select` statement could in theory return thousands of rows, which isn't generally good for users or the back-end data source or infrastructure. Allowing users to filter the data that they can view would be a better, more usable solution. To do this, a method generally needs three things for each column that you want to be able to filter: a `FilterDescriptor`, a `Parameter`, and also the SQL statement or stored procedure to make use of the parameter/filter, as shown in listing 2.8.

**Listing 2.8   How to create a filter descriptor**

```
<FilterDescriptors>
      <FilterDescriptor Type="Comparison" Name="ProductId" />
      <FilterDescriptor Type="Wildcard" Name="Name">
      <FilterDescriptor Type="Wildcard" Name="ProductNumber" />
</FilterDescriptors>
```

You can see from our earlier SQL `select` statement that we have a `FilterDescriptor` defined for each part that makes up our `where` clause. The type of filter has a lot to do with how the user interface looks. If you choose the type to be `Comparison`, you're presented with the filter options in the Business Data Web Parts and the item picker control. In figure 2.2, you can see how the filters are used by the information workers.

**Figure 2.2   The use of the filter descriptor in a Data List Web Part**

If you choose `Wildcard`, you're presented with a screen like the one shown in figure 2.3.

You may think that choosing `Wildcard` for all string filters would make sense, but there seems to be a problem with using a wildcard filter and the general wildcard character. If you have your filter set to `Contains` and you enter the filter value to be %, you'd expect it to return all the data. This isn't the case, and you'll find that no data is visible. If you do want this type of func-

**Figure 2.3   The effect of using a wildcard filter in your application definition file**

tionality, you should choose `Comparison` as the type of filter. With this filter for a string column, you'll find that the wildcard symbol will work as expected, with the small caveat still that % won't return all data.

### 2.1.5   *Parameters*

Parameters are big within application definition files, as they describe the values you're passing in to filter at the back-end data source, as well as the data that the back end is returning to you. We'll therefore break this up further into input parameters and output parameters.

**INPUT PARAMETERS**

For each parameter described in a SQL statement or stored procedure, we also need to define it in our definition file. These parameters may or may not also be filter descriptors—more on the why not later! Let's look at our first parameter, as shown in listing 2.9.

**Listing 2.9   How to create an input parameter for an entity**

```
<Parameter Direction="In" Name="@ProductId">          ◁─┐ Direction and name
    <TypeDescriptor TypeName="System.Int32"                of parameter
                    Name="ProductID"
                    AssociatedFilter="ProductId"
                    IdentifierName="[ProductID]">
        <DefaultValues>
            <DefaultValue MethodInstanceName="dbo.[Product]Finder"
                          Type="System.Int32">1</DefaultValue>
        </DefaultValues>
    </TypeDescriptor>
</Parameter>
```

While this input parameter initially seems complex, once you understand it, it'll seem easy. The first part to mention is the name of the parameter. This maps to the name given to a parameter in either our SQL statement or stored procedure.

The direction is marked as In, meaning this is a value we're going to pass in to our query or stored procedure.

Within our parameter, we have a TypeDescriptor element. A TypeDescriptor is a way of defining the parameter's data type. For input parameters, they're generally only a single level deep, but we'll soon see that, for Out parameters, type descriptors can be multilevel and get quite complex.

Back to looking at our particular type descriptor, we can see here we have a TypeName, which casts the values as a particular .NET framework type. If the parameter you're passing in is being used against a column that's also marked as an Identifier, you must mark it as such by adding the IdentifierName in the type descriptor. This isn't necessarily used in the finder method, but we'll see why it's important in a SpecificFinder method shortly.

If this parameter is something for which a user can dynamically supply a value, this will be achieved by matching the parameter with a filter descriptor. We do this by adding an AssociatedFilter attribute to the parameter's type descriptor with the value matching a filter descriptor.

Within our TypeDescriptor element for our input parameter, we have some DefaultValues elements. Our SQL statement could contain one, two, or three parameters, for example, username, age, city. The user may want to filter only by username, so—to allow the statement to be executed with just this one user-entered filter—default values are described that can be substituted in if they're not supplied by the user. You'll see our DefaultValue element has a MethodInstance attribute. Method instances are defined at the end of a method, which we'll cover shortly. For now just remember that your DefaultValue element will need a MethodInstance element. Our DefaultValue also has to have a type, such as System.Int32. Again, this is a .NET type, the same as the TypeName of our main Parameter element.

Input parameters won't be directly mapped to filter descriptors for SpecificFinder methods. This is because the parameter that's used to return a unique row by the SpecificFinder is only really ever used internally by the BDC, and not in the user interface. In fact, it only really makes sense to create filter descriptors for the Finder method.

So that covers input parameters. Pretty simple, huh? Now we come to output parameters—quite a scary beast!

**OUTPUT PARAMETERS**

The Business Data Catalog utilizes the ADO.NET data access classes to retrieve data and return it to the SharePoint front end. The classes it utilizes are

`DataReader` and `DataRecord`, and these must be defined in the return parameter. Let's take a look at XML, shown in listing 2.10.

**Listing 2.10   An example output parameter for an entity**

```
<Parameter Direction="Return" Name="dbo.Product">
    <TypeDescriptor TypeName="System.Data.IDataReader, System.Data,
➡ Version=2.0.3600.0, Culture=neutral, PublicKeyToken=b77a5c561934e089"
                    IsCollection="true"
                    Name="dbo.ProductDataReader">
        <TypeDescriptors>
            <TypeDescriptor TypeName="System.Data.IDataRecord, System.Data,
➡ Version=2.0.3600.0, Culture=neutral, PublicKeyToken=b77a5c561934e089"
                        Name="dbo.ProductDataRecord">
            <!-- Listing 2.11 goes here -->

            </TypeDescriptor>
        </TypeDescriptors>
    </TypeDescriptor>
</Parameter>
```

Defining the data that's being returned by your query/stored procedure/web method is about the most complex-looking piece of XML in your application definition files. How complex it'll be also depends on the type of BDC method. For example, if you're defining a finder method, it'll be returning many records of data, so you need to define a `DataReader` and `DataRecord` in your XML. But a `SpecificFinder` method will only be returning a single row of data and therefore only needs the `DataRecord` level.

Once you have the `DataRecord` level in your XML, you need to define each individual field that's being returned. At the most basic level, you need to define the name of the field coming back and the data type, as shown in listing 2.11.

**Listing 2.11   How to create a `DataRecord` within your application definition file**

```
<TypeDescriptors>
    <TypeDescriptor TypeName="System.Int32"
                    Name="ProductID"
                    IdentifierName="ProductID" />
    <TypeDescriptor TypeName="System.String" Name="Name" />
    <TypeDescriptor TypeName="System.String" Name="ProductNumber" />
    <TypeDescriptor TypeName="System.Decimal" Name="ListPrice" />
</TypeDescriptors>
```

If the data field that's coming back is one of your identifier's columns, you need to mark it with the correct identifier name. In our example, this is the `ProductId` field.

There are a number of other attributes that can be set for each `TypeDescriptor` field being returned:

- `Name`—This should match the name of your field as it's being returned from the data source.
- `TypeName`—This is the .NET data type as returned by your data source. Depending on your data source, you may need to translate the data source type to the relevant .NET data type.
- `IdentifierName`—As detailed previously, if the column being brought back is an identifier, it should be marked as such. This is so the BDC Web Parts know which columns to pass around in association relationships, and for search functionality.
- `IdentifierEntityName`—This is used within association methods. (See later section.)
- `AssociatedFilter`—If you have a filter associated with a column, it must be named the same as the column or use the `AssociatedFilter` property to associate the method with the column.

Of course, not every database column being returned has a nice name that your users would understand, and in a multilingual deployment, users in different locations will want localized column names. This is achieved by adding the `Localized` element to each type descriptor column being returned, as shown in listing 2.12.

**Listing 2.12   How to create localized names or aliases**

```
<TypeDescriptor TypeName="System.String" Name="Name">
    <LocalizedDisplayNames>
        <LocalizedDisplayName LCID="1033">Product Name</LocalizedDisplayName>
    </LocalizedDisplayNames>
</TypeDescriptor>
```

As you can tell, you can add as many different `LocalizedDisplayName` elements to a type descriptor as you like, modifying the Locale ID (LCID) to the relevant country code. There is one type of `Property` element you can add to a `TypeDescriptor` that's being used to describe a returned column—`ShowInPicker`, as shown in listing 2.13.

**Listing 2.13   How to create a `ShowInPicker` property**

```
<TypeDescriptor TypeName="System.String" Name="ProductNumber">
    <Properties>
        <Property Name="ShowInPicker" Type="System.Boolean">true</Property>
```

```
        </Properties>
    </TypeDescriptor>
```

This is used in the data picker that's part of the Business Data column and is used in lists and libraries. By default, this picker will only show the Identifier columns for an entity, but if you mark a `TypeDescriptor` with the `ShowInPicker` property, it'll appear as shown in figure 2.4. You only need to use the `ShowInPicker` property in your finder method. In other BDC method types, it has no relevance.

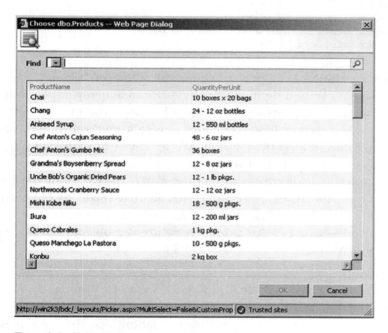

**Figure 2.4** Using the `ShowInPicker` property

Another interesting thing about the data picker is the search area at the top. To be able to search your data, you must create filters for your entity. No filters means no filtering of data, even though the controls to do this are still displayed—a common support question!

**METHOD INSTANCES**

The final thing you need to do with your method is let the BDC know what method type you've just described. This is done by adding the `MethodInstances` element to the end of your method description, as shown in listing 2.14.

**Listing 2.14  How to create a method instance in your application definition file**

```
<MethodInstances>
               <MethodInstance Name="dbo.ProductFinder" Type="Finder"
➥ReturnParameterName="dbo.Product"
➥ReturnTypeDescriptorName="dbo.ProductDataReader"
➥ReturnTypeDescriptorLevel="0" />
</MethodInstances>
```

As you'll see here, the XML fragment begins with a `MethodInstances` element. This indicates that a method defined in your ADF can actually implement more than one BDC method. This statement is true; by clever use of parameters and default values for the parameters, you could enable a method to act as both a finder and a specific finder BDC method. We've found though that an ADF is always much easier to understand if you keep the BDC methods separate.

The most important attribute of our method instance is obviously the `Type`. As discussed previously, the types we're interested in that relate to out-of-the-box BDC functionality are `Finder`, `SpecificFinder`, and `IdEnumerator`. The `ReturnParameterName` and `ReturnTypeDescriptorName` are the objects described previously that will return data to us.

**ASSOCIATION METHODS**

Using the BDC List Web Part and the BDC Related Data List Web Part, you can display a parent/child relationship, which is similar to a one-to-many relationship. A good example of this may be a customer/orders relationship, where you may want to click on a customer and see a list of orders that customer made. In database terms, this occurs when you have a primary key in Customers that links to a foreign key in Orders. Typically both of these columns would be called CustomerId, and you can see how they're joined in a database by the diagram in figure 2.5.

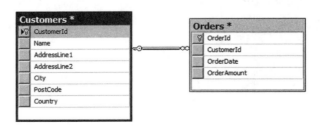

Figure 2.5  A relationship diagram in SQL, and how you should mirror that to create associations in your application definition file

When we have our Customer and Orders defined as BDC entities, we need to know how we're going to pass a primary key value from one entity to the other. This is done by passing identifier values from the parent entity to the child entity; the child entity uses these identifier values to return related records.

The first important decision is where you should place your association method. Should it go in the Customer entity or the Orders entity? The answer is it can go in either, but best practice is to place it in the child entity, this being Orders. It becomes impossible to build multiple cascading associations if you place the association method in the parent entity (for example, you want to relate Customers > Orders > Products).

Let's look at the association method shown in listing 2.15.

**Listing 2.15  How to create associations within your application definition file**

```
<Method Name="Getdbo.OrdersFordbo.Customers">
  <Properties>
    <Property Name="RdbCommandText" Type="System.String">Select
➡dbo.[Orders].[OrderId],dbo.[Orders].[CustomerId],dbo.[Orders].
➡[OrderDate] ,dbo.[Orders].[OrderAmount] FROM dbo.[Customers],
➡dbo.[Orders] Where dbo.[Customers].[CustomerId]=dbo.[Orders].
➡[CustomerId] and dbo.[Customers].[CustomerId]=@CustomerId
➡</Property>
    <Property Name="RdbCommandType" Type="System.String">Text</Property>
  </Properties>
  <Parameters>

    <Parameter Direction="In" Name="@CustomerId">          Specifying input
                                                           parameter as unique ID

      <TypeDescriptor TypeName="System.Int32" Name="[CustomerId]"
➡IdentifierName="[CustomerId]" IdentifierEntityName="dbo.Customers" />
    </Parameter>
    <Parameter Direction="Return" Name="dbo.Orders">
      <TypeDescriptor TypeName="System.Data.IDataReader, System.Data,
➡Version=2.0.3600.0, Culture=neutral, PublicKeyToken=b77a5c561934e089"
➡IsCollection="true" Name="dbo.OrdersDataReader">
        <TypeDescriptors>

          <TypeDescriptor TypeName="System.Data.IDataRecord, System.Data,
➡Version=2.0.3600.0, Culture=neutral, PublicKeyToken=b77a5c561934e089"
➡Name="dbo.OrdersDataRecord">
            <TypeDescriptors>                            Strongly typed
              <TypeDescriptor  TypeName="System.Int32"   type descriptors
                        Name="OrderId"
                        IdentifierName="[OrderId]"
                        IdentifierEntityName="dbo.Orders" />
              <TypeDescriptor  TypeName="System.Int32"
                        Name="CustomerId"
                        IdentifierName="[CustomerId]"
```

```
                            IdentifierEntityName="dbo.Customers" />
            <TypeDescriptor TypeName="System.String" Name="OrderDate" />
            <TypeDescriptor TypeName="System.Decimal" Name="OrderAmount" />
          </TypeDescriptors>
        </TypeDescriptor>
      </TypeDescriptors>
    </TypeDescriptor>
  </Parameter>
  </Parameters>
</Method>
```

In this example, we'd be following the best practice and placing the `association` method in the child entity—our `Order` entity.

As you can see, our `association` method looks like a finder method. It returns a `DataReader` and `DataRecords`. The input parameter is the primary key that the query needs so that it can filter the orders coming back by a particular customer. You'll notice that this has an identifier name, but our `Order` entity won't have an identifier called `Order`. This is where the attribute `IdentifierEntityName` comes in, as the BDC knows it wants to get the `Identifier` value from this particular entity. This also means that the order of the entities in your application definition file is important. The Business Data Catalog imports an application definition file in an interpreter-type manner, line by line. If, during the import, the BDC comes across an entity with an association method that refers to an `IdentifierEntityName` where the entity has yet to be imported, the import process will error. This means your parent entity must appear before what will be the child entity.

Your input parameter needs to be marked with the parent identifier name. In addition, the column name being returned as a type descriptor—which is the foreign key column—needs to be marked to match up with the parent identifier. You can see this in our example in listing 2.16.

The one thing you'll notice is missing from our method is a `MethodInstance` element. This is because association methods don't have them—simple as that. So if you see a method with no `MethodInstance` tags, it's either meant to be an association method, or it's an error!

There's one final thing to get associations working in order to display a parent/child relationship. At the end of our application definition files, outside of all our entity definitions, we need to define how our entities are linked together using `Associations` tags, as shown in listing 2.16.

**Listing 2.16   Setting the parent/child relationship**

```
<Associations>

    <Association AssociationMethodEntityName="dbo.Orders"
➥AssociationMethodName="Getdbo.OrdersFordbo.Customers"
➥AssociationMethodReturnParameterName="dbo.Orders"
➥Name="dbo.CustomersTodbo.Orders" IsCached="true">
      <SourceEntity Name="dbo.Customers" />
      <DestinationEntity Name="dbo.Orders" />
    </Association>
</Associations>
```

This isn't too hard to explain, but we'll break it down into its individual sections:

- `AssociationMethodName`—A unique name for this association. This name will appear in the Related Data Web Part, so it's best to give it a name that users will understand.

- `AssociationMethodEntityName`—The name of the entity that contains the association method the BDC should execute.

- `AssociationMethodReturnParameterName`—The name of the return parameter that describes our data that is coming back for our association method.

Each association also has at least two elements:

- `SourceEntity`—The name of the parent entity. Usually this is a single entry, but occasionally it may be a list of entities if you have a two-parents–to-child relationship (for example, `Customer` and `Location` > `Orders`).

- `DestinationEntity`—The name of the child entity.

Now that we've identified the elements of an association and how to configure associations, it's worth explaining some of the most common problems that are found with associations.

**PROBLEMS WITH ASSOCIATIONS**

Associations are great and work really well—until you get to an entity that has a *composite key*. A composite key is a primary key that's made up of multiple columns. Having an entity based on a database table that has a composite key isn't a problem, as the entity will just contain multiple identifiers, each identifying one of the columns in the composite key. This becomes a problem when this entity is the parent in an association relationship. This is because the Business Data Catalog will try to pass all the identifiers through to the association method, when your association method may only expect one identifier (as usually happens with one-to-many relationships).

If you're working with an entity that needs to have multiple identifiers, you could do the following:

1  Create your original entity with multiple identifiers (composite key). This entity will be used for search.

2  Create a copy of the entity in step one (named differently), but with only a single identifier—basically the one you want to be the filter for your association method.

You could do this with BDC Meta Man by using the original table, then creating a view for the second step that only returns the key column you're interested in.

### 2.1.6  Business Data Catalog actions

Easily displaying your line-of-business data within SharePoint is a fantastic start, but you may want to perform certain actions with your data from the SharePoint user interface. Some examples include:

- Creating or updating data
- Viewing location information on a map
- Emailing a contact

Actions are defined at the entity level after all methods have been defined. Figure 2.6 shows an example of an action.

The attributes are pretty self-explanatory. The URL is the most significant, as this is where your users will be navigated to when they click the action link. You may want the link to be dynamically generated so users are navigated to a particular page's record. This is achieved using query strings and ActionParameter definitions. Here's an example of a Url value:

http://crm/customer.aspx?customeriD={0}

The query string value {0} is dynamically replaced by the BDC field that's defined in your action parameter. If you have a URL that has a number of query string values, their locations within the URL can be defined using {0}, {1}...{n}, with the ActionParameters index number relating to the number within the brackets.

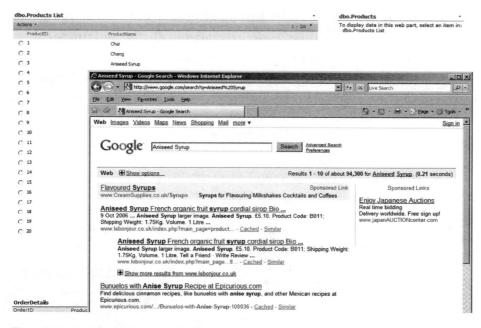

**Figure 2.6  A custom action of a Google search**

## 2.2  *Creating an application definition file*

Now that we've discussed the application definition file, let's walk through the real-world steps for how to create and import your ADF. As we mentioned at the start of this chapter, you probably won't want to write one of these files by hand. So we'll use the Lightning Tools BDC Meta Man tool to configure our ADF. We'll then upload it to the Shared Services Provider so that we can begin to use our business data within SharePoint. In order for these steps to work, you'll need the Northwind database installed in SQL Server. The Northwind database can be found here:

http://www.microsoft.com/downloads/details.aspx?FamilyID=06616212-0356-46A0-8DA2-EEBC53A68034&displaylang=en

For this exercise to work, we're going to use the free version of BDC Meta Man to generate an application definition file.

   **1**  To download BDC Meta Man, open your browser and navigate to www.lightningtools.com.

2   On the home page under Latest Releases, download BDC Meta Man.

3   Once the file has downloaded, extract the Zip file and run `Setup.exe`.

4   BDC Meta Man will begin the install process.

5   Once BDC Meta Man is installed, launch BDC Meta Man. When you run the program, choose the Try It option, which will give you access to the developer version.

6   When BDC Meta Man launches, click the Connect to Data Source button.

7   Choose SQL Server.

8   Type your server name and instance for your SQL Server in the format `ServerName\InstanceName`, or just `ServerName` if you don't have multiple instances.

9   Choose your authentication type. I'm using Windows Authentication because my SQL Server is set to Mixed Mode, as shown in figure 2.7.

10  To connect to the data source and display the available databases, click Connect.

11  You should see a list of databases on the left side of your screen.

12  Expand Northwind to see the list of objects within the Northwind database.

13  To create a `Products` entity, drag the dbo.Products table onto the design surface.

14  To create a `Categories` entity, drag the dbo.Categories table onto the design surface.

**Figure 2.7   The Connect to Data Source dialog box, with authentication set to Windows Authentication**

15  To create an association between the two entities, drag the CategoryID from the Categories table onto the CategoryID field in the Products table to create an association, as shown in figure 2.8.

16  To modify the methods and actions of the entity, right-click the `dbo.Products` entity and choose Edit Entity.

17  Click the Actions tab to configure an action.

18  Click Add Predefined Action to add the Google Search Action.

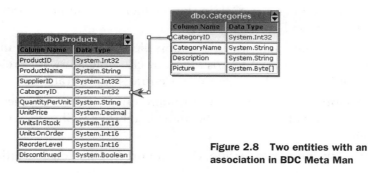

**Figure 2.8   Two entities with an association in BDC Meta Man**

**19**  Select the Google Search Action, then set your column to search as `Pro-ductName`, as shown in figure 2.9.

**20**  Click Save to save your changes.

**21**  In BDC Meta Man, click Configuration, Settings from the Menu Bar to set the Output Filename.

**22**  Set your application definition file name—for example, c:\AppDefs\Prod-ucts.xml.

**23**  Click Save to save the changes.

**24**  Click the green Run icon in the top left corner to generate the XML.

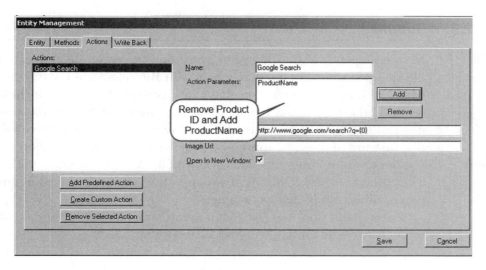

**Figure 2.9   The Entity Management dialog box in BDC Meta Man, demonstrating how to create a Custom Action**

25   Click Yes to open the XML in the browser. You can now review the application definition file.

26   To upload the application definition file, close the browser and navigate to SharePoint Central Administration by choosing Start, All Programs, Microsoft Office Server, SharePoint 3.0 Central Administration.

27   In SharePoint Central Administration, on the left pane, click your Shared Services Provider. It should be immediately below Shared Services Administration.

28   In the Business Data section, click Import Application Definition.

29   Browse to the file that was generated—for example, c:\appdefs\products.xml.

30   Click Import to finish the import.

31   The application definition file should import successfully.

Now that the application definition file is imported, you'll be able to start using the Business Data Catalog. Occasionally, you may receive errors at this point. Common errors include incorrect associations that don't match the relationships in the back-end database, or sometimes permission errors.

In appendix C of this book, we'll explore how to generate an ADF for a web service. This will include creating the web service to connect to the data source.

## 2.3   Summary

In this chapter, we've explored in detail how to create the application definition file that populates the meta database with Business Data Catalog properties. We explored how to configure database connection information, including the LOB system and LOB system instance. We learned how to define entities, including type descriptors, parameters, methods, associations, and actions. Once we created the file, we learned how to import it into the Shared Services Provider.

Once you've configured the ADF, you'll want to configure the security. Who can actually see the data? We'll explore all of the authentication and authorization options within the next chapter.

Throughout this book, we'll explore other examples of how to connect to different sources, including SAP, Siebel, and web services.

*Security*

3

**This chapter covers**

- Defining authentication
- Working around the double hop issue
- Exploring Single Sign-On and the Business Data Catalog
- Configuring LOB application permissions
- Configuring entity permissions

Recently I decided to move to the United States from the United Kingdom. I already had a passport, but in order to live and work in the United States, I needed to apply for a visa. This is a good analogy of how authentication and authorization work in both SharePoint and your back-end data source. My passport simply provides customs and immigration with information about me (my credentials); my visa, which is printed inside my passport, provides me with permissions to live and work within the United States. The same applies to Share-Point and the back-end data source. Every user has a username and password that form his credentials. Any roles that the user has, or permissions applied to that user, allow him to carry out a particular task (for example, being able to read a table or create an item in a SharePoint list). So authentication represents who you are, whereas authorization represents what you can do.

41

SharePoint supports several different authentication mechanisms, which we'll discuss in the authentication section of this chapter.

In addition to SharePoint having to authenticate you and provide you with permissions, if you're going on to access data through the BDC, you'll have to be authenticated and granted permission to the line-of-business system as well. We can't allow just any SharePoint user to view all of the data in a back-end database. Therefore, we also have to specify how we're going to authenticate and authorize each and every SharePoint User, so that when they view or search the back-end database, only the appropriate confidential information is allowed to be viewed.

Every database or data source usually contains its own security model, its own authentication mechanisms, and its own permissions/role model. The Business Data Catalog provides authentication properties that allow you to take advantage of the back-end security model, providing multiple types of authentication and permission inheritance from the data source. But BDC also provides the ability to security trim on the front end as well as the back end. This is sometimes referred to as a pain in the neck, because it almost seems that you're granting permissions twice to the data source—once in the back end and once in the front end. But it does mean that somebody who can access data via the company's LOB system may not need or shouldn't be granted permission to the same data via SharePoint. Therefore each LOB application, and each entity, can have further permissions set for SharePoint users from within SharePoint.

In this chapter, we'll explore the different authentication mechanisms that the Business Data Catalog allows us to use, and we'll explore permissions on the web application and the entity. We'll also explore Single Sign-On, and how Single Sign-On can enable us to overcome the double hop issue in Microsoft Office SharePoint.

## 3.1    *Authentication*

Let's begin by looking at how SQL authentication works. We can set the SQL Server to use SQL Server Authentication (Mixed Mode) or Windows Authentication (Integrated). Windows Authentication is usually preferred and recommended, because we don't have to pass usernames and passwords in connection strings or store them in configuration files, which is considered to be a security risk. Using Windows Authentication, we simply pass a token across to the database server, which in turn authenticates us. The token contains an algorithm that informs SQL to authenticate us.

Microsoft Office SharePoint Server can also be configured to allow various types of authentication. It boils down to using Basic Authentication, Forms Authentication, or Integrated Windows Authentication (IWA). Basic Authentication is used for environments where we need to authenticate with a Microsoft Office SharePoint Server through a firewall, such as on an extranet, but would ideally require SSL (Secure Sockets Layer) so that the username and password aren't sent as clear text. Integrated Windows Authentication works well on an intranet when access to IIS and SQL is available on the internal network, and we've been authenticated by Active Directory. Forms Authentication is useful for internet use; we can control accounts and permissions via an ASP.NET database similar to what we'd do in a typical ASP.NET web application.

If your SQL Server is configured for Windows Authentication, you can select either `PassThrough` or `RevertToSelf` in your application definition file.

If you're using Single-Sign On, a third option exists that allows us to connect BDC data sources using Single Sign-On. This is called Windows Credentials. All three have pros and cons, as well as different uses that will be discussed throughout this chapter. First, we'll explore Integrated Windows Authentication and the implications of using NTLM (NT LAN Manager) or Kerberos.

### 3.1.1  *Integrated Windows Authentication*

SharePoint 2007 supports two methods of Integrated Windows Authentication: NTLM and Kerberos. Integrated Windows Authentication uses the security features of Windows clients and servers. Unlike Basic or Digest Authentication, it doesn't initially prompt users for a username and password. When connecting to IIS from the browser, the credential information from the client is passed to the web server via a cryptographic exchange, and information is sent to the web server as a hash. If the user credentials aren't recognized, the user is challenged to enter a username and password.

Integrated Security is best suited to intranet environments where it's known that Internet Explorer is used as the browser, or other browsers can be configured for IWA. Also, it's not always possible to authenticate over Integrated Authentication through a firewall.

NTLM is probably the most widely used protocol in SharePoint, as NTLM is easy to configure. NTLM is the default protocol when installing SharePoint, so it usually doesn't require you to do anything. With NTLM, the domain name, username, and hashed password are sent across the network to the domain controller, which in turn authenticates the user. There are disadvantages to using NTLM versus Kerberos, one of which specifically has to do with authenticating against a database.

NTLM can only pass your credentials and the hashed password from Internet Explorer to the IIS Server. Usually, the SQL Server that you're trying to access is stored on another computer unless you're running in a small farm environment where SQL is local to the IIS Server. NTLM can't pass your credentials to the SQL Server, because it only allows one hop (IE to IIS) for security reasons. You'll also find that connecting to the Active Directory via an ASPX page isn't possible using NTLM, as that would also require a second hop. Figure 3.1 illustrates this.

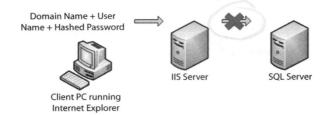

Domain Name + User
Name + Hashed Password

IIS Server      SQL Server

Client PC running
Internet Explorer

**Figure 3.1    The double hop issue when NTLM is used as an authentication protocol**

There are a couple of workarounds for this issue. You can use Kerberos instead of NTLM when using Integrated Windows Authentication, use `RevertToSelf` in your ADF instead of `PassThrough` (this is recommended), or use Single Sign-On, which is described later in this chapter. If you already have SharePoint installed, it isn't a straightforward process to upgrade from NTLM to Kerberos, just so you can access remote databases using Integrated Windows Authentication.

It's sometimes necessary to access the database using the context of the logged-on user. You do this by specifying the authentication in the ADF as `PassThrough`. `PassThrough` attempts to pass the logged-on SharePoint user's credentials to IIS, and then on to SQL. Of course, if NTLM is being used and your database is on a different server than SharePoint, this simply isn't possible. But you can change the `Authentication` setting in the ADF file to connect using `RevertToSelf` instead of `PassThrough`.

Setting the authentication mode to `RevertToSelf` allows you to connect to the database as the Application Pool Identifier. This occurs after you've already passed your user credentials over to the IIS Server, meaning that the Application Pool ID credentials are only passed one hop: from the IIS Server to the SQL Server. The downside to this is that every user who logs on to SharePoint will always connect to the database as one account, and not her own context. If we were using the Data Form Web Part or a custom web part to access this data source, that would concern me, as I'd need to write a security module ensuring that users who weren't supposed to see the data didn't see it. But with BDC, even if we connect as the Application Pool ID, we can still trim the permissions on the entity by setting up explicit BDC permissions. We can say who's allowed to view and execute each entity.

Figure 3.2 displays a screenshot from the Shared Services Provider BDC settings that allow us to set permissions on each entity. The choices are Edit, Execute, Select in Clients, and Set Permissions. Therefore, we may be accessing SharePoint as User A, and the database as the Application Pool ID, and then hide the confidential information from User A from within SharePoint. This can make a lot of sense in most business applications, such as Microsoft Dynamics GP or CRM. Security trimming takes place not only in the back end, but also in the front end. So we shouldn't assume that confidential information won't be displayed to users based on database permissions alone. Figure 3.2 displays the Add Users/Groups page when assigning permissions to entities.

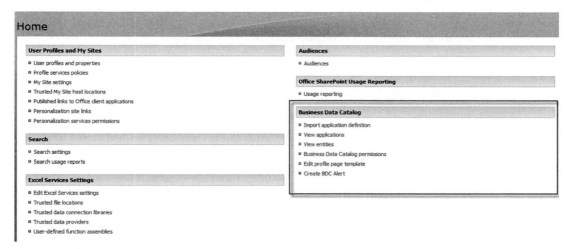

**Figure 3.2   The BDC settings on the SSP Administration page**

Another way to avoid having to switch to Kerberos is to use SSO (Single Sign-On). Although solving the double hop issue isn't the sole intention of SSO, it does help. The purpose of SSO is to map credentials so that User A actually connects to the database as User B. This is useful for back-end systems that use different login names. You can also map a domain group and all of its members to a single account that accesses the database. This is why the double hop issue isn't a problem for SSO. The SSO Service runs on the SharePoint Web Front-End Server. So you authenticate with IIS, and then another set of credentials is used between IIS and the SQL database.

### 3.1.2   *Configuring Single Sign-On*

To configure SSO on your server, you need to follow these steps:

1   Ensure that the Microsoft Single Sign-On Service is running on every WFE (SharePoint Web Front-End). If you intend to use BDC Searching, you'll also need to make sure that the Microsoft Single Sign-On Service is running on the index server as well.

2   Navigate to SharePoint Central Administration where the rest of the configuration of SSO will take place. We'll need to configure the settings for SSO, which includes specifying the Single Sign-On Administrative Account, the Enterprise Application Definition Administrative Account, and the time-out settings for Single Sign-On tickets.

3   Create the encryption key that you'll use to encrypt the credentials stored in the SSO database. Make sure the encryption key is backed up.

4   Create an application definition. This isn't the same as an application definition file for BDC. Application definition in SSO refers to the back-end database that you'll be connecting to.

5   Configure the credential mapping for the Enterprise Application Definition.

#### STEP 1: CONFIGURE THE SINGLE SIGN-ON SERVICE

1   On each SharePoint Web Front-End Server, Index Server, or Excel Services Server, choose Start, Administrative Tools, Services. Right-click Microsoft Single Sign-On Service and choose Properties.

2   Under the General tab, in the Startup Type field, change the startup type to Automatic.

3   Click the Log On tab and change the account to use the following settings:

   - A domain user account (not group)

   - A MOSS farm account

   - A member of the Local Administrators group on the Encryption Key Server

   - Must have DB_Creator & Security Administrators roles on the SQL Server for SharePoint

   - Must be the Single Sign-On Administrative Account or a member of the SSO Admin group

4   Click OK.

Figure 3.3 displays the Single Sign-On Service dialog box where the username and password for the service are set.

**STEP 2: MANAGE THE SETTING FOR SINGLE SIGN-ON**

1 Navigate to SharePoint Central Administration by choosing Start, Administrative Tools, SharePoint 3.0 Central Administration.

2 Click the Operations tab.

3 In the Security Configuration section, click Manage Settings for Single Sign-On.

4 Click Manage Server Settings in the Server Settings section.

5 Set the Single Sign-On Administrative Account, which will be able to create, edit, and delete application definitions for SSO. This account must be an Individual Domain User or a Global Domain Group Account. It must also be the same as the Configuration Account if you've specified a user account. If you specify a global group, then it must be the same group that contains the configuration account. Set this in the format `DomainName\AccountName`.

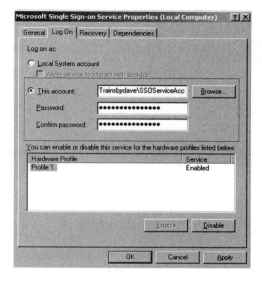

Figure 3.3   The Single Sign-On Service Log On Properties where you need to change the account used

6 Set the Enterprise Application Definition Administrator Account. The user/ group here will be able to configure the credential mapping for each application definition. Configure this in the format `DomainName\AccountName`.

7 Set the SQL Server database name, including the instance name if one exists, for example, MOSS01\OfficeServer or MOSS01.

8 Set the Ticket Time-Out, or leave it alone. (SSO issues a ticket when a request is made by an authorized user. The ticket includes the encrypted username and password of the authenticated user, as well as the time-out. The time-out is set to two minutes by default, which is recommended.)

9 Finally, set the number of days to keep audit records. The default is 10 days.

**STEP 3: MANAGE THE ENCRYPTION KEY**

You can only have one Encryption Key Server, where the encryption key is generated. This server is where you first enabled the Single Sign-On Service in step 1.

The encryption key is used to encrypt the credentials stored in the SSO database for each user. Make sure that you have a backup of the encryption key and re-create it periodically. The recommended period is 90 days.

1   From the Manage Single Sign-On page, click Manage Encryption Key.

2   Click Create Encryption Key.

3   Ensure that the check box is selected to Re-encrypt all credentials using the new encryption key.

4   Optionally back up the encryption key.

**STEP 4: CREATE AN APPLICATION DEFINITION**

Each database you want to set up SSO for is referred to as an *application definition*. The application definition is the mapping of credentials for each user or group that can authenticate with the database. To configure the application definition:

1   On the Manage Single Sign-On page, choose Manage Settings for Enterprise Application Definitions from the Enterprise Application Definition Settings section.

2   Choose New Item to create a new application definition.

3   Type a display name for the application definition—for example, Adventure Works. This will display in places such as the Data Form Web Part.

4   Type the application name (in our example, Adventure Works). This is what you'll use to connect to the data source using your BDC application definition file (ADF), or in the Data Form Web Part properties.

5   Type a contact email address—usually the SSO Administrator.

6   The Account Type field depends on the results that you require. You can select from Group, Individual, or Group Using Restricted Account.

- *Group*—Select Group if you want a domain group to access the database using a particular account. For example, if you want your sales department to access the database as one user, choose this option. You'll then be able to map the credentials for that group, such as DOMAIN-NAME\Sales > DOMAINNAME\SalesUser. The sales user will have the permissions on the database tables that are required by salespeople. For example, the DOMAINNAME\Sales group may have read permissions on the Customers, Orders, and Order Details tables, but no permissions on the Suppliers table.

- *Individual*—Select Individual if you want to map the credentials for a user account to another user account. For example: DOMAINNAME\Brett

> DOMAINNAME\Administrator. When using the Data Form Web Part, if the user doesn't have stored credentials when trying to access the database, she'll be prompted the first time, and then credentials will be stored for her so that she isn't prompted again.

- *Group Using Restricted Account*—Choose this option if you're going to use a group such as DOMAINNAME\Domain Users, so that all users will be able to access the database via SSO. The group name will still access the database with a specific user account. This option uses a different API than the other two options to access the database. It's worth noting that Share-Point Designer and Excel Services don't support this option.

7 Set the authentication type depending on your SQL Server Authentication. If you're using Mixed Mode in SQL, you'll need to have the Authentication Type check box cleared. If you're using Windows Authentication, this option will need to be checked.

8 If you're using Windows Authentication on your Oracle Server, check the setting The Same Applies to Oracle. Note that the account that accesses the database will be authenticated using Windows Authentication, not the user who's logged in to SharePoint.

9 *Logon Account Information*—This provides the ability to set up all the required information to access the data source. For example, if accessing a SQL Server, you may only need to prompt for username and password, so you can proceed with the default settings for Field 1 and Field 2. But you may also want to prompt for additional information, especially if you've created your own web part that requires information to access the data source. For example, if you're using Oracle, you may set Field 1 to Oracle User Name, Field 2 to Oracle Password, and Field 3 to Oracle Database Name. If you're using a group account rather than an individual account, you can set the credentials in the next step. (This has to be performed by an SSO Administrator.)

10 Click OK.

**STEP 5: MANAGE ACCOUNT INFORMATION FOR AN ENTERPRISE APPLICATION DEFINITION**

You perform this next step if you're using one of the two group options. You can also configure individual credential mapping using this option. Alternatively, users can be prompted for credentials when using the Data Form Web Part instead of BDC. Because we're using BDC and more than likely group credentials, we'll go through the steps:

1  From the Manage Single Sign-On page, choose Manage Account Information for an Enterprise Application Definition.

2  Select the Required Enterprise Application Definition from the Enterprise Application Definition field.

3  Enter the group account name for the group you intend to set the credentials for. In this example, we're using TRAINSBYDAVE\Sales.

4  Click the Set button.

5  You'll be taken to a page where you can provide the username and password for the account that will access the data source.

6  Click OK.

**STEP 6: EDIT THE APPLICATION DEFINITION FILE TO INCLUDE SSO**

Finally, you'll need to create your application definition, as outlined in chapter 2 of this book. You can automatically apply the SSO settings using the BDC Meta Man interface. But if you created your application definition file by hand, or used another tool, you'll need to configure the following in your ADF to support SSO:

1  Add the following property to specify which SSO application definition to use:

```
<Property Name="SsoApplicationId"
Type="System.String">AdventureWorks</Property>
```

2  Add the following property to set the SSO provider class:

```
<Property Name="SsoProviderImplementation"Type="System.String">
➥Microsoft.SharePoint.Portal.SingleSignon.SpsSsoProvider,
➥Microsoft.SharePoint.Portal.SingleSignon, Version=12.0.0.0,
Culture=neutral, PublicKeyToken=71e9bce111e9429c</Property>
```

3  Save the changes.

Once you've followed all the preceding steps, you should find that you can surface your business data in the Business Data Web Parts using Integrated Windows Authentication even though your database is more than one hop away. If none of these options is suitable for your organization, you could consider using Kerberos. We'll discuss Kerberos in the next section.

### 3.1.3  *Kerberos*

When SharePoint is using Kerberos as an Integrated Windows Authentication protocol, the double hop issue shouldn't be a problem as long as you've set up your trusts correctly. With Kerberos, we can even go beyond two hops, as long as the trusts are configured correctly.

Kerberos uses a ticketing technique. When a user logs on to the network, he is issued a Kerberos Ticket (TGT). The client uses the ticket to connect to the IIS Server and provides the ticket. The IIS Server can then use the ticket to connect to the SQL Server using the client's credentials.

In order for this to be successful, the service account on the IIS Server will need to be configured for Constrained Delegation to the SQL Server. The web server can then request a ticket to connect to the SQL Server on the client user's behalf.

### CONFIGURING KERBEROS

Within this section, we'll look at how to configure Kerberos for SharePoint 2007. Initially we'll look at your first task, which is to configure some service principal names (SPN) for the SharePoint Service Account in Active Directory (AD). In MOSS, you'll probably find that you have several accounts, each doing a specific role such as:

- Server Farm Account
- SQL Service Account
- SSP Service Account
- MOSS Search Account
- Default Content Access Account
- User Profile Access Account
- Application Pool Account

The SPN is used to make sure that specific accounts can only delegate a specific service on the client's behalf. To set up the SPNs, you need to download a utility from microsoft.com called SetSPN.exe. A sample SPN command would be `Set-spn.exe -A HTTP/%PORTALFQDN% %DOMAIN\AppPoolAccount%`.

Trust would also need to be set up for each of the computer accounts, and for some of the service accounts for delegation. This will allow the accounts to delegate on the client's behalf. To set this up, you'll need to open Active Directory, and for each account user or computer, right-click it, choose Properties, select the Delegation tab, and choose Trust this user/computer for delegation to any service (Kerberos).

If MOSS is being set up from scratch, during the setup you can configure Kerberos. But if you're switching from NTLM to Kerberos, you need to:

1  Open Microsoft SharePoint Central Administration.
2  Click the Application Management tab.
3  Select the web application that you're configuring.
4  Click Default.
5  Set the authentication to Negotiate (Kerberos), as shown in figure 3.4.
6  Open a command prompt and type IISRESET.

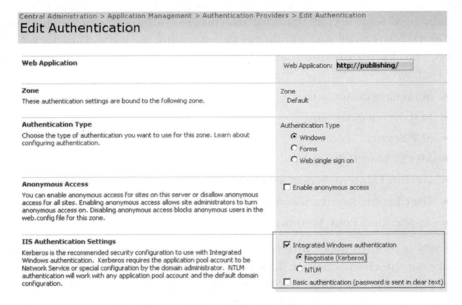

**Figure 3.4   The section of the Authentication Providers screen where Kerberos is selected**

Then you'll need to enable Kerberos on your SSP by running the following STSADM command: STSADM.exe -o SetSharedWebServiceAuthn -negotiate.

The last step is to configure the Component Services:

1  Open the Component Services on your Web Front-End Server by navigating to Component Services, Computers, My Computer.
2  Click Properties, Default Properties, Default Impersonation Level = Delegate, as shown in figure 3.5.
3  Navigate to My Computer, DCOM Config, IIS, WAMREG Admin Service.

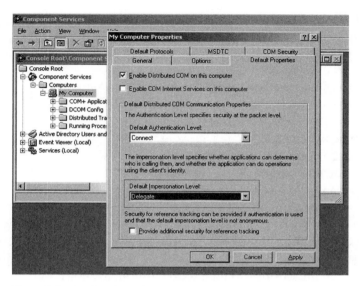

**Figure 3.5   Setting the Default Impersonation Level on your machine**

4  Click Properties for the IIS WAMREG Service.

5  Click the Security tab, and then click Edit Launch and Activate Permissions.

6  Grant Local Activation permissions to the Application Pool ID.

You should find that, once Kerberos has been set up correctly, you can use pass-through authentication in your application definition file, even though your SQL Server is on a different machine than the IIS Server.

We've now covered most scenarios when it comes to authentication. Let's now look at how we can trim security permissions using LOB application-level permissions and entity-level permissions.

## 3.2   *Permissions*

One of the concerns about surfacing any form of data in a client application is security, especially if we're accessing the database with a specific user account that has read access to every table in the database. This is the situation if you use `RevertToSelf`, which is what many BDC users do to get around the double hop issue. This in turn means that every user in SharePoint will have read rights to every table in the database. Fortunately, the BDC has provided a way to trim the permissions on the front end. Assume that we have one LOB system instance that's made up of 10 entities with associations. It might be the case that User A should have permission to read all 10, or maybe he should only be able to read some of them. You can set the permission on the LOB system instance and then push down those permissions to each entity, or you can break the inheritance and set specific permissions on each entity. You can also configure the permissions for the entire Business Data Catalog. This can be configured at three levels, as illustrated in figure 3.6.

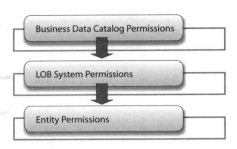

**Figure 3.6   The three levels in which permissions can be applied in MOSS**

You can configure these permissions via the Shared Services Provider Administration page. Navigate to SharePoint Central Administration, and then select your SSP Administration page from the Quick Launch. On the bottom right side of the screen, you'll see the Business Data Catalog option, as shown in figure 3.7.

SharedServices1 > Business Data Catalog Applications > NorthwindLOBSystem > Manage Permissions
**Manage Permissions: NorthwindLOBSystem**

Use this page to control access to NorthwindLOBSystem

Add Users/Groups   |   ✖ Remove Selected Users   |   Modify Permissions of Selected Users   |   Copy all permissions to descendants

| | User/Group Name | Rights |
|---|---|---|
| ☐ | WIN2K3\administrator | Edit, Execute, Selectable in clients, Set Permissions |
| ☐ | WIN2K3\brett | Edit, Execute, Selectable in clients, Set Permissions |

**Figure 3.7   The Manage Permissions page on the LOB system**

By editing the permissions, you can add each user or groups of users, and then select the required level of permission, of which there are four to choose from, as shown in figure 3.8:

- *Edit*—Update and delete objects and create child objects. Users with this right on the Business Data Catalog itself can import application definitions. Applies to all objects.

- *Execute*—Execute a method instance. Users with this right can view instances of an entity that has finder methods. Applies to method instances, which are descendents of entities.

- *Select in Clients*—Select an entity when configuring Business Data Web Parts, columns, or other clients. Applies to entities.

- *Set Permissions*—Applies to all objects.

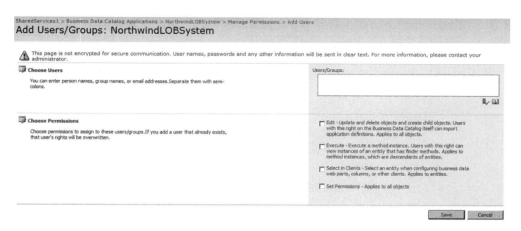

**Figure 3.8  The Add Users/Groups page, where you can set permissions on the LOB system**

Exactly the same permissions can be applied to entities as well. Note in figure 3.9 that you can apply permissions from any level to the descendents. For example, you could set all permissions at the Business Data Catalog level, and then push the permissions down to the LOB systems, and then down to the entities.

**Figure 3.9  The Copy all permissions to descendants option**

Security in the Business Data Catalog is something that can also be configured using the BDC API. Examples will be shown in the Business Data Catalog object model chapter of this book (chapter 8). In the next section, we'll discuss the BDC Web Parts and how you can surface the data on your SharePoint sites. Upon adding a web part on the page, you'll notice the errors that are displayed should you not have permission to execute the returned entity. One of the main advantages of the BDC is that you can add AD groups, authenticated users, and your Share-Point groups when configuring the BDC permissions. All of the permissions can also be set up in the application definition file. You'll notice that, if you export an ADF from SharePoint, your configured permissions are included. This helps when moving your ADF from staging to production.

## 3.3    *Exercise: employing RevertToSelf authentication*

In this exercise, we'll explore the application definition file security settings and modify the XML file to use `RevertToSelf` instead of `PassThrough` authentication.

1   Edit the application definition file that we created in chapter 2 (c:\App-Defs\Products.xml) in Visual Studio or Notepad. (If Visual Studio isn't available, I like to use XML Notepad 2007, which can be downloaded from http://www.microsoft.com/downloads/details.aspx?familyid=72d6aa49-787d-4118-ba5f-4f30fe913628&displaylang=en.)

2   On line 12 of the file, you should see that the authentication mode is set to `PassThrough`.

3   Make sure that you log in to SharePoint as a user who doesn't have permission to the Northwind database. We'll refer to this user as User A.

4   Navigate to a SharePoint site, and add a Business Data List Web Part.

5   Configure the web part to point to the `Products` entity. (You should find that an error is returned, as you don't have permissions to view that table.)

6   Log in to SharePoint as another user (we'll refer to that user as User B), and you should be granted permission to the data in the web part. (This proves that your SharePoint user account is being passed through to the database.)

7   Now change the XML file to use `RevertToSelf`. Use Find and Replace if necessary, as there will only be one instance.

8   Log back on to SharePoint as User A or User B. Neither user should be able to see the data.

9   You can now grant User B permission to the products data by using security trimming. Open SharePoint Central Administration.

10  Click the Shared Services Provider page, which can be found in the Quick Launch area on the left side of your screen.

11  In the Business Data Catalog section, click View Entities.

12  Click the drop-down on the `Products` entity and choose Manage Permissions.

13  Click Add Users/Groups.

14  Add User B and select Execute Permission.

**15** Test the web part by logging on as User A and User B. Only User B should be able to see the data, even though both are accessing the database as the Application Pool ID.

You should now see how `RevertToSelf` allows you to connect to the LOB system as a specific user (the Application Pool Account). This overcomes the double hop issue, as well as allows you to use connection pooling. Even though we're connecting to the LOB system as one specific user, you can see how you can then trim the results using BDC security trimming. The security trimming will be applicable everywhere in SharePoint, including in search results.

## 3.4 Summary

Within this chapter, we explored one of the biggest problems that occurs when accessing your data—the double hop issue. If you follow Microsoft's best practices, you'll be using Trusted Security on your back-end database, you won't have SQL Server and your SharePoint Web Front-End Server on the same machine, and you'll use Integrated Windows Authentication configured for SharePoint. This means you'll suffer from the double hop issue. We looked at ways of overcoming this issue with BDC, which included using `RevertToSelf`, Single Sign-On, or Kerberos.

We also explored how permissions on the Business Data Catalog, LOB systems, and entities can be applied using your Shared Services Provider. This means that we don't have to worry too much about security if we use `RevertToSelf`. We'll be able to trim permissions on the data itself.

Now that the security is in place, we'll look at the Business Data Catalog Web Parts. We'll explore each of the out-of-the-box BDC Web Parts in the next chapter, and then later on in the book (in chapter 9), we'll explore how to create our own custom web parts.

# Out-of-the-box
# BDC Web Parts

Displaying business data in web parts is probably one thing that everyone using the Business Data Catalog will want to do. The out-of-the-box web parts for the Business Data Catalog have been well thought out and are really functional. But most people we've spoken with don't realize how simple it is to customize those existing web parts. There's so much more functionality that we can add to them without writing any code, simply using Microsoft Office SharePoint Designer. If you still can't get the results you're after, you can create your own custom web parts that present the business data in your own way. We'll learn this in chapter 9 of this book.

Microsoft Office SharePoint Server 2007 Enterprise Edition (MOSS) ships with numerous Business Data Web Parts that enable us to display business data in various formats, and provide an interface to the entity actions. In chapter 2 of this book, we learned how to configure entities, associations, actions, and filters. This is where all of that stuff comes into play! The most commonly used web part from the Business Data Catalog Web Parts is the Business Data List, which displays business data in a data grid format. Others include web parts that display data in a columnar format (one row at a time). Also included are web parts specific to Profile pages, which we'll be discussing in this chapter. One of the most versatile web parts is the Data Form Web Part that ships with Microsoft Office SharePoint Designer. We'll use this web part to connect to our business data, as it allows for more customization than the Business Data List Web Part. In this chapter, we'll explore all of the Business Data Catalog Web Parts that come with MOSS Enterprise, and we'll explore the Data Form Web Part in SharePoint Designer. First, let's explore the purpose of the out-of-the-box web parts.

## 4.1 The purpose of the out-of-the-box web parts

In this section, before we look at data form web parts, custom web parts, or third-party web parts, let's explore what web parts we get out of the box with MOSS 2007.

Most of the BDC Web Parts are shown in figure 4.1, highlighted with a rectangle. All of these web parts are flexible, offering the ability to customize them with your own Extensible Stylesheet Language (XSL) code and connect them to other web parts for parent/child or master/detail scenarios. Figure 4.1 displays the available BDC Web Parts in the Add Web Parts dialog box.

> **NOTE** The three web parts that appear at the bottom of the Business Data section don't have anything to do with the Business Data Catalog, but refer to obtaining business data from other portals or Excel spreadsheets.

Let's first explore using the Business Data List Web Part. We'll demonstrate how to configure it to display data, and later in this module, how to further customize it within SharePoint Designer.

### 4.1.1 Business Data List Web Part

The Business Data List Web Part simply displays an entity (refer to chapter 1 for more on entities) in a data grid format, providing everyday data grid functionality such as sorting/grouping and filtering. Via the web part's properties, you can

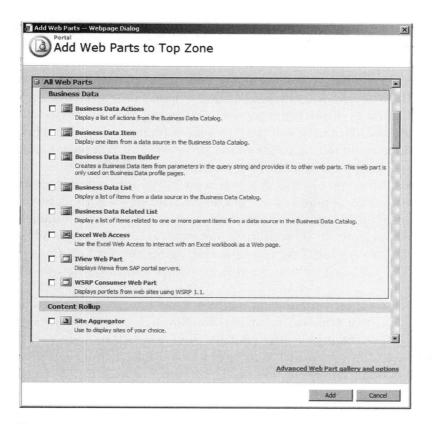

**Figure 4.1    The Business Data section of the Add Web Parts dialog box**

further customize it by using the provided XSL Editor tool, add additional parameters for connections, and optimize the web part by configuring caching.

The first thing to do when you've added the web part to your page is follow the hyperlink to open the Tool pane and modify its properties. The first property to set is referred to as Type. Type is a more user-friendly term for entity. So Type can refer to a table, stored procedure, or view, but basically it has the same meaning as entity.

The Type property has a Check Types button and a Browse button. The Browse button is useful, as you can explore the full catalog of types offered to you by the Business Data Catalog.

In figure 4.2, you can see a business data grid that has been configured to show the data from the `Production.Products` entity from the Adventure Works database.

Once you've configured the web part, depending on the number of columns that you returned in your entity, you're likely to have a wide web part, because the web part defaults to displaying every column and will grow to incorporate them. We can make an adjustment and choose which columns to display by clicking the Edit View link in the top right side of the web part. This link only displays when the web part page is in Edit mode.

In the Edit view, you can specify which items you want to retrieve. Set your item limit, specify which columns you want to display, and set the sorting, filtering, and pagination options. In our example, we're going to reduce the number of columns to two, in order to simply display the `ProductID` and `Name` columns. Note that you can also set the Title column, which gives you an Edit Control Block menu on the specified column to link you to the Profile page, as shown in figure 4.3.

Once you click the hyperlink or the View Profile menu item, you're taken to the Profile page that BDC creates for you. The Row ID is passed as a query string to the Profile page. The Profile page contains the Business Data Item Web Part and the Business Data Item Builder Web Part, which displays all of the columns and values in a column format for that particular row. The View Profile page can be seen in figure 4.4.

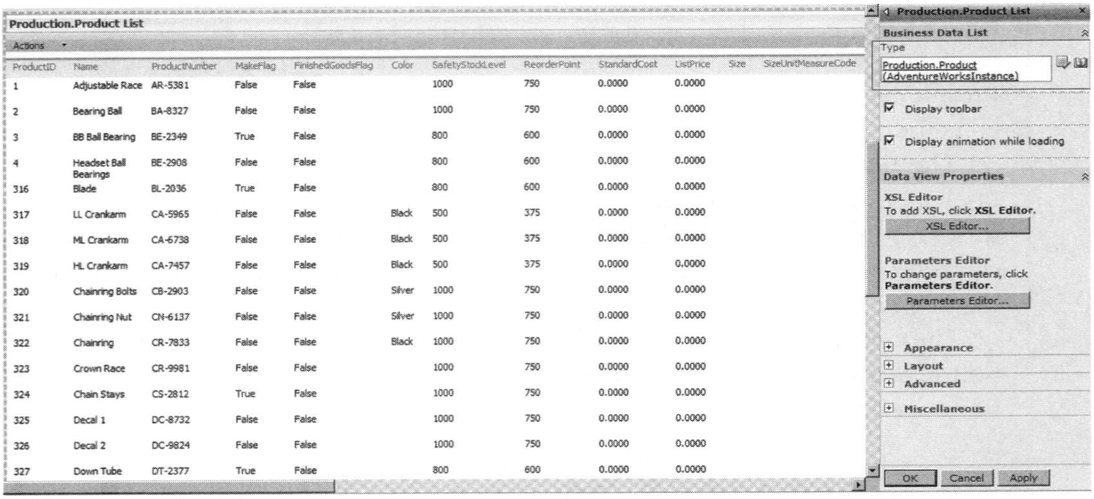

**Figure 4.2    The Business Data List Web Part and the Tool pane with the `Type` property set**

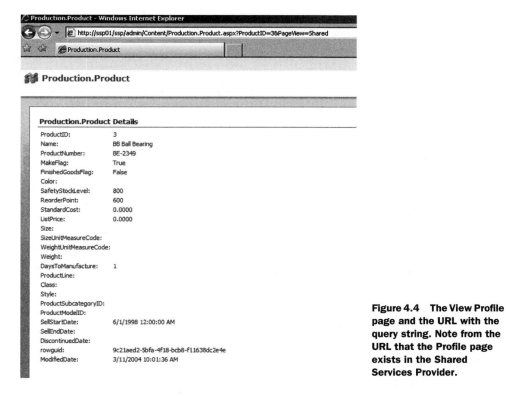

**Production.Product List**

| Actions ▾ | |
|---|---|
| ProductID | Name |
| 1 | Adjustable Race |
| 2 | Bearing Ball |
| 3 | BB Ball Bearing |
| 4 | Headset Ball Bearings |
| 316 | Blade |
| 317 | LL Crankarm ▾ |
| 318 | 🖳 View Profile |
| 319 | HL Crankarm |
| 320 | Chainring Bolts |
| 321 | Chainring Nut |

**Figure 4.3   The Title column with the Edit Control Block menu. The Title column is specified in the Edit View page of the Business Data List.**

**Production.Product Details**

| ProductID: | 3 |
|---|---|
| Name: | BB Ball Bearing |
| ProductNumber: | BE-2349 |
| MakeFlag: | True |
| FinishedGoodsFlag: | False |
| Color: | |
| SafetyStockLevel: | 800 |
| ReorderPoint: | 600 |
| StandardCost: | 0.0000 |
| ListPrice: | 0.0000 |
| Size: | |
| SizeUnitMeasureCode: | |
| WeightUnitMeasureCode: | |
| Weight: | |
| DaysToManufacture: | 1 |
| ProductLine: | |
| Class: | |
| Style: | |
| ProductSubcategoryID: | |
| ProductModelID: | |
| SellStartDate: | 6/1/1998 12:00:00 AM |
| SellEndDate: | |
| DiscontinuedDate: | |
| rowguid: | 9c21aed2-5bfa-4f18-bcb8-f11638dc2e4e |
| ModifiedDate: | 3/11/2004 10:01:36 AM |

**Figure 4.4   The View Profile page and the URL with the query string. Note from the URL that the Profile page exists in the Shared Services Provider.**

If you set up actions in your entity as well, these will also display in the Edit Control block for the Title field. Note that, as part of our BDC entity, we configured MSN and Google Search actions so that we can search the product name in Google, as shown in figure 4.5.

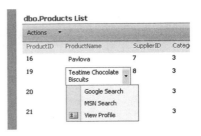

**Figure 4.5   The MSN Search and Google Search actions in the Title Field Edit Control Block menu**

You can also configure connections between the Business Data Web Parts. In the next section, we'll use two web parts to demonstrate web part connections. We'll explore the Business Data Item Web Part and the Business Data Related List Web Part.

### 4.1.2   *Business Data Item Web Part*

We've already seen the Business Data Item Web Part in action on the Profile page. But rather than being driven away from the web part page that contained your Business Data List Web Part, you may want to remain on the same page, but still view all of the columns for the selected row. This scenario would allow you to click a product name from the Business Data List Web Part, and then see detailed product information in the Business Data Item Web Part.

To configure the Business Data Item Web Part, follow these instructions:

1   Click Site Actions, Edit Page on a web part page.

2   In the Web Part zone on the right side of the page, click Add a Web Part.

3   From the Business Data section, check the Business Data Item Web Part.

4   Click the Open the Tool Pane link from within the Business Data Item Web Part.

5   In the `Type` property, click the Address Book icon, and then select the entity that you require. (I'm using `Production.Product` from the Adventure-Works database as an example.)

6   Leave the Item property blank, as we'll pass through an item using Web Part Connections.

7   Click OK.

8   Click the Edit button in the Business Data List Web Part, and choose Connections, Send Selected Item To, Entity Name (in our case, `Production.Product`).

9   Exit the Edit mode.

**10**  You should notice that, in your Business Data List Web Part, each row has a radio button. Click one of the radio buttons to fire the connection.

Figure 4.6 shows the results from these two selected web parts.

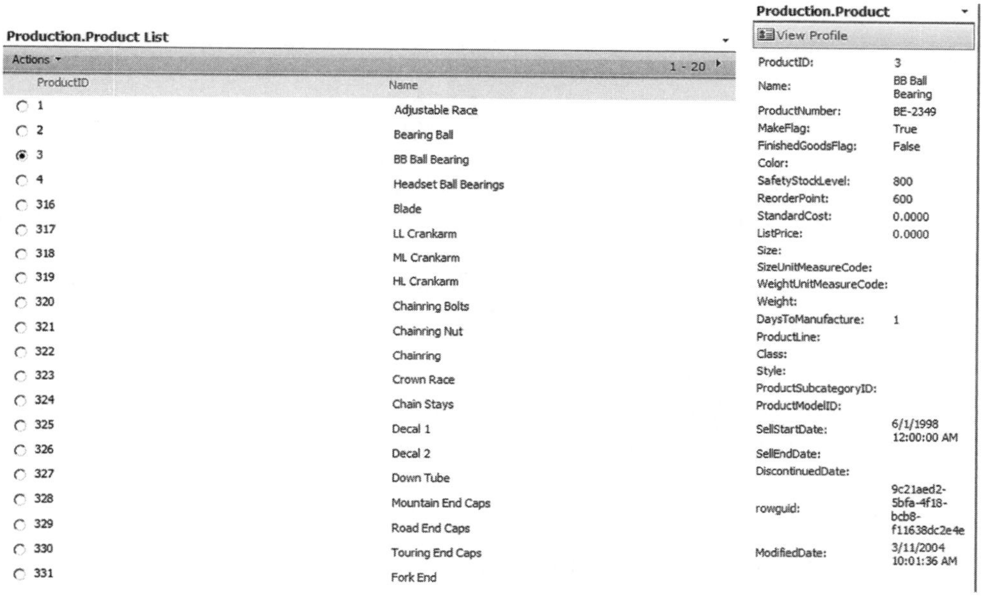

**Figure 4.6  Two connected web parts—the Business Data List Web Part connected to the Business Data Item Web Part**

Web parts can also be connected to the Business Data Filter Web Part. We'll explore the Business Data Filter Web Part in the next section.

### 4.1.3  Business Data Filter Web Part

The Business Data Filter Web Part is used in conjunction with a SharePoint list. You can use the Business Data Filter Web Part to filter what's shown in a Share-Point list or library. A good example would be selecting a customer in the Business Data Filter Web Part, and having the results of Document Libraries, Contact Lists, Task Lists, and so on filtered for the selected customer. Figure 4.7 displays the Business Data Catalog Filter Web Part.

The Business Data Filter Web Part can provide connections to multiple web parts at the same time. As long as each web part is configured to consume a filter

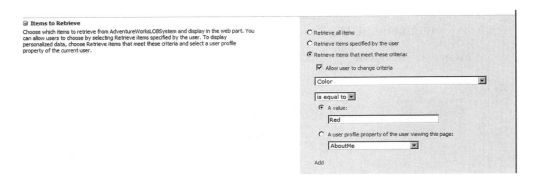

**Figure 4.7    Business Data Catalog Filter Web Part configured to filter lists by the selected product name**

from a Business Data Filter Web Part, the filtered data will display. To add and configure a Business Data Filter Web Part, follow these steps:

1  Click Site Actions, Edit Page.

2  In the Web Part zone on the left side of the page, click Add a Web Part.

3  Click the Open the Tool Pane link to display the Tool pane.

4  In the Filter Name property, type the name of the filter—for example, `Color`.

5  Choose an entity for the Entity property.

6  Set the Value and Description columns to a column you want to pass—for example, Color.

7  Click OK.

8  From your Business Data List Web Part, click Edit.

9  Click Connections, Get Filter Values From.

10  Choose your Filter Web Part.

11  Map the Consumer field to the Provider field—for example, Color.

12  You can now provide a value in the Business Data Filter Web Part, which will in turn filter the Business Data List Web Part.

Figure 4.8 displays the Filter Web Part connected to the Business Data List Web Part.

There are three other web parts to discuss briefly before moving on to customizing web parts with Microsoft Office SharePoint Designer and XSL. The next web part we'll talk about is the Business Data Actions Web Part.

color

Red

**Production.Product List**

| Actions ▾ | 1 - 20 ▶ |
|---|---|

| ProductID | Name |
|---|---|
| ○ 706 | HL Road Frame - Red, 58 |
| ○ 707 | Sport-100 Helmet, Red |
| ○ 717 | HL Road Frame - Red, 62 |
| ○ 718 | HL Road Frame - Red, 44 |
| ○ 719 | HL Road Frame - Red, 48 |
| ○ 720 | HL Road Frame - Red, 52 |
| ○ 721 | HL Road Frame - Red, 56 |

**Figure 4.8   The Business Data Filter Web Part connected to the Business Data List Web Part**

## 4.1.4 Other out-of-the-box BDC Web Parts

The Business Data Actions Web Part allows you to choose an entity, a row (identified by a unique ID, either set in the Property pane or passed via a web part connection), and a list of actions that you want to see.

The actions are displayed in a bulleted list, list, or toolbar. Personally, I prefer to use actions on my data directly from the Business Data List Web Part, because it displays the Actions button on the toolbar with a drop-down list of actions that can be performed on each row. It can also be configured to display them in the Title Columns Edit Control block, as we saw earlier in the chapter. But when designing your own business data page or site, it may be useful to have a separate web part.

Another useful web part is the Business Data Item Builder. The purpose of this web part is to grab a query string from the page's URL and pass the ID of the selected row to the Business Data Item Web Part. It is merely a joining web part.

The final web part is the Business Data Related List Web Part. If you have associations between two entities in your application definition file, you can use the Business Data Related List Web Part to provide a parent/child view of the data. This is done using web part connections between itself and a Business Data List Web Part. The Business Data List Web Part is usually the provider (the "one" side of a join), and the Business Data Related List Web Part is the consumer (the "many" side of the join). A good example of where this is useful would be to display customer information in the Business Data List Web Part, and related orders for each customer in the Business Data Related List Web Part. You can configure the Related List Web Part by specifying the entity and the related entity in the Web Parts tool pane, as shown in figure 4.9

Once the web part is configured for the correct entity, you
simply need to connect them as
you would any other connected
web parts. From the Business Data
List Web Part, click the drop-
down list, and provide a connection to the Related List Web Part.
The end result will be as shown in
figure 4.10. Click a radio button
and it will filter the related list for
the selected item.

Now that we've discussed each
web part, let's talk about customizing the data that's displayed in the
web part. This can be done in two
ways: using Microsoft Office
SharePoint Designer or using XSL.

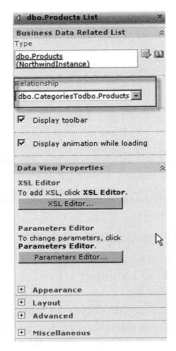

**Figure 4.9
The configuration
of the Related List
Web Part**

## 4.2    *Using SharePoint Designer with the Business Data List Web Part*

The Business Data Catalog Web Parts look a little plain out of the box. Using
Microsoft Office SharePoint Designer or XSL, you can pimp them up a bit and
end up with a good-looking web part that also provides more functionality than
the standard BDC Web Parts. The nice thing about Microsoft Office SharePoint
Designer is that it generates XSL for you while you point and click your way to a
nice-looking web part. Occasionally, you'll find you just can't achieve what you
want to using SharePoint Designer, so we like to use SharePoint Designer first,
then tweak the web part using XSL.

In this example, we're going to use a Business Data List Web Part that's consuming a `Production.Products` entity from the Microsoft SQL Adventure Works
sample database.

The `Production.Product` entity consists of too many columns to display in one
horizontal web part, and takes up too much space onscreen. Therefore, we're
going to remove some of the columns before we apply any formatting:

**dbo.Categories List**

Actions ▾

| | CategoryID | CategoryName | Description |
|---|---|---|---|
| ○ | 1 | Beverages | Soft drinks, coffees, teas, beers, and ales |
| ○ | 2 | Condiments | Sweet and savory sauces, relishes, spreads, and seasonings |
| ◉ | 3 | Confections | Desserts, candies, and sweet breads |
| ○ | 4 | Dairy Products | Cheeses |
| ○ | 5 | Grains/Cereals | Breads, crackers, pasta, and cereal |
| ○ | 6 | Meat/Poultry | Prepared meats |
| ○ | 7 | Produce | Dried fruit and bean curd |
| ○ | 8 | Seafood | Seaweed and fish |

**dbo.Products List**

Actions ▾

| ProductID | ProductName | SupplierID | CategoryID | QuantityPerUnit | UnitPrice | UnitsInStock | UnitsOnOrder | ReorderLevel | Discontinued |
|---|---|---|---|---|---|---|---|---|---|
| 16 | Pavlova | 7 | 3 | 32 - 500 g boxes | 17.4500 | 29 | 0 | 10 | False |
| 19 | Teatime Chocolate Biscuits | 8 | 3 | 10 boxes x 12 pieces | 9.2000 | 25 | 0 | 5 | False |
| 20 | Sir Rodney's Marmalade | 8 | 3 | 30 gift boxes | 81.0000 | 40 | 0 | 0 | False |
| 21 | Sir Rodney's Scones | 8 | 3 | 24 pkgs. x 4 pieces | 10.0000 | 3 | 40 | 5 | False |
| 25 | NuNuCa Nuß-Nougat-Creme | 11 | 3 | 20 - 450 g glasses | 14.0000 | 76 | 0 | 30 | False |
| 26 | Gumbär Gummibärchen | 11 | 3 | 100 - 250 g bags | 31.2300 | 15 | 0 | 0 | False |
| 27 | Schoggi Schokolade | 11 | 3 | 100 - 100 g pieces | 43.9000 | 49 | 0 | 30 | False |
| 47 | Zaanse koeken | 22 | 3 | 10 - 4 oz boxes | 9.5000 | 36 | 0 | 0 | False |
| 48 | Chocolade | 22 | 3 | 10 pkgs. | 12.7500 | 15 | 70 | 25 | False |
| 49 | Maxilaku | 23 | 3 | 24 - 50 g pkgs. | 20.0000 | 10 | 60 | 15 | False |
| 50 | Valkoinen suklaa | 23 | 3 | 12 - 100 g bars | 16.2500 | 65 | 0 | 30 | False |
| 62 | Tarte au sucre | 29 | 3 | 48 pies | 49.3000 | 17 | 0 | 0 | False |
| 68 | Scottish Longbreads | 8 | 3 | 10 boxes x 8 pieces | 12.5000 | 6 | 10 | 15 | False |

**Figure 4.10   Business Data List Web Part connected to the Business Data Related List Web Part**

1   Click Edit in the top right corner of the web part that you just added.

2   Choose Modify Shared Web Part or Modify My Web Part.

3   You'll notice that an Edit View link is available. Click Edit View, as displayed in figure 4.11.

On the Edit View page, you can deselect some of the columns that you don't want to see. We've changed the view so that we only see

**Figure 4.11   The Edit View hyperlink that enables you to configure the Business Data List Web Part. This only displays while in Edit mode of the web part page.**

the Name, Product Number, Color, Reorder Point, List Price, and Standard Cost columns.

The web part displays the data that we wanted to see, but none of the data is formatted. Using SharePoint Designer, we'll first format the Standard Cost and List Price columns into their appropriate currency. To begin editing your web part, follow these steps:

1  Start Microsoft SharePoint Designer by clicking Start, All Programs, Microsoft Office, Microsoft Office SharePoint Designer.

2  Open the site that contains your BDC List Web Part by choosing File, Open Site.

3  In the Site Open dialog box, type the URL for your site, such as http://servername/sitename.

4  Double-click the Default.aspx file in the folder list.

5  Your site should now be open and ready for editing.

Now that you have your web part page opened in SharePoint Designer, you can completely configure the Business Data List Web Part to do almost anything. Let's first look at formatting the data differently.

### 4.2.1   *Number formatting*

The Business Data List Web Part doesn't display numbers in the data grid with any specific formatting. Therefore, in this example, we're going to change the formatting of the two price fields in the `Production.Product` entity. The first change we're going to make is to the Standard Cost column. Currently the value is just displayed as a general number. To format this into a currency value:

1  Click one of the numbers in the Standard Cost column. A grey button with a > symbol will appear next to your cursor, as shown in figure 4.12.

2  Click the grey button. A small submenu will appear, where you can configure the number formatting.

3  Choose Currency, as shown in figure 4.13.

| StandardCost | ListPrice |
| --- | --- |
| 0.00 | 0.00 |
| 1.01 | 1.01 |
| 2.02 | 2.02 |
| 3.03 | 3.03 |
| 4.04 | 4.04 |
| 5.05 | 5.05 |
| 6.06 | 6.06 |
| 7.07 | 7.07 |

**Figure 4.12   The Business Data List Web Part in Microsoft Office SharePoint Designer displays sample data.**

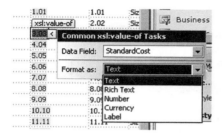

Figure 4.13   The cell being edited, and the format of the cell being chosen within Microsoft Office SharePoint Designer

4   Change the format for the Price columns to display the $ symbol prior to the value, as shown in figure 4.14.

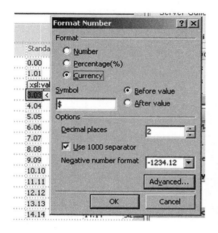

Figure 4.14   The Format Number dialog box, which can be used to format column values in SharePoint Designer for the BDC List Web Part

5   Choose OK.

6   Click the Save icon on the toolbar to save your changes. If you get a warning message about the site becoming customized from the Site Definition, choose OK.

7   The color formatting is like most other Microsoft Office tools. You can high-light cells of data in the table, then apply a formatting change to them. SharePoint Designer also allows you to do conditional formatting on your BDC data.

8   Format the data grid.

9   Highlight the entire table in the BDC List Web Part.

10   Choose Format from the menu at the top of the page.

**11** Choose Borders and Shading.

**12** Select the Shading tab, as shown in figure 4.15.

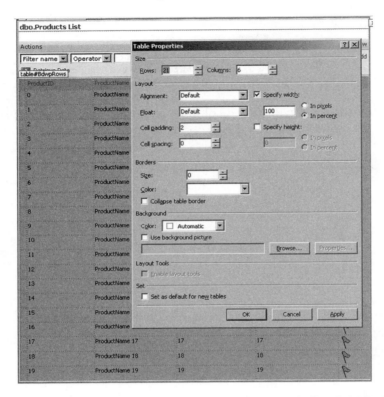

**Figure 4.15   The Web Part Formatting Options dialog box in SharePoint Designer**

**13** Apply foreground and background colors. You may also want to remove the background image.

The web part is now beginning to take shape, with formatted numbers as well as conditional formatting. All of this can be modified further with XSL if required. In figure 4.16, you can see the final result.

**dbo.Products List**

| ProductID | ProductName | UnitsInStock | ReorderLevel | Unit Price | KPI |
|---|---|---|---|---|---|
| 1 | Chai | 39 | 10 | $20.00 | |
| 2 | Chang | 17 | 25 | $19.00 | |
| 3 | Aniseed Syrup | 13 | 25 | $10.00 | |
| 4 | Chef Anton's Cajun Seasoning | 53 | 0 | $22.00 | |
| 5 | Chef Anton's Gumbo Mix | 0 | 0 | $21.35 | |
| 6 | Grandma's Boysenberry Spread | 120 | 25 | $25.00 | |
| 7 | Uncle Bob's Organic Dried Pears | 15 | 10 | $30.00 | |
| 8 | Northwoods Cranberry Sauce | 6 | 0 | $40.00 | |
| 9 | Mishi Kobe Niku | 29 | 0 | $97.00 | |
| 10 | Ikura | 31 | 0 | $31.00 | |
| 11 | Queso Cabrales | 22 | 30 | $21.00 | |
| 12 | Queso Manchego La Pastora | 86 | 0 | $38.00 | |
| 13 | Konbu | 24 | 5 | $6.00 | |
| 14 | Tofu | 35 | 0 | $23.25 | |
| 15 | Genen Shouyu | 39 | 5 | $15.50 | |
| 16 | Pavlova | 29 | 10 | $17.45 | |
| 17 | Alice Mutton | 0 | 0 | $39.00 | |
| 18 | Carnarvon Tigers | 42 | 0 | $62.50 | |
| 19 | Teatime Chocolate Biscuits | 25 | 5 | $9.20 | |
| 20 | Sir Rodney's Marmalade | 40 | 0 | $81.00 | |

**Figure 4.16   The completed, formatted web part**

### 4.2.2   *Conditional formatting*

Conditional formatting enables us to apply formatting to a cell value or an entire row depending upon a condition. You can apply a background color to the row or cell, or change the foreground color. You can also hide or show values based upon a condition. The condition can come from a hardcoded value, or you can compare two columns returned from the same entity. For example, you can choose to view only products where the value for Products In Stock is less than the value for Reorder Point.

To apply and configure conditional formatting, follow these steps:

1  Using conditional formatting, we want to display in red all the products that we need to reorder.

2  Highlight whatever you want the formatting to apply to: a value, a group of column values, or an entire row.

3  Right-click the highlighted area and choose Conditional Formatting from the menu.

4  The Conditional Formatting window will appear on the top right corner of the SharePoint Designer Window.

5  Click Create.

6  Click Apply Formatting.

7  Configure your condition. For our example, we want products where SafetyStockLevel is less than ReOrderPoint, as shown in figure 4.17.

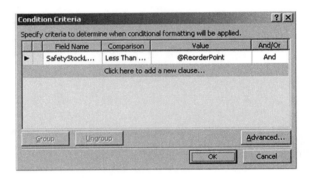

**Figure 4.17  The Condition Criteria dialog box used in SharePoint Designer for applying conditional formatting**

8  Click OK.

9  The Formatting window will appear.

10 Change the font color to red.

11 Click OK.

12 Choose Save from the menu in SharePoint Designer.

13 Test your changes by refreshing the browser window.

The conditional formatting displays the SafetyStockLevel in an alternate color, as shown in figure 4.18. This can be applied to the cell, row, or even to an object such as an image in a column.

| ProductID | ProductName | UnitsInStock | ReorderLevel | Unit Price | KPI |
|---|---|---|---|---|---|
| 1 | Chai | 39 | 10 | $20.00 | |
| 2 | Chang | 17 | 25 | $19.00 | |
| 3 | Aniseed Syrup | 13 | 25 | $10.00 | |
| 4 | Chef Anton's Cajun Seasoning | 53 | 0 | $22.00 | |
| 5 | **Chef Anton's Gumbo Mix** | 0 | 0 | **$21.35** | |
| 6 | Grandma's Boysenberry Spread | 120 | 25 | $25.00 | |
| 7 | Uncle Bob's Organic Dried Pears | 15 | 10 | $30.00 | |
| 8 | Northwoods Cranberry Sauce | 6 | 0 | $40.00 | |
| 9 | Mishi Kobe Niku | 29 | 0 | $97.00 | |
| 10 | Ikura | 31 | 0 | $31.00 | |
| 11 | Queso Cabrales | 22 | 30 | $21.00 | |
| 12 | Queso Manchego La Pastora | 86 | 0 | $38.00 | |
| 13 | Konbu | 24 | 5 | $6.00 | |
| 14 | Tofu | 35 | 0 | $23.25 | |
| 15 | Genen Shouyu | 39 | 5 | $15.50 | |
| 16 | Pavlova | 29 | 10 | $17.45 | |
| 17 | **Alice Mutton** | 0 | 0 | **$39.00** | |
| 18 | Carnarvon Tigers | 42 | 0 | $62.50 | |
| 19 | Teatime Chocolate Biscuits | 25 | 5 | $9.20 | |
| 20 | Sir Rodney's Marmalade | 40 | 0 | $81.00 | |

**Figure 4.18   The completed web part with conditional formatting**

### 4.2.3 *Modifying the columns using Microsoft SharePoint Designer*

Using SharePoint Designer, you can manipulate the data in the data grid and perform calculations on it. We're going to insert a new column into the table on our web part to calculate the list price, including tax:

1 Click your cursor somewhere in the List Price column.

2 From the menu at the top of the SharePoint Designer window, choose Table, Insert, Column to the Right, as shown in figure 4.19.

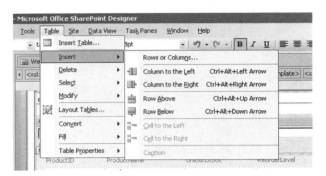

**Figure 4.19   The Table menu in SharePoint Designer, and inserting a new column into the Business Data List Web Part**

3    A small column will appear.

4    Type a title for your column—for example, `Total Price`.

5    Right-click in the first cell under the column name.

6    Choose Insert Formula from the menu.

7    In the Insert Formula dialog box, enter an XPath expression—for example, `@ListPrice*1.08`—as shown in figure 4.20.

8    Format your new value as currency and to two decimal places, as we did earlier in this chapter.

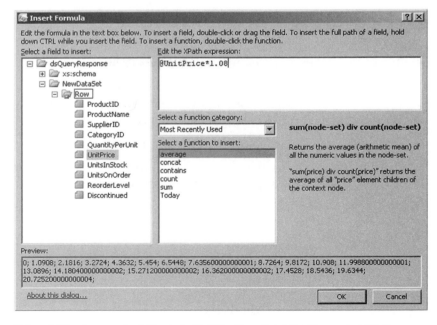

**Figure 4.20   A new calculation being built in SharePoint Designer using XPath**

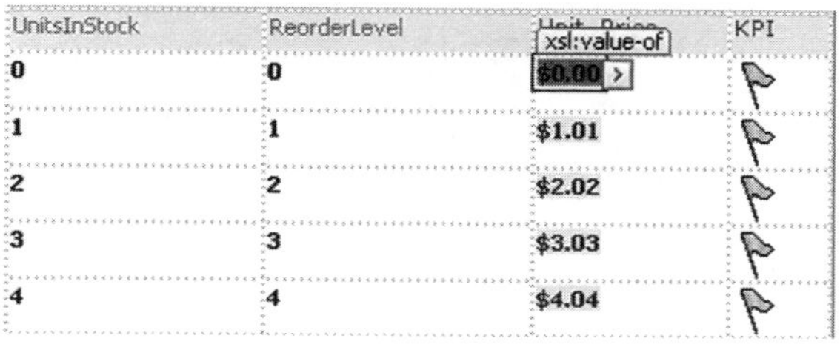

**Figure 4.21   The completed new column containing a calculation**

You can see in figure 4.21 that the values are now displayed with the dollar symbol. This makes the data far more readable.

## 4.3   *Sorting, grouping, and filtering*

You can specify sorting and grouping options in the Business Data List Web Part, but you can't do so in the default Web Part view. You have to click the Edit View link and then specify the sort and filter options. Using the Data Form Web Part, you can enable a Sort, Group & Filter toolbar that's always present in the web part. This allows users to configure the options in the toolbar on the fly. To enable users to filter, group, and sort the data displayed in your web part, you can enable the Sort, Group & Filter toolbars. To do this:

1  Select your Business Data List Web Part.

2  In the top right corner of the web part, click the grey button.

3  Choose Data View Properties.

4  Check the boxes so that you can see the Sort, Group & Filter toolbar, and also select View footer, which we'll be using later on.

5  Click OK.

6  Save your changes to the site, and refresh your browser.

The toolbar shown in figure 4.22 displays the Sort by, Group by, and Filter options. This is a great addition to any Business Data List Web Part, as it means users have a lot more control over the data that they can see.

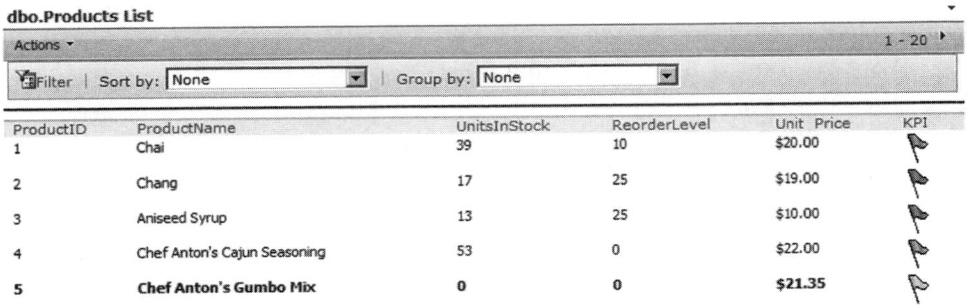

dbo.Products List

| Actions ▾ | | | | | 1 - 20 ▸ |
| --- | --- | --- | --- | --- | --- |

Filter | Sort by: None ▾ | Group by: None ▾

| ProductID | ProductName | UnitsInStock | ReorderLevel | Unit Price | KPI |
| --- | --- | --- | --- | --- | --- |
| 1 | Chai | 39 | 10 | $20.00 | |
| 2 | Chang | 17 | 25 | $19.00 | |
| 3 | Aniseed Syrup | 13 | 25 | $10.00 | |
| 4 | Chef Anton's Cajun Seasoning | 53 | 0 | $22.00 | |
| 5 | **Chef Anton's Gumbo Mix** | 0 | 0 | **$21.35** | |

**Figure 4.22    The completed web part with Sort by, Group by, and Filter options**

### 4.3.1  *The View footer*

The View footer is useful for summary data. It's a simple area below the grid where you can type text or perform aggregate functions. When using pagination, you can't tell how many items are in the list, therefore a count of the items is useful. You can also use other aggregate functions in the footer such as Sum, Min, Max, and Average on any column in the entity. You should already see that there's a count of the number of items returned from your data. To see other aggregate information:

1   Type a label in the footer, such as `Average List Price`.

2   Drag the List Price field from the Fields list on the right side of your page, as shown in figure 4.23.

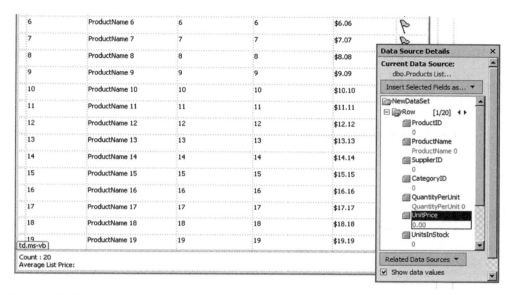

**Figure 4.23** You can drag columns from your data source into the footer section of your Business Data List Web Part, and then format it to display aggregate information.

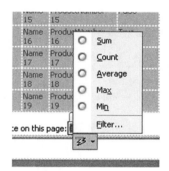

3 Click the yellow bolt of lightning to choose an aggregate function, as shown in figure 4.24.

4 Select Average.

5 Format the value as currency, as we did earlier.

The aggregate functions are useful for providing summary information to the user, such as how many items are in a view, or a sum of this month's sales. You might want to use this area to simply display an image or text. Now that we've configured the web part in SharePoint Designer, you may want to tweak it further by manually modifying the XSL.

**Figure 4.24** The above image displays the available aggregate functions in the Business Data List footer.

### 4.3.2 *Tweaking the XSL*

If you don't have SharePoint Designer, you still have the ability to format web parts using XSL. This can be done using just the browser. Also, some things that you may want to do to your BDC List Web Part aren't possible using SharePoint Designer, but can be done using XSL. To do this:

1   Using SharePoint in Internet Explorer, click Site Actions, Edit Page.

2   On your web part, click the drop-down and choose Modify Shared Web Part.

3   In the Web Part properties, click the XSL Editor button.

4   You can then manipulate the web part using XSL, as shown in figure 4.25.

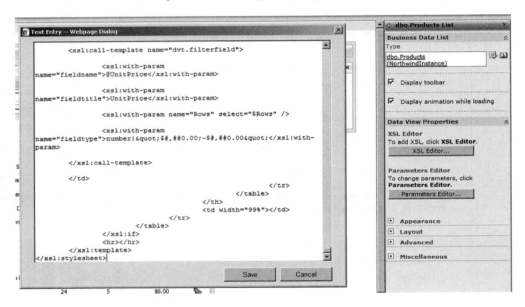

**Figure 4.25   XSL formatting options within the Web Part properties in the browser**

**NOTE**   Once you've made all the changes you're going to make using Share-Point Designer, right-click your Default.aspx file and choose Reset to SharePoint Designer. This avoids unghosting, and your site will now receive changes made to the site definition upon upgrading of Share-Point or installing a service pack. Note that your web part still retains the changes that we made.

## 4.4   *Exercise: joining two web parts*

In this exercise, we'll join two web parts for our Products and Categories tables in Northwind. To perform this exercise, we'll be using the Categories and Products entities from the Northwind database. Please make sure that you have these entities configured prior to adding the web parts. Chapter 2 explains how to create the entities.

**Third-party web parts**

Many organizations require more functionality from BDC Web Parts. There are a few third-party companies offering web parts for download that save your development time. You can obtain for instance a BDC Mapper Web Part, KPI (Key Performance Indicator) Web Part, and BDC Calendar Web Part from www.lightningtools.com. Other companies such as Dundas Charts also offer more expensive (but more functional) BDC Chart Web Parts. We'll learn how to create your own custom web parts in a later module.

1  Create a new blank site by choosing Site Actions, Create Site.

2  Type `Products` as the site name.

3  Type `products` as the URL.

4  Choose the Blank Site template.

5  Choose Site Actions, Edit Page.

6  Choose Add a Web Part in the Web Part zone on the left.

7  Select the Business Data List Web Part and the Business Data Item Web Part.

8  Edit the properties of the Business Data Item Web Part.

9  Select the `Categories` entity and choose OK.

10  Edit the Related Items Web Part: choose the `Products` entity to display, and select the `Categories` entity as the relationship item.

11  Choose OK.

12  Connect the web parts by choosing Edit, Connections, Send Selected Item To, `dbo.Products`, as shown in figure 4.26.

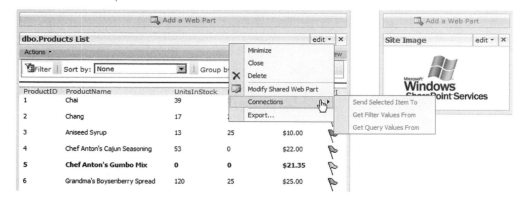

**Figure 4.26  How to connect the two web parts to provide master/detail or summary/detail scenarios**

Now that the web parts are connected, you can navigate the data more easily by selecting a product category such as Beverages, which will then fire a connection to the consuming web part, which in turn filters all of the beverage products. You can see how to connect the web parts in figure 4.26.

## 4.5   *Summary*

In this chapter, we explored how to use all of the out-of-the-box Business Data Web Parts to display business data. We described each web part and explored how to connect web parts to display data in a more meaningful way. We learned how to configure the Business Data List Web Part and the Business Data Item Web Part, and use their out-of-the-box functionality to display our line-of-business data.

The last section of this chapter explored how to customize the out-of-the-box Business Data List Web Part using SharePoint Designer. This enables us to format and perform calculations on the business data while in the grid.

In chapter 5, we'll explore the Business Data column and see how that allows us to use business data within SharePoint lists and libraries.

# 5

# Using the Business Data field type in lists and libraries

**This chapter covers**

- Demonstrating the use of business data in lists and libraries
- Creating custom list columns that display BDC data
- Using data throughout Office via the Document Information panel
- Customizing the Document Information panel with InfoPath
- Building a custom field type that lists BDC entities

The Business Data field type is a type of field you can create, just like a Single Line of Text, Currency, or Date Time field type. Only it allows you to look up data from the LOB system and then store the data as metadata in a list item or document. We're going to explore the out-of-the-box functionality of this field type, as well as look at improving it using InfoPath. We'll then look at how to over-come additional issues by creating our own field type.

Throughout this book so far, we've discussed the issue of having islands of data within an organization. The Business Data column within MOSS Enterprise resolves another part of that puzzle when bringing those islands of data back together. Organizations have invested large sums of money in applications such as Microsoft Dynamics GP, CRM, and NAV. Those applications store information in back-end databases such as Customers, Employees, Orders, and Product Informa-tion. This data is all stored in tables. What about the documents associated with that data, though? We may send letters, proposals, and invoices to our customers; send purchase orders to our suppliers; and store résumés against our employees. We're also trying to educate our users to store such documents in SharePoint doc-ument libraries. So the fact that the Business Data field type allows us to associate documents that are stored in document libraries with records in our databases should be another advantage to storing documents in SharePoint document libraries and not in the file system. This isn't limited to just document libraries, either. You can use the Business Data column in all lists and libraries, thereby allowing documents, InfoPath forms, pictures, announcements, contacts, and so on all to be associated with a unique record in the line-of-business system.

When you use the Business Data column in a document library, you'll also find that the columns are displayed to you in the Document Information panel throughout Office 2007. This Document Information panel can be customized using Microsoft Office InfoPath to provide further logic or validation of the data entered. The Document Information panel is shown later in this chapter.

Within this chapter, we'll also explore how you can create your own field type to extend the functionality of the out-of-the-box Business Data field type, thereby providing you with a drop-down list from which to select your ID column, instead of having to know the ID. For example, if you wanted to find a particular customer such as Lightning Tools, you may not know the customer ID and therefore have to look it up. It would be far better to see a drop-down list displaying the company name, but storing the customer ID. Let's first of all explore the out-of-the-box functionality.

## 5.1   The Business Data field type

Within a list or library, there are lots of different field types that you can choose from, including Single Line of Text, Multiple Lines of Text, Date Time, and so forth. If you're using MOSS and have the Enterprise features enabled within your site, you can also use the Business Data column. We're going to explore the Business Data field type, exploring how it should be used, its limitations, and how to overcome those limitations using Microsoft Office InfoPath 2007. We'll then explore how to create your own custom field type using Visual Studio.NET.

**NOTE**    You can enable Enterprise features for a site by choosing Site Actions, Site Settings, and then choosing Site Features under the Site Administration column.

So let's suppose for a moment that you're using Microsoft Dynamics CRM for your customer relationship management, but you store customer proposals in a document library within SharePoint. Without the Business Data field type, you could prompt users of the Customers table to associate their documents with a customer, but either the users would need to type the company name, or you'd need to create a choice field or lookup for them to select from. If the data is already in the CRM database, the Business Data field type could look up those columns for you. Why is this so useful? It means we can filter, sort, and group our documents reliably by customer name or customer ID, or in fact any field from the Customers table that we decide to display within the document library. The information is stored as metadata within the document library, but can be refreshed should the back-end data change. For example, if a customer changes its name and we've modified the record in the back-end database, we could refresh the Company Name column in SharePoint to pick up the change automatically.

Storing business data within SharePoint lists and libraries also means that they can form the basis for web part connections, so that you can filter document libraries from another web part, such as a Business Data List Web Part or a List View Web Part. It also means that workflows can be based on the business data.

One major drawback of the Business Data field type is that it can't be used within a content type, and can't become a Site column. This is a limitation, as you may want to reuse your column elsewhere in other lists/libraries or create different content types, such as Customer, Supplier, Employee, and so on. This would really increase the benefits of the Business Data field type, as it would mean different line-of-business data could be displayed depending on the type of document. For example, if we were storing a proposal, we may want to see Customer Name, Contact Name, and Phone Number. If we were storing a commission claim, we may be storing employee information such as Employee ID, Name, and Department. One way around this issue is to create your own custom field type, which provides richer controls, such as a drop-down list to look up column values. The custom column could also be used in Site columns or content types.

### 5.1.1   *Using the Business Data field type*

Using the Business Data field type is straightforward. You need to ensure that you have the Enterprise features activated, and then you can add a Business Data field type to any SharePoint list or library. The Business Data field type is great for working with a document library.

Take the following steps to associate documents in a document library with customers that are stored in a back-end database:

1  Navigate to a team site or create a new team site.

2  Create a new document library called `Proposals` by choosing Site Actions, Create.

3  Choose Document Library from the Libraries column.

4  Type the name `Proposals` in the Name field and then choose Create.

5  Open the document library by clicking Proposals in the Quick Launch menu.

6  Choose Settings from the Document Library toolbar.

7  Choose Create Column.

8  In the Name field, type `Customer`.

9  Select Business Data as the field type.

10  You may get an error, as shown in figure 5.1, if Enterprise features aren't enabled on your Office SharePoint Server. This is likely if you're working in a team site. You can activate the Enterprise features by navigating to Site Actions, Site Settings and clicking Site Features. Find the appropriate feature and choose Activate.

11  In the Type attribute, click the Address Book icon to look up your Customers entity.

12  Choose which field you want to display in the library. It would be better to display the company name than the customer ID.

13  Note that you can also display other columns from the same entity within the library. In figure 5.2, we're selecting the Contact Name and Phone fields.

14  Click OK.

15  Note that the columns you selected are now displayed as columns within the default view of the document library.

16  Click New, New Document to create a new blank Word document.

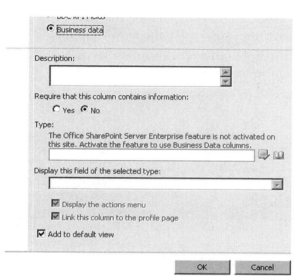

**Figure 5.1 The attributes for a Business Data column being created. Note that the error message is pointing out that the Office Enterprise feature needs to be enabled to use the Business Data column.**

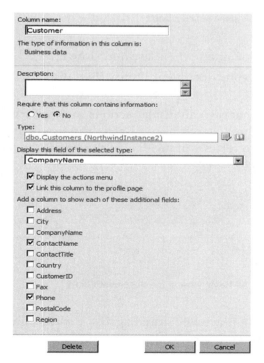

**Figure 5.2 The Business Data field being created, and the attributes to display other column values from the same row in the database**

17    If you're using Word 2007, you'll notice that the Document Information panel displays soon after you create the new document.

18    In the Customer ID column, type a customer ID such as ALFKI, and click the Check Names button beside the Customer ID field.

19    You should notice that the other columns are then displayed also, as shown in figure 5.3.

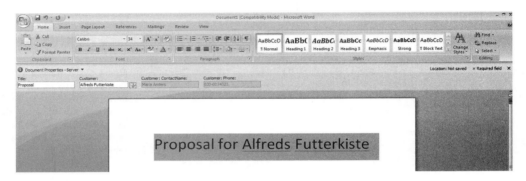

**Figure 5.3    The Document Information panel in Word 2007**

20    Type some text in the document, then save and close it.

21    You should notice that your document library then displays the new document and the metadata.

22    Note within figure 5.4 that you can display actions such as View Profile from the Customer ID column. There's also a Refresh indicator in the column heading, allowing you to refresh all the data in the view if the back-end data has changed.

**Figure 5.4    The properties set in the All Items view of the document library**

The data from the LOB system is actually stored against the document, and is no longer linked at this point. You'll notice that the data can be refreshed by clicking the Refresh icon. This will refresh every document in the document library;

unfortunately, you can't just choose to refresh one document. When you click the Refresh indicator, you're taken to a page that says that this process could take a few minutes. If you have thousands of documents, it could take a very long time to requery all of the metadata and refresh the documents.

You'll also notice the drop-down arrow next to the customers' names in the Customer column. This is optional, but allows you to call one of the actions for this entity. The default action, View Profile, will be displayed along with any other actions that you've configured, such as a Send Email action. It would be useful to create an action that takes you into the Customers view for that customer in the LOB system application. For example, we could click View Customer for Alfreds Futterkiste, which could in turn open up CRM and would take us to that particular customer's page.

### 5.1.2 The ShowInPicker property

When you edit the properties for a document in the document library, you're provided with an Address Book icon next to the Business Data column that provides a list of data to choose from. This can be seen in figure 5.5.

This dialog box will only display 200 items from your entity. If there are more than that, you get a red error message explaining that only 200 entries can be

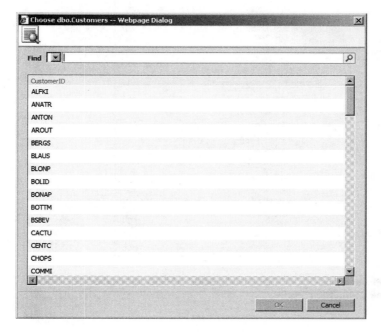

**Figure 5.5  The dialog box when editing the value for a Business Data field from within the SharePoint UI**

displayed. Therefore, you must create some filters on the finder method in the application definition file, including a default value for the filter. Note at the top of the dialog box that you can choose a filter using the Find drop-down list, and then enter a value. This will limit the choices so that you can easily select a row to store as your value. It's worth noting that, even if you don't have a filter in place, the filter controls still display, which can confuse your users.

Another problem is that only the Identifier columns are displayed. You can set the ShowInPicker property within your ADF for any other columns you want to display, making it easier to then select the correct information. Figure 5.6 displays a Picker dialog box with the company name and contact name rather than just the customer ID.

Configuring the ShowInPicker property for each column is a huge benefit to users when they're looking up an item using the Chooser control shown in figure 5.6. In the next section, you'll see just how useful this information becomes once it's configured. For example, you can use it for filtering, sorting, and Share-Point workflows.

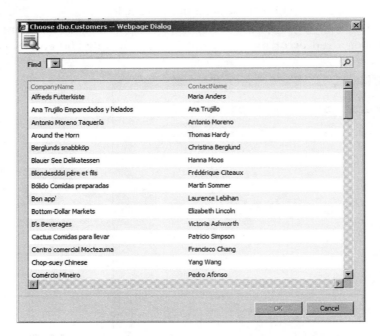

**Figure 5.6   The Picker dialog box with the ShowInPicker property set on the CompanyName and ContactName fields**

### 5.1.3 *The Business Data column with a view*

Business Data columns will always appear as read-only in any view that you create. This includes Data Sheet views or Microsoft Access views. You can change other metadata for the document, but not metadata that's based on the business data. We want it that way so that the data displayed is always accurate and in sync with the back-end database.

While in the view, the business data can be used for filtering, sorting, and categorizing. You can click the drop-down on the column header just like you can in any other column. This gives you the opportunity to categorize your documents by customer, or by contact name, for example. Filtering on these columns makes finding the documents you're looking for quick and easy.

Figure 5.7 displays a categorized view of the document library, with the customer name serving as the category header. This makes it easy to expand and collapse your customers to get to all of the documents that belong to a particular customer.

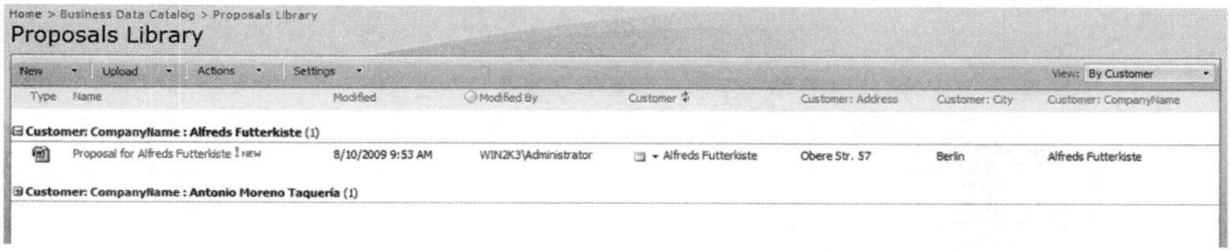

**Figure 5.7   A custom view of the document library with documents grouped by a Business Data field**

Another useful view change you could make is to create a view so that each sales representative can only see her own customers' documents. This can be done easily using the view filtering capabilities and the [Me] keyword, as shown in figure 5.8. As each person logs on to SharePoint and displays this view, she'll see all of the documents for customers that the logged-on user manages.

The Business Data column can also serve within your custom workflows. Using the SharePoint Designer workflows, you may want to email a customer, informing her that her shipment has been sent. The creation of a shipment document in a document library could be the trigger for the workflow, which in turn picks up the business data to populate the email and to be used in the conditions of the workflow. Figure 5.9 displays the Business Data column being used in a SharePoint Designer workflow condition.

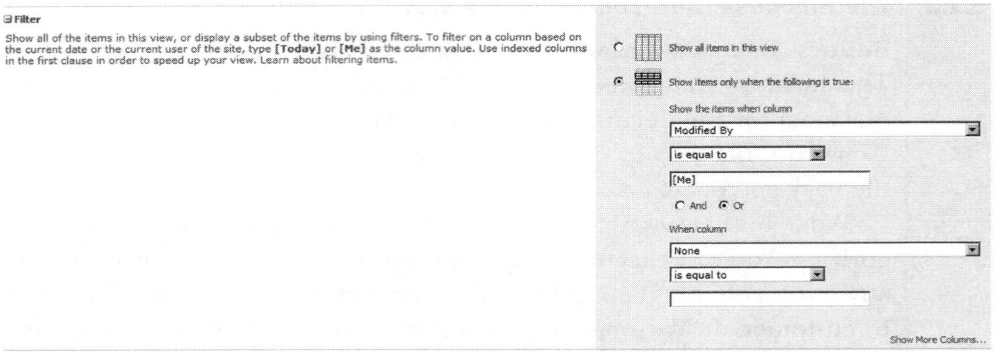

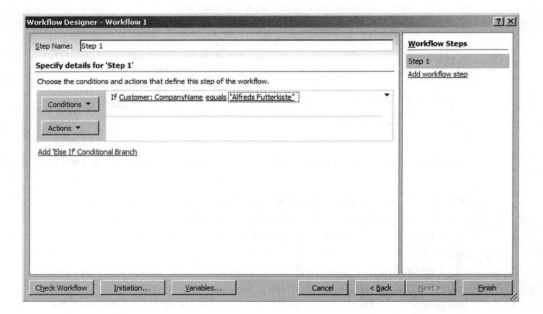

**Figure 5.8**   **The view properties allow you to filter on business data. In this example, the [Me] keyword is used to show only your accounts as a sales representative.**

**Figure 5.9**   **A dialog box from SharePoint Designer. Note that Business Data fields can form your conditions to control the flow of a document.**

You can also use the Business Data columns within your lists and libraries as a basis for web part connections. The screenshot in figure 5.10 displays an unmodified Contacts list that provides filter values to a document library. The Company column from the Contacts list is connected to the Customer field (Business Data field type) in the document library.

You can connect as many web parts as you like in this way, as long as they have values in common. Imagine accessing a team site, clicking a customer, and then seeing orders from that customer, proposals for that customer, financial data for that customer, and so forth. All of this can be done without any programming at all. Figure 5.10 displays a SharePoint Contacts list, connected to a document library named Proposals to provide filtering.

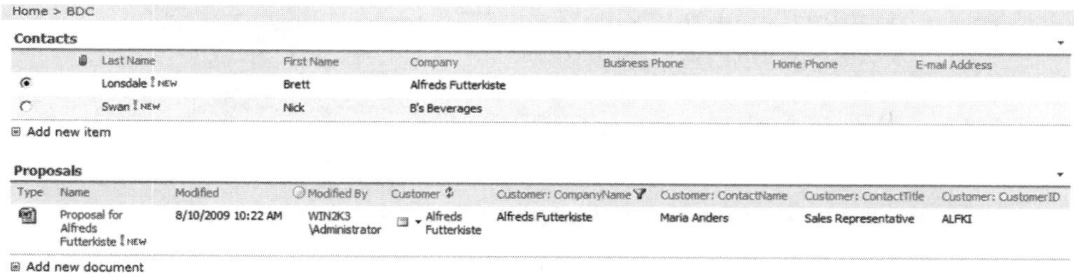

**Figure 5.10　Two connected web parts. They're connected using the Business Data field (Customer)**

## 5.2　*Customizing the Document Information panel with InfoPath 2007*

Before we jump into Visual Studio to create a custom field type, one thing worth exploring is InfoPath 2007. In addition to making useful forms to collect data, we can also create our own Document Information panels. Let's explore how to improve the Document Information panel for a document library that uses a Business Data field.

The out-of-the-box Document Information panel is quite basic. You need to know the primary key value or unique value to enter in the Business Data field so that the data can be resolved. But you can customize the ID field to make the text box a drop-down. We can do this simply by using InfoPath to create a new Document Information panel.

1   Create a new document library called `Proposals`.

2   Create a new column in the document library called `Customer`.

3   Choose the Business Data field type.

4   In the Type field, choose your Customers entity. (We're using Northwind Customers.)

5   Choose Customer ID as the display field.

6   Choose Company Name, Address, and City as the other display columns. Your screen should look like figure 5.11.

7   Open Microsoft InfoPath 2007.

8   Select Design a Form Template.

9   Choose XML or Schema, and click OK.

10   Type the URL for your Proposal list—for example, http://win2k3/bdc/Proposals/.

11   Click Next, then choose Document. (Document is the content type used in your document library.)

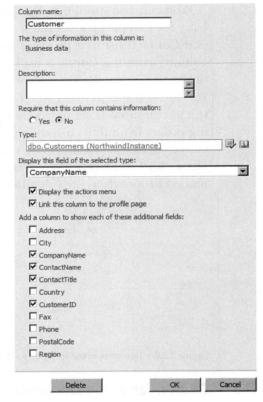

**Figure 5.11   What your screen should look like when following these steps**

12   You should end up with the Document Information panel opened up in InfoPath, as in figure 5.12.

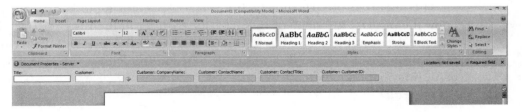

**Figure 5.12   The Document Information panel in InfoPath**

13   Right-click the Customer text box control in InfoPath, and choose Change
     To, Drop Down-List, as shown in figure 5.13.

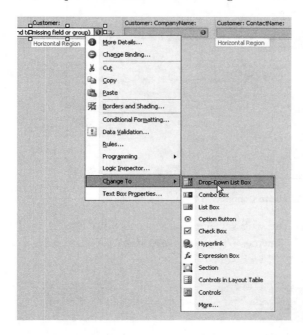

**Figure 5.13    The Change To
option for the Customer field**

14   Right-click the Customer drop-down list and choose Drop-Down List Proper-
     ties.

15   Choose Lookup Values from an External Data Source.

16   We're going to use a web service (BDC wrapper) to return the entity, but
     you could connect directly if you wish. We prefer to use a web service as the
     data source, but you can see the available choices in figure 5.14.

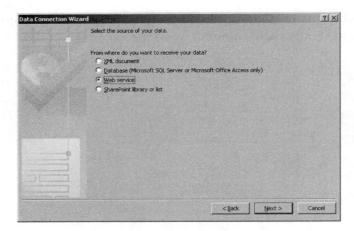

**Figure 5.14    The Add Data Connection Wizard dialog box**

**17**  Type the URL of the web service that returns your BDC data. (Chapter 8 covers creating web services to expose BDC data.) Figure 5.15 displays the URL entered for the BDC web service.

**Figure 5.15    We point the data connection at a web service.**

**18**  Set the LOBSystemInstance and Entity parameters to the LOB system and entity that contain your data, as shown in figure 5.16.

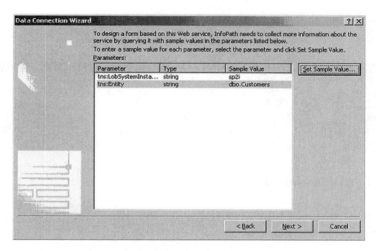

**Figure 5.16    Set the parameters for the web service.**

19  Set the Display and Value properties. In this example, the Display property
will be `CompanyName`, and the Value property is `CustomerID`. You can see the
configuration of this dialog box in figure 5.17.

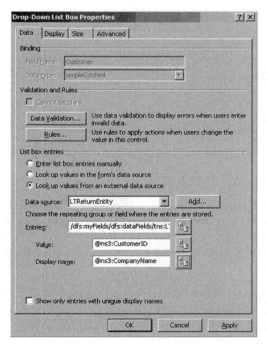

**Figure 5.17    Configure the Display and
Value properties.**

**20**  Click OK.

**21**  Your completed form should look like figure 5.18.

**Figure 5.18   The completed InfoPath 2007 form**

**22**  Publish the form by choosing File, Publish. (You'll also be prompted to save; please do so.)

**23**  Choose the default option to publish it to the list or content type.

**24**  Click Next, and then Publish.

**25**  Try the form out by creating a new document from within the document library.

**26**  You should now be able to select a customer from the drop-down, and the other values will be resolved based on the option that you choose, as shown in figure 5.19.

**Figure 5.19   The finished Document Information panel being used in Word 2007 with a drop-down list box instead of a text box**

**NOTE**    There are many other things that you could do with the InfoPath Document Information panel. For example, you could use conditional formatting to hide columns that aren't required depending on the type of document created. You can also perform calculations and change controls for richer controls.

This process can also be used to get around the content type issue. A Business Data column can't be used in a content type, as this isn't supported. But you could create a content type with all of the Site columns that you need, with the exception of the Business Data columns, then add the content type to your document library before adding the Business Data columns directly to the library. You can now modify the InfoPath for the content type, but then change the XML source to be that of the document library. This will allow you to add the controls from the document library onto the InfoPath form for the content type. The result is that your Document Information panel now displays Business Data columns and the columns from the content type. You can create one of these for each content type that's used within the library. Now that we've customized the Document Information panel using InfoPath 2007, you might want to totally change the way that the Business Data column works. In this case, you'll need to create a custom field type.

## 5.3 *Creating a SharePoint custom field type*

If you're trying the preceding technique using InfoPath and you find it to be too much like hard work—let's face it, some companies will have many InfoPath forms to change—you could consider creating your own field type to replace the out-of-the-box Business Data field type. The custom field type still only overcomes one issue, though. It means that you could use business data in a Content Type or Site column.

Custom field types allow you to create your own type of field. Some developers create these so that they can extend the functionality of the existing field types. For example, the Single Line of Text field offers basic field validation. You have a setting of Required or Maximum Length. You can't verify if what the user has entered fits a particular input mask, such as a telephone number, ZIP code, or email address. So you can inherit from these field types in order to generate your own added customizations.

We could use a custom field type, allowing you to look up field values from a BDC entity in a drop-down list. To create the field type:

1 Create a new VS.NET Class Library called `MyCustomFieldType`.

2 Add a reference to Windows SharePoint Services and `System.Web`. This will be required so that we can create controls.

3 Rename `Class1.cs` to be `BDCField.cs` and choose Yes to refactor your code.

4 Because this field type is going to be placed in the Global Assembly Cache, you'll need to provide a strong name, which can be done through the project properties. Also in the `AssemblyInfo.CS` file, change the dynamic version to a static version, such as 1.0.0.0.

**5** Add `using` statements as shown in listing 5.1, and press Ctrl-Shift-B to compile.

**Listing 5.1   The `using` statements for the BDCField class**

```
using Microsoft.SharePoint;
using Microsoft.SharePoint.WebControls;
```

**6** Add the following constructors shown in listing 5.2 to the class.

**Listing 5.2   The constructors for the BDCField class**

```
    private const int numberOfFields = 1;

public BDCField(SPFieldCollection fields, string fieldName)
        : base(fields, fieldName) { }

        public BDCField(SPFieldCollection fields, string typeName, string
    displayName)
        : base(fields, typeName, displayName)
    {
    }
```

**7** Compile and make note of the public key token (`sn -Tp "$(TargetPath)"`) for later use. Listing 5.3 provides the complete BDCField class, which returns the WebControl.

**Listing 5.3   The complete BDCField class**

```
using System;
using System.Collections.Generic;
using System.Text;

using Microsoft.SharePoint;
using System.Diagnostics;

namespace MyCustomFieldType
{
  public class BDCField : Microsoft.SharePoint.SPFieldMultiColumn   ◁──┐
  {
      public BDCField(SPFieldCollection fields, string fieldName)
          : base(fields, fieldName) { }

          public BDCField(SPFieldCollection fields, string typeName, string
➡  displayName)
          : base(fields, typeName, displayName)
      {
      }

      // Returns a WebControl as the field control's UI
      //public override Microsoft.SharePoint.WebControls.BaseFieldControl
➡  FieldRenderingControl
      //{
```

**Inherits from SPFieldMultiColumn to provide multiple values**

```
    //get
    //{
        //return new BDCFieldControl();
    //}
    }

    }
}
```

8 Add a TEMPLATE folder to the VS.NET project for the 12 hive content, as shown in figure 5.20.

9 Add an XML folder to the TEMPLATE folder.

10 Add a new XML file to the XML folder called fldtypes_BDCField.xml.

11 Add the XML shown in listing 5.4 to the fldtypes_BDCField.xml file. (Note the filename has to be prefixed with fldtypes.) The XML provides the properties for the field type.

**Figure 5.20  The structure of your TEMPLATE folder to mimic that of the 12 hive**

---

**Listing 5.4  The XML required for the 12\Template\XML folder**

```xml
<?xml version="1.0" encoding="utf-8" ?>
<FieldTypes>
  <FieldType>
    <Field Name="TypeName">MyCustomFieldType</Field>
    <Field Name="ParentType">MultiColumn</Field>
    <Field Name="TypeDisplayName">BDC Field</Field>
    <Field Name="UserCreatable">TRUE</Field>
    <Field Name="FieldTypeClass">
      MyCustomFieldType.BDCField,
      MyCustomFieldType,
      Version=1.0.0.0,
      Culture=neutral,
      PublicKeyToken=[TOKEN]
    </Field>
  </FieldType>
</FieldTypes>
```

12 Replace the [token] in FLDTYPES_BDCField.xml with your public key token from step 7.

13 Type the post-build event shown in listing 5.4 into the VS.NET project's Post-Build Events field. This will copy the DLL (Dynamic Link Library) into the GAC (Global Assembly Cache) including the PDB (program database) so that you can step through your code. The Global Assembly Cache resides in C:\windows\assembly and consists of DLLs that receive full permissions to do

anything. It's possible to drag a DLL into the GAC but not the PDB, meaning that the code can't be debugged. This post-build event will copy the DLL and the PDB into the GAC for you, as shown in listing 5.5.

**Listing 5.5   The post-build event so that the DLL and PDB go automatically into the GAC**

```
cd "$(ProjectDir)"                              Sets up variables for application
                                                pool and target path
"%programfiles%\Microsoft Visual Studio 8\SDK\v2.0\Bin\GacUtil.exe"
⮑/if    "$(TargetPath)" /nologo
"%systemroot%\system32\iisapp.vbs" /a "[YourAppPool]" /r

xcopy "TEMPLATE" "%CommonProgramFiles%\Microsoft Shared\web server
⮑extensions\12\TEMPLATE\" /ys        Xcopies TEMPLATE      Xcopies DLL to Global
                                     folder to 12 hive     Assembly Cache
REM xcopy "$(TargetDir)*.pdb"
    "%systemroot%\Assembly\GAC_MSIL\CustomFieldTypes.VEField\1.0.0.0__
⮑[token]\" /ys
REM MakeCab.exe /f WSP.ddf ◁    Calls MakeCab to create WSP—
                                currently commented out
```

**14** Replace [token] in the Post-Build Events field with your public key token from step 7.

**15** Replace [YourAppPool] with your application pool name.

**16** Press Ctrl-Shift-B to compile the VS.NET project and deploy the bits.

**17** Test the new field by creating an instance of it in a SharePoint list. But we're not finished yet. Figure 5.21 displays the new custom field type.

**18** Add a new class called BDCFieldValue to help represent the custom field type's value. The BDCFieldValue class will be a useful helper class so that we can manipulate the returned value. This is useful in multicolumn field types.

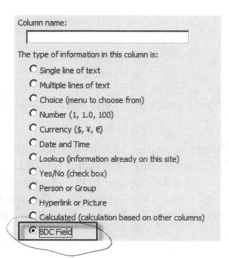

Figure 5.21   The BDC Field available when creating a new field in a SharePoint list

**19** Type the code from listing 5.6 into the `BDCFieldValue` class. This class exposes a property for each column used in our field type. In listing 5.6, we provide the property to store the field value for the one field. We can increase the number of fields if required. An example would be a field type called Address, made up of multiple fields such as Address, City, and Zip.

**Listing 5.6   The complete BDCFieldValue**

```csharp
using System;
using System.Collections.Generic;
using System.Text;

namespace MyCustomFieldType
{
   public class BDCFieldValue :
➥ Microsoft.SharePoint.SPFieldMultiColumnValue
   {
       private const int numberOfFields = 1;

       public BDCFieldValue()
          : base(numberOfFields) { }

       // New field in the SPFieldCollection
       public BDCFieldValue(string value)
          : base(value) { }

       public string ColumnValue
       {
           get { return this[0]; }
           set { this[0] = value; }
       }

   }
}
```

**20** Add a new class called `BDCFieldControl` to represent the custom field types web control.

**21** Add a reference to `Microsoft.SharePoint.Portal.dll`.

**22** Type the code from listing 5.6 into the `BDCFieldControl` class. This code uses the BDC API to access the data stored in the entity. It then iterates through each row to populate the drop-down list control. Each field type has three states: New, Read, and Edit. When the state is New or Edit, we populate the drop-down list with choices. When it's Read, we display the selected value in a label. Listing 5.7 contains the code that provides you with the BDCFieldControl class.

**Listing 5.7   The complete BDCFieldControl class**

```
using System;
using System.Collections.Generic;
using System.Text;
using System.Web.UI.WebControls;
using System.Web.UI;
using Microsoft.SharePoint.WebControls;
using Microsoft.Office.Server.ApplicationRegistry.Administration;
using Microsoft.Office.Server.ApplicationRegistry.Infrastructure;
using Microsoft.Office.Server.ApplicationRegistry.MetadataModel;
using System.Data;

using Microsoft.SharePoint;
using Microsoft.Office.Server.ApplicationRegistry.Runtime;
namespace MyCustomFieldType
{
    public class BDCFieldControl :
➥ Microsoft.SharePoint.WebControls.BaseFieldControl
    {
        // Module level variables
        protected BDCFieldValue fieldValue = null;
        Label tmpEntity = new Label();
        Label tmpColumn = new Label();

        protected DropDownList ColumnValue = null;

        protected Label lblColumnValue = null;

        protected LiteralControl br = null;
        public override object Value
        {
            // Runs when a user Saves a list item containing this
➥ field type
            // Passes the value entered by the user back to the Field class
            get
            {
                EnsureChildControls();

                fieldValue.ColumnValue = ColumnValue.SelectedValue.Trim();

                return fieldValue;
            }
            // Runs when a list item containing this field type is
➥ displayed
            // Takes the value from the Field class for presentation in the
    Control
            set
            {
                EnsureChildControls();
                fieldValue = value as BDCFieldValue;

                // set only fires in Edit mode
```

```
                    // Place the existing values into the TextBoxes so that the
user can edit them

                ColumnValue.Items.Add(fieldValue.ColumnValue);
                ColumnValue.Text = fieldValue.ColumnValue;

            }
        }
        protected override void CreateChildControls()
        {
            base.CreateChildControls();

            // If the FieldMetadata Field has been created
            if (Field != null)
            {
                switch (base.ControlMode)
                {
                    // Display mode is handled by a CAML RenderPattern
                    case SPControlMode.Display:

                        lblColumnValue = new Label();

                        break;
                    case SPControlMode.Edit:

                        ColumnValue = new DropDownList();
                        ColumnValue.Width = 200;
                        this.Controls.Add(ColumnValue);

                        br = new LiteralControl("<br />");

                        this.Controls.Add(br);

                        break;
                    case SPControlMode.New:
                        Microsoft.Office.Server.
ApplicationRegistry.MetadataModel.LobSystem adWorksLobSystem =
Microsoft.Office.Server.ApplicationRegistry.MetadataModel.
ApplicationRegistry.GetLobSystems()["NorthwindLOBSystem"];

    Microsoft.Office.Server.ApplicationRegistry.MetadataModel.LobSystemInsta
    nce
    myIns = adWorksLobSystem.GetLobSystemInstances()
["NorthwindInstance"];
                        Microsoft.Office.Server.ApplicationRegistry.
MetadataModel.Entity myEntity = myIns.GetEntities()["dbo.Products"];
                        FilterCollection fc = myEntity.GetFinderFilters();
                        IEntityInstanceEnumerator
prodEntityInstanceEnumerator = myEntity.FindFiltered(fc, myIns);
                        DataTable dtResults = null;
                        dtResults =
BuildDataTable(myEntity.GetFinderView().Fields);
                        ColumnValue = new DropDownList();

                        while (prodEntityInstanceEnumerator.MoveNext())
```

```
                    {
                        IEntityInstance IE =
    prodEntityInstanceEnumerator.Current;
                        DataRow dr = dtResults.NewRow();
                        BoundField colName = new BoundField();
                        foreach (Field f in
    myEntity.GetFinderView().Fields)
                        {
                            if (IE[f] != null)
                            {

                                dr[f.Name] = IE[f];

                            }
                        }

                        // Add the Rows to the Data Table
                        dtResults.Rows.Add(dr);

                        ColumnValue.DataTextField =
    dtResults.Columns["ProductName"].ToString();

                        ColumnValue.DataValueField =
    dtResults.Columns["ProductName"].ToString();
                        ColumnValue.DataSource = dtResults;
                        ColumnValue.DataBind();

                    }

                    ColumnValue.Width = 200;
                    this.Controls.Add(ColumnValue);
                    br = new LiteralControl("<br />");
                    this.Controls.Add(br);

                    break;
                }
            }
        }
        private static DataTable BuildDataTable(FieldCollection
    fieldCollection)
        {
            DataTable dt = new DataTable();
            // Go through each field, and get the columns, and build a
    field
            foreach (Field f in fieldCollection)
            {
                DataColumn dc = new DataColumn(f.Name,
    Type.GetType(f.TypeDescriptor.TypeName));
                dt.Columns.Add(dc);
            }
            return dt;
        }
    }
```

**23** The `Rendering` class can be used to present the data in any way, shape, or form. In listing 5.8, we just return the `BDCControl` class.

**Listing 5.8   The complete BDCFieldType class**

```
using System;
using System.Collections.Generic;
using System.Text;

using Microsoft.SharePoint;
using System.Diagnostics;

namespace MyCustomFieldType
{
  public class BDCField : Microsoft.SharePoint.SPFieldMultiColumn
  {
      public BDCField(SPFieldCollection fields, string fieldName)
        : base(fields, fieldName) { }

        public BDCField(SPFieldCollection fields, string typeName, string
  displayName)
      : base(fields, typeName, displayName)
    {
    }

    // Returns a WebControl as the field control's UI
    public override Microsoft.SharePoint.WebControls.BaseFieldControl
  FieldRenderingControl
    {
      get
      {

        return new BDCFieldControl();
      }
    }

  }
}
```

**24** You should now be able to build and test your new field type. The results should resemble the image shown in figure 5.22.

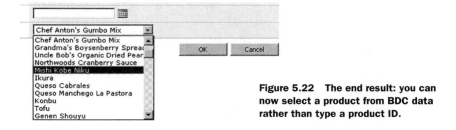

**Figure 5.22   The end result: you can now select a product from BDC data rather than type a product ID.**

## 5.4    *Summary*

In this chapter, we explored the Business Data field type, its limitations, and how to use it out of the box. We then overcame some of its limitations using InfoPath. InfoPath allowed us to customize the Document Information panel that's displayed throughout Office when setting metadata. By modifying it, we were able to provide a drop-down list so that users can select a row from the database rather than having to enter a unique ID. We then explored how you could use Visual Studio to create a new Business Data field type of your own. Whereas this is a basic example, it should give you food for thought. By creating your own custom field type, you can overcome all of the limitations of the out-of-the-box Business Data field type, and also present the data in any way, shape, or form. A good example would be to present address details for a customer in a Virtual Earth map.

The next chapter involves configuring and customizing search. Using the MOSS Search Center, we'll be able to allow our users to search line-of-business data without having to use the line-of-business application. Using the MOSS Search Center for all of your line-of-business data makes more sense than having users learn multiple applications.

# Configuring BDC search

6

**This chapter covers**

- Configuring the ADF to allow searching
- Setting up crawling
- Building a custom Search page
- Exploring the search web parts
- Manipulating the Search API

MOSS 2007 has a fantastic search facility that can not only search documents, list items, and pages stored within SharePoint, but can also search public folders, file shares, and the Business Data Catalog. This gives you a powerful search tool in SharePoint that searches your back-end databases as well. The results link to the Profile page, where all of your actions on the entity will be available.

One of the plus points of the Business Data Catalog is the ability to index and search the back-end database as well as display the data in web parts. MOSS provides additional content sources that can be indexed and searched, whereas WSS is limited to only searching the current site collection. MOSS allows the following content sources: external websites, SharePoint websites, files, Exchange, and business data. In addition to those, you can create or use third-party protocol handlers to allow more content sources. An example of this is Lotus Notes. A Lotus Notes protocol handler was available in SharePoint 2003, which allowed SharePoint to search Lotus Notes databases. Although the Lotus Notes protocol handler is still available for MOSS, the Business Data Catalog has superseded it, because BDC can also connect to Notes databases via ODBC.

Searching business data via MOSS is invaluable to businesses that want to search across all of their islands of data. As we've said before, within most businesses, you'll find islands or little pockets of data all over the network. MOSS can index and search them all—and the fact that you can also search products such as CRM or Siebel makes this an extremely powerful tool.

Within this chapter, we're going to concentrate on the Business Data Catalog search, how to configure it, and then how to customize the Search Results pages in the Search Center. First, as a brief reminder, let's explore how to configure the application definition file for search. (This was covered in detail in chapter 2.)

Configuring search for the BDC takes many steps, and therefore we've summarized them in figure 6.1.

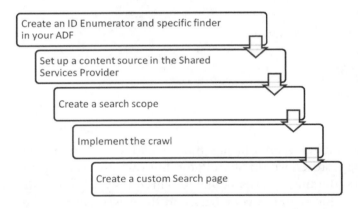

**Figure 6.1   The steps to configuring the BDC search and indexing**

Once you've followed this process, you'll be able to successfully search your business data. There's still a lot more you could do by customizing the Search Results pages and manipulating the Search API.

## 6.1    *Configuring the ADF to allow searching*

The first bridge to cross with BDC search is to configure the application definition file to allow the indexing of data. This is done by creating an `IDEnumerator` and a specific finder method. You'll probably recall from chapter 2 that the specific finder method has the responsibility of returning all columns for a particular row, and that the row is identified using a unique identifier. This is often a primary key or other unique column. The IDEnumerator only returns the Identifier column. The ID Enumerator gets called first; every ID value is returned for the Identifier. This is then followed by the specific finder, which returns all of the other columns for each row that was identified.

Each entity can only have one IDEnumerator. If you don't create an IDEnumerator, you won't be able to search the business data for that particular entity.

**NOTE**     If you don't want to crawl an entity, you can just omit the IDEnumerator method.

Each IDEnumerator will only return Identifier columns. If you return other columns, these will be ignored by the Business Data Catalog. Examples of an ID Enumerator and specific finder can be seen in listing 6.1.

**Listing 6.1    Configuring an ID Enumerator in the application definition file**

```
<Method Name="dbo.[Customers]IDEnumerator">          ⤺   IDEnumerator in
        <Properties>                                       application definition file
            <Property Name="RdbCommandType"
➡Type="System.String">Text</Property>

            <Property Name="RdbCommandText" Type="System.String">
➡Select [CustomerID] from dbo.[Customers]</Property>
        </Properties>                                  Input parameter
        <Parameters>                                   required for crawling
            <Parameter Direction="Return" Name="dbo.[Customers]IDs">  ⤺
              <TypeDescriptor TypeName="System.Data.IDataReader,
➡System.Data, Version=2.0.3600.0, Culture=neutral,
➡PublicKeyToken=b77a5c561934e089" IsCollection="true"
➡Name="dbo.[Customers]IDs">
                <TypeDescriptors>
                  <TypeDescriptor TypeName="System.Data.IDataRecord,
➡System.Data, Version=2.0.3600.0, Culture=neutral,
➡PublicKeyToken=b77a5c561934e089" Name="dbo.[Customers]">
                    <TypeDescriptors>
                      <TypeDescriptor TypeName="System.String"
➡Name="CustomerID" IdentifierName="[CustomerID]" />
                    </TypeDescriptors>
                  </TypeDescriptor>
                </TypeDescriptors>
              </TypeDescriptor>
            </Parameter>
        </Parameters>
        <MethodInstances>
          <MethodInstance Name="dbo.[Customers]EnumeratorInstance"
```

```
⇒Type="IdEnumerator" ReturnParameterName=" dbo.[Customers]IDs" />
        </MethodInstances>
      </Method>
```

The specific finder method is used by the Search and Index service, as well as providing other functionality, such as selecting a specific record in the Business Data columns within a list or a library. It's used to display a single row from an entity. An example of how to create a specific finder in your application definition file is shown in listing 6.2.

**Listing 6.2   Configuring the specific finder method (each column strongly typed)**

```
<Method Name="Production.[Product]SpecificFinder">
  <Properties>
    <Property Name="RdbCommandText" Type="System.String">
⇒Select [ProductID],[Name],[ProductNumber],[MakeFlag],
⇒[FinishedGoodsFlag],[Color],[SafetyStockLevel],[ReorderPoint],
⇒[StandardCost],[ListPrice],[Size],[SizeUnitMeasureCode],
⇒[WeightUnitMeasureCode],[Weight],[DaysToManufacture],[ProductLine],
⇒[Class],[Style],[ProductSubcategoryID],[ProductModelID],[SellStartDate],
⇒[SellEndDate],[DiscontinuedDate],[rowguid],[ModifiedDate]
⇒From Production.[Product] Where ([ProductID]=@ProductID)
    </Property>
<Property Name="RdbCommandType" Type="System.Data.CommandType">Text</
    Property>
  </Properties>
        <Parameters>
          <Parameter Direction="In" Name="@ProductID">
            <TypeDescriptor TypeName="System.Int32"
⇒Name="[ProductID]" IdentifierName="[ProductID]" />
          </Parameter>
          <Parameter Direction="Return" Name="Production.[Product]">
          <TypeDescriptor TypeName="System.Data.IDataReader, System.Data,
⇒Version=2.0.3600.0, Culture=neutral, PublicKeyToken=b77a5c561934e089"
⇒IsCollection="true" Name="Production.[Product]DataReader">
              <TypeDescriptors>
                <TypeDescriptor TypeName="System.Data.IDataRecord,
⇒System.Data, Version=2.0.3600.0, Culture=neutral,
⇒PublicKeyToken=b77a5c561934e089" Name="Production.[Product]DataRecord">
                  <TypeDescriptors>
                    <TypeDescriptor TypeName="System.Int32"
⇒Name="ProductID" IdentifierName="[ProductID]" />
                      <TypeDescriptor TypeName="System.String" Name="Name"
⇒/>
                      <TypeDescriptor TypeName="System.String"
⇒Name="ProductNumber" />
                      <TypeDescriptor TypeName="System.Boolean"
⇒Name="MakeFlag" />
                      <TypeDescriptor TypeName="System.Boolean"
```

```
⇒Name="FinishedGoodsFlag" />
                        <TypeDescriptor TypeName="System.String"
⇒Name="Color" />
                        <TypeDescriptor TypeName="System.Int16"
⇒  Name="SafetyStockLevel" />
\\ Truncated for the purpose of the book.
                    </TypeDescriptors>
                  </TypeDescriptor>
                </TypeDescriptors>
              </TypeDescriptor>
            </Parameter>
          </Parameters>
          <MethodInstances>
            <MethodInstance Name="Production.[Product]SpecificFinder"
⇒Type="SpecificFinder" ReturnParameterName="Production.[Product]"
⇒  ReturnTypeDescriptorName="Production.[Product]DataReader"
⇒ReturnTypeDescriptorLevel="0" />
          </MethodInstances>
        </Method>
```

If you want to perform an incremental crawl on the data (index the data on items that have changed rather than all items) as well as a full crawl, you'll need to record the last modified date/time stamp. You can do this by returning the date/time in the Identifier and then setting the __BdcLastModifiedTimestamp property in the IDEnumerator method.

Once you've created and imported your application definition file, you have some configuring to do in the Shared Services Provider. We'll need to create a content source and a search scope. (The content source explains to the search which BDC entity we need to include in the results, and the search scope allows you to minimize the results shown to that particular entity.) Optionally, you can customize the Search page. We'll explore this toward the end of the chapter. Now that we understand the changes we need to make to the application definition file, let's look at the changes we'd need to make using SharePoint Central Administration to set up searching.

## 6.2 Setting up crawling

Crawling is the process in which items are discovered by iterating through them and adding them to the search index. To set up crawling, we need to create two things in the Search Settings section of the Shared Services Provider Administration page. The first item to create is a *content source*. The content source is a pointer to the data that you want returned from the search. For example, you could create a content source that points to a file share on the network, or a particular website on the internet. In this case, we'll create a content source to point at an entity.

The second item to create is a *search scope*. The search scope allows you to restrict the items returned from the search index to a specific content source rather than returning items from all sources. For example, if I perform a search on the word "Bike," and I only want to return items from the Products entity, and not the Customer entity or even a website, I can specify that I only want items returned from the Products content source for that given scope.

First, let's explore the steps involved in creating a content source:

1  Open SharePoint Central 3.0 Administration by clicking Start, Administrative Tools, SharePoint 3.0 Central Administration.

2  Click the Shared Services Provider that will appear on the Quick Launch menu on the left side.

3  In the Search section, click Search Settings.

4  Click Content Sources & Crawl Schedules.

5  Click New Content Source.

6  Type a name for your content source in the Name text box—for example, Products.

7  Select the Business Data radio button from the Content Source Type field.

8  Select the LOB System Instance from the Applications section.

9  Optionally set up a crawl schedule.

10  Check the Start Full Crawl Now check box.

The completed Add Content Source page is shown in figure 6.2.

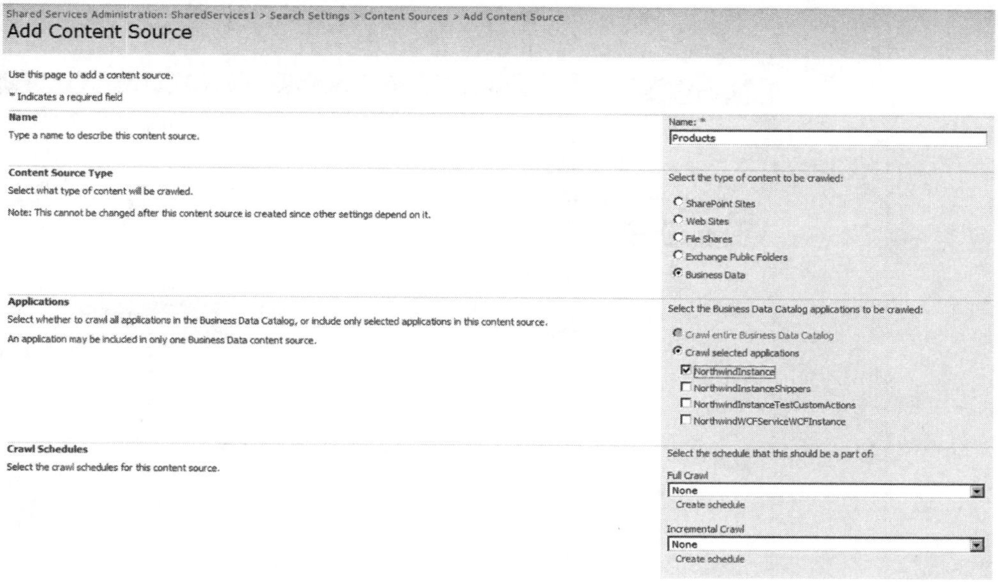

**Figure 6.2  The completed Add Content Source page**

Once you've clicked OK, the crawl should begin to take place. The crawl has been known to generate errors at this point. Usually it's because the default SharePoint search account doesn't have the required permissions in the content database. You can set the search account via the Office SharePoint Server Search service properties in the Services snap-in on your server, as shown in figure 6.3.

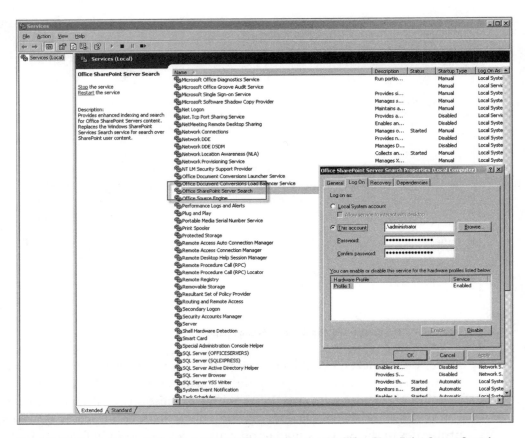

**Figure 6.3    The Services window and the Log On properties for the Office SharePoint Server Search**

To see whether your crawl failed, on the Edit Control block of the content source, choose View Crawl Log. This will tell you whether the crawl was successful, as shown in figure 6.4.

Once you've created the content source, you can move on to creating the search scope, which is useful if you want to search your entity independently of the other search scopes. The search scope is configured by following these steps:

1  On the Search Settings page, within the Scopes section, click View Scopes.

2  Click New Scope.

3  Type a title and description of your scope—for example, `Products` and `Products Desc`.

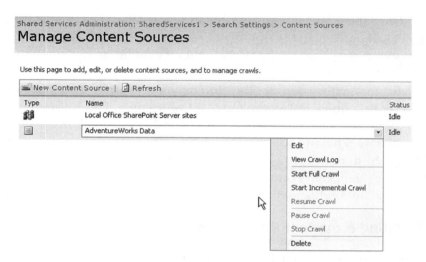

**Figure 6.4   The Edit Control block of the Content Sources page**

4   Click the radio button to specify the name of your new Search page.

5   Type a name such as `products.aspx`.

6   Navigate back to the Search Settings page.

7   Click Start Update Now to retrieve the items.

8   Create a rule from the Search page to populate the search scope. You can see the Add Scope Rule page in figure 6.5.

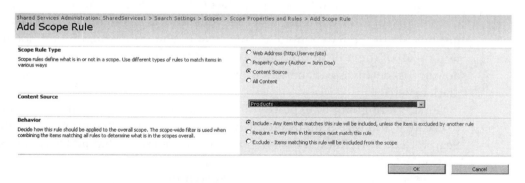

**Figure 6.5   The Add Scope Rule, which sets the rule for the content source**

Once the scope has finished updating, you should see that it has some items in it. This should equal the number of rows in the entity. You can now test the results by performing a search in MOSS, although you'll see the results on the All Sites tab in the Search Center.

In the next section, we'll create our own Search Results page in the Search Center that only displays the results of your entity. This is useful, as you could set up a tab to search all customers, and another tab to show all suppliers. Or you could have a tab for both, so that all the data from an application such as CRM is displayed under the same tab. The important thing is to separate your BDC data from regular SharePoint data and the other content sources. The next stage is optional but useful, and that's to build your own custom Search page.

## 6.3  *Building a custom Search Results page*

MOSS provides Search Results pages by default to show the results of People Search or All Items search. It also provides a template so that you can create your own pages for displaying search results. The Search Results pages are created from a page layout called `SearchResults.aspx`, which lives in the Master Pages & Page Layouts gallery within your site collection. Every page layout in MOSS obtains its field controls from a content type. The content type used for the out-of-the-box Search Results page is Welcome page. It's possible to create your own content type and page layout if you want to heavily customize the structure of the Search Results page. Content types can be created using features, code, or the user interface. Content types, page layouts, and features all deserve an entire chapter on their own, but because this would distract from the focus on BDC, we'll just talk about them in general in this section. You can, however, find documentation on all of them by downloading the SDK for MOSS (http://www.microsoft.com/downloads/details.aspx?FamilyID=6D94E307-67D9-41AC-B2D6-0074D6286FA9&displaylang=en).

First, we're going to explore the out-of-the-box Search Results page, and how to create it and wire it up by modifying the web parts and creating tabs within the Search Center. We'll then explore each of the web parts that make up the page in section 6.4.

The reason for creating a separate Search Results page is to isolate our results from our LOB system to just one tab. This allows us to focus on results from the back-end database rather than mixing them up with results from documents, lists, and other scopes in MOSS. To create the custom Search page, follow these steps:

1 Navigate to the Search Center in MOSS by clicking on the Search tab.

2 Choose Site Actions, Create Page.

3 Type the title of the page such as `Products`, along with a description.

4 Type the URL, which should be the same as the URL that you created when setting up your search scope. For our example, we're using `products.aspx`.

5 Select the (Welcome Page) Search Results Page page layout, and then click Create.

Once the page is created, we simply need to set some properties in the web parts. On the new Search page, you'll find a web part called Search Core Results. Click the Edit drop-down arrow and choose Modify Shared Web Part. Expand the Miscellaneous section, and type the name of the scope that you created. In our case, the name of the scope was `Products`. You can test your page by navigating to it and performing a search. The results should look like figure 6.6.

**Figure 6.6   The custom Search page with the results displayed from the Products entity in BDC**

We now have a working Search Results page for our LOB system. Let's now polish this off by adding a tab next to the All Sites and People tabs in the Search Center. This is easy. First, click the All Sites tab, choose Site Actions, Edit Page, and then click the Add New Tab link. The only items that you need to provide here are the tab name, page URL, and a tool tip. The tab name in our case is `Products`, and our page is `products.aspx`. You need to repeat this process for each of the existing Search Results pages in your Search Center. Figure 6.7 displays the new Products tab directing the results to the `Products.aspx` page.

Now that we have a fully working page, let's explore the web parts that make up this page and how we can go about tweaking them to suit our requirements.

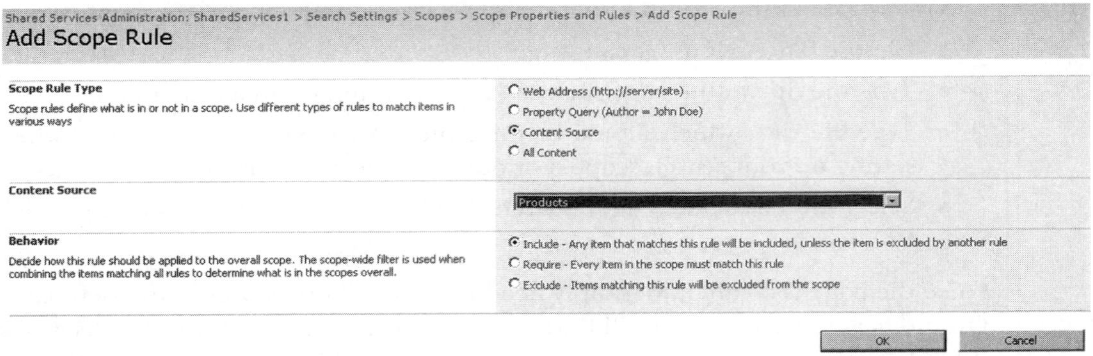
Shared Services Administration: SharedServices1 > Search Settings > Scopes > Scope Properties and Rules > Add Scope Rule
Add Scope Rule
Scope Rule Type
Scope rules define what is in or not in a scope. Use different types of rules to match items in various ways
Web Address (http://server/site)
Property Query (Author = John Doe)
Content Source
All Content
Content Source
Products
Behavior
Decide how this rule should be applied to the overall scope. The scope-wide filter is used when combining the items matching all rules to determine what is in the scopes overall.
Include - Any item that matches this rule will be included, unless the item is excluded by another rule
Require - Every item in the scope must match this rule
Exclude - Items matching this rule will be excluded from the scope
OK
Cancel

**Figure 6.7 The new Products tab in the Search Center**

## 6.4 Exploring the search web parts

There are nine web parts that make up the Search Results page. We've already set one property in the Search Core Results Web Part to make our search operable. In this section, we'll explore all of the search web parts and some of the useful property settings that are available. We'll also see how you can customize some web parts to display results in a different way.

### 6.4.1 Search Box Web Part

The Search Box Web Part allows the user to type in a keyword to perform the search. Out of the box, the web part simply provides us with a Query text box and a Search button. But we can display other controls such as a Scopes drop-down list, allowing the user to change the scope during the search. The Scopes Drop-down Mode property has several choices. The default is to not display the Scopes drop-down. You can also show the Scopes drop-down as default to the `s` parameter in the URL. This means that you can pass the default scope from a parameter in your URL when you link to the Search page. The other options are whether you want to include contextual scopes, either with or without a default.

You can also customize the Query box. You can include a label for the control to help users understand the types of values that they can enter. You can also set a default value, which is useful to display an example of a valid search, and also change other properties of the Query box, such as the width.

Inside the Miscellaneous property section, we need to set the Target Search Results page URL so that the results of the search are shown on the current page. In this example, we've set it to `Products.aspx`.

### 6.4.2  Search Summary Web Part

The Search Summary Web Part displays the "Did you mean" text. For example, if we performed a search such as "Read Bike," it would suggest "Red Bike." One other relevant property is the Cross-Web Part Query ID. This is useful if you place these search web parts on another site, such as a team site. You may want a default Search Results page to display, in which case you'd need to set a unique Cross-Web Part Query ID so that all the web parts pass the same queries, rather than receiving the query from the user.

### 6.4.3  Search Action Links Web Part

The Search Action Links Web Part provides the Search Results page with links such as Alert Me, RSS, and View by Modified Date. Using the properties, you can display or hide the links based on your requirements.

### 6.4.4  Search Best Bets Web Part

The Search Best Bets Web Part is a powerful feature. In some ways, it's similar to that of a pay-per-click ad on Google or MSN Search. You can identify keywords that your business searches on regularly, and always make sure that a result is displayed in the Search Best Bets Web Part. To create a best-bet keyword for BDC, go to the Search Keywords option in the Site Collection Settings column on the Site Settings page. Add a new keyword and direct it at the Profile page containing the keyword that you want to display. Figure 6.8 shows a best bet in the Search Best Bets Web Part for the keyword *freewheel*.

**Figure 6.8   A keyword best bet being displayed in the Search Best Bets Web Part**

The Search Best Bets Web Part can also be configured. You can choose how many best bets to display, turn on or off the best bets title keyword, and also configure the XSL if you want to completely change the look and feel of this web part. You could turn off the best bets if you prefer your users to use the mainstream results.

### 6.4.5  Search Statistics Web Part

This web part simply displays the number of results, and the amount of time it took to display the results. Both of these can be turned on or off depending on whether you want to display them.

### 6.4.6  Search Paging Web Part

The Search Paging Web Part is a control that allows users to navigate through the pages of results. This can be customized so that different numbers of pages are displayed in front of the Next and Previous arrows. You may also display a custom image in place of the > or < symbols.

### 6.4.7  Search High Confidence Results Web Part

The Search High Confidence Results Web Part can be configured to show the results from keyword best bets. By default, it doesn't do this. The only real place where this web part is useful is on a People search, because it displays information from a person's profile.

### 6.4.8  Search Core Results Web Part

The Search Core Results Web Part is the web part that actually displays the results from your search. It has many properties that allow you to change the way the results are displayed. Within the Results Display/Views section, you can choose how many results per page you want to display, choose how many sentences to display in the summary, and set the Highest Result page, which defaults to 1,000 results. The Results Query Options section allows you to remove duplicates, enable search stemming, and permit noise words. The most interesting property is Selected Columns, which allows you to change the XSL in order to pick which columns you want to display in the web part. In the next section, we'll explore the Data View properties of the web part and how we can change the results.

## 6.5  Modifying the core Search Results page

Search pages are based on a page layout, which means that a page instance can't be modified within SharePoint Designer. This is frustrating when you want to use SharePoint Designer to modify how your search results are being displayed. But you can still get your search results into SharePoint Designer so that you can modify the way they're displayed. This involves a very effective workaround. Those of you who are fully versed in XSL will find that you can simply modify the XSL while in the browser. For the rest of you, SharePoint Designer is certainly your friend here. The first thing to do is get some search results so that you can see some useful sample data to start modifying. To do that, navigate to the Search Center, select the tab that you created earlier (in our case, the Products tab), and perform a search. I performed a search on the word "bike," which gave me plenty of results, as shown in figure 6.9.

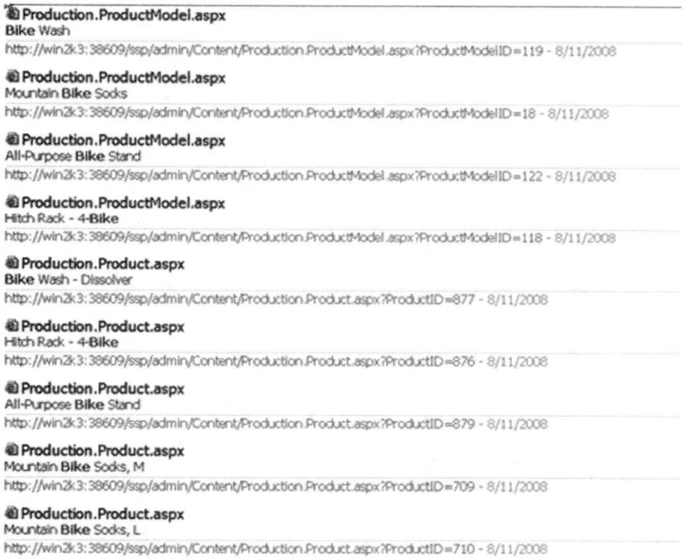

**Figure 6.9   Search results using the out-of-the-box XSL**

We need to get our hands on the XML for those results. Remember, this is purely so that we have some sample data in SharePoint Designer. To get to the XML, replace the out-of-the-box XSL for the Core Results Web Part with the XSL in listing 6.3.

**Listing 6.3   Code for a basic view of the Core Results Web Part**

```
<?xml version="1.0" encoding="UTF-8"?>
<xsl:stylesheet version="1.0" xmlns:xsl="http://www.w3.org/1999/XSL/
    Transform">
<xsl:output method="xml" version="1.0" encoding="UTF-8" indent="yes"/>
<xsl:template match="/">
<xmp><xsl:copy-of select="*"/></xmp>
</xsl:template>
</xsl:stylesheet>
```

Once you've done this, your Search Core Results Web Part will look like figure 6.10.

Results by Relevance | View by Modified Date | Alert Me! | RSS

Results **1-10** of 15. Your search took 3.35 seconds.                                                    1 2 Next>

```
<All_Results>
  <Result>
    <id>1</id>
    <workid>1159</workid>
    <rank>682</rank>
    <title>Production.ProductModel.aspx</title>
    <author></author>
    <size>0</size>
    <url>http://win2k3:38609/ssp/admin/Content/Production.ProductModel.aspx?ProductModelID=119</url>
    <urlEncoded>http%3A%2F%2Fwin2k3%3A38609%2Fssp%2Fadmin%2FContent%2FProduction%2EProductModel%2Easpx%3FProductModelID%3D119</urlEncoded>
    <description></description>
    <write>8/11/2008</write>
    <sitename>71d66c55-f373-4f36-8db8-853f1288d69f</sitename>
    <collapsingstatus>0</collapsingstatus>
    <hithighlightedsummary>
      <c0>Bike</c0> Wash </hithighlightedsummary>
    <hithighlightedproperties>
      <HHTitle>Production.ProductModel.aspx</HHTitle>
      <HHUrl>http://win2k3:38609/ssp/admin/Content/Production.ProductModel.aspx?ProductModelID=119</HHUrl>
    </hithighlightedproperties>
    <contentclass></contentclass>
    <isdocument>0</isdocument>
    <picturethumbnailurl></picturethumbnailurl>
    <imageurl imageurldescription="File with extension: aspx">/_layouts/images/html16.gif</imageurl>
  </Result>
  <Result>
    <id>2</id>
    <workid>1134</workid>
    <rank>682</rank>
    <title>Production.ProductModel.aspx</title>
    <author></author>
    <size>0</size>
    <url>http://win2k3:38609/ssp/admin/Content/Production.ProductModel.aspx?ProductModelID=18</url>
    <urlEncoded>http%3A%2F%2Fwin2k3%3A38609%2Fssp%2Fadmin%2FContent%2FProduction%2EProductModel%2Easpx%3FProductModelID%3D18</urlEncoded>
    <description></description>
    <write>8/11/2008</write>
    <sitename>71d66c55-f373-4f36-8db8-853f1288d69f</sitename>
    <collapsingstatus>0</collapsingstatus>
    <hithighlightedsummary>Mountain <c0>Bike</c0> Socks </hithighlightedsummary>
    <hithighlightedproperties>
      <HHTitle>Production.ProductModel.aspx</HHTitle>
      <HHUrl>http://win2k3:38609/ssp/admin/Content/Production.ProductModel.aspx?ProductModelID=18</HHUrl>
    </hithighlightedproperties>
    <contentclass></contentclass>
    <isdocument>0</isdocument>
    <picturethumbnailurl></picturethumbnailurl>
    <imageurl imageurldescription="File with extension: aspx">/_layouts/images/html16.gif</imageurl>
  </Result>
  <Result>
    <id>3</id>
    <workid>1082</workid>
    <rank>681</rank>
    <title>Production.ProductModel.aspx</title>
    <author></author>
```

**Figure 6.10   The Search Core Results Web Part—raw XML**

Now that we have the results in such a format, we can highlight them, copying and pasting them into a TXT file. The next thing we can do is create a new team site in SharePoint; it doesn't matter what you call it, as this is a temporary site. Once the team site is created, edit the site in SharePoint Designer, as shown in figure 6.11. Insert a Data View Web Part into the left Web Part zone and expand the XML Files section, browsing to the TXT file that you just created. You'll notice that you have a handful of columns that can be modified. You can also drag and drop additional columns into the table using the Data Source window on the right side of your screen.

**NOTE**    Of course, you don't need to create a table at all; it would be best practice to use divs.

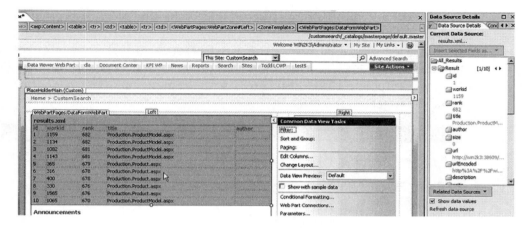

**Figure 6.11** Using SharePoint Designer, you can now modify the Data Form Web Part to display your results exactly as you want them to appear.

As you become familiar with the Data Form Web Part, you'll find that there are many things you can do, such as create hyperlink values, sort and group, apply conditional formatting, and so on. For everything you do using the Designer client, it creates XSL for you behind the scenes. That XSL can then be copied and placed into your Search Core Results Web Part.

Once you've finished editing, save the changes to the site using SharePoint Designer. You can now edit the Data Form Web Part in the browser on your site, click the XSL Editor button, and then copy and paste the contents into your Search Core Results Web Part.

In addition to the Search pages being fully customizable, you can also use the search capabilities of MOSS and the BDC outside of SharePoint. You can therefore use MOSS as a search engine, but expose the results to another .NET application. We'll explore this in the following section.

## 6.6 The Search API

SharePoint's API is useful to .NET programmers, because almost the entire API is available for you to use in your own applications, including the Search API. Maybe you simply want to tweak the search capabilities—for example, allow wildcard searches and use operators such as >, <, Contains, and Like. Alternatively, you may actually want to view the results in your own custom web part or expose them outside of SharePoint. The Search API isn't specific to BDC, but it's still useful to know that you have the option of using search results in other applications.

There are two query classes that you can use: Microsoft.Office.Server.Search.Query.FullTextSqlQuery and Microsoft.Office.Server.Search.Query.KeywordQuery. The FullTextSQLQuery class is more powerful, but the KeywordQuery class is simpler to use. We'll be concentrating on the FullTextSqlQuery class. Listing 6.4 is an example of some code that would allow you to search the BDC.

**Listing 6.4    A sample of the Search API code**

```
ResultTableCollection results = null;
        using (FullTextSqlQuery query = new
➥FullTextSqlQuery(ServerContext.Current))
        {
              query.StartRow = 0;
              query.RowLimit = 10;
              query.HighlightedSentenceCount = 3;
              query.EnableStemming = true;
              query.TrimDuplicates = true;
              query.Culture = CultureInfo.GetCultureInfo(1033);
              query.KeywordInclusion = KeywordInclusion.AnyKeyword;
              query.SiteContext = new Uri("http://win2k3");
                  // query.AuthenticationType =
➥QueryAuthenticationType.NtAuthenticatedQuery;
              query.QueryText = "SELECT Title FROM Scope() WHERE
➥FREETEXT(defaultproperties, 'Bike') ORDER BY Title";
              results = query.Execute();
              Console.Write(results.Count.ToString());
              Console.ReadLine();
        }
```

As you can see, the properties of the query object allow you to change the results that you receive, by specifying the RowLimit, stemming, and HighlightedSentenceCount. It's also worth noting that you need to ensure that your authentication type is handled. If you're using Integrated Windows Authentication, you can use NtAuthenticatedQuery. If you're using Basic Authentication, you can use PluggableAuthenticatedQuery.

The defaultproperties keyword references the default set of properties to include in the ranking algorithm. This is also recommended for optimal ranking of results.

Something else that should be at the forefront of your mind is security within the search results.

### 6.6.1 *Security trimming the search results*

Within the security chapter of this book, we spoke about security trimming on your BDC data using the BDC permissions, as well as the permissions on the LOB system. Enterprise Search also takes advantage of these permissions so that users won't see results from an entity that they don't have permission to see.

An access check is performed by the query engine against the user's identity and removes any items that the user shouldn't see. One concern is that, in many applications, security trimming is done in the front-end application and not the back end, or that you have unusual security requirements such as using search results from an HR database that's only available between 9 a.m. and 5 p.m. Take Microsoft CRM for example: a sales person can view just the customers that her account manages, not the customers that her colleagues manage. This occurs even though all of the customers live within the same table in the relational database.

Out-of-the-box search would allow all customers to display within the search results, as Enterprise Search is unaware of the Microsoft CRM front end. But you can implement your own custom security trimming by creating a class that implements the `ISecurityTrimmer` interface from the `Microsoft.Office.Server.Search.Query` namespace. There are two methods that have to be used: `Check-Access` and `Initialize`. Within the `Initialize` method of this class are two parameters—`NameValueCollection` and `SearchContext`—that represent the SSP service. These values are specified when you register the search trimmer, and are called when the worker process for the web application is fired. Within the class, a `CheckAccess` method is called at least once for each search query, but can be called many times. Using the `CheckAccess` method, you can obtain the currently logged-on user and determine whether that user should be allowed to execute the `CrawlURL`.

The `CheckAccess` method then returns true or false using a bit array depending on whether the logged-on user is allowed to execute the `CrawlURL`. There are two parameters for this method: `System.Collections.Generic.IList`, which contains the URL for each content item from the search results that matches the crawl rule, and `System.Collections.Generic.IDictionary`, which can be used to track check access calls multiple times for the same search query.

A third method is available but optional, called `CheckLimit`. This is good for performance reasons, as you can limit the number of crawl URLs that are checked.

The DLL that you've created will have to be deployed to the Global Assembly Cache, and is then registered using a `STSADM` command as shown:

```
stsadm -o registersecuritytrimmer -ssp SharedServices1 -id 1 -typeName
➡"NameSpace, Type, Version=1.0.0.0, Culture=neutral,
➡PublicKeyToken=<token>" -rulepath http://*
```

**NOTE**     The BDC doesn't support indexing unstructured data, such as files in a document management system.

## 6.7   *Summary*

In this chapter, we've explained how to set up BDC search using the application definition file and the IDEnumerator. We've also explored the settings in the Shared Services Administration page that we'd need to set in order to create a content source and a scope. Later, once we proved that we could see results, we looked at how to create your own Search page, and explained the purpose of each search-related web part and how we could use XSL or SharePoint Designer to customize the results. Finally, we explored exposing the search using the Search API.

In the next chapter, we're going to explore how the BDC can be used to import user profiles from data sources such as human resources databases, and use the information to populate your SharePoint user profile. This will allow you to use MOSS services such as audience targeting within SharePoint, using HR user-profile information as the criteria when populating your audiences.

# MOSS user profiles 7

**This chapter covers**

- Describing MOSS user profiles
- Using audience targeting
- Extending the MOSS user profile with BDC
- Working with audiences

Every user in SharePoint has a user profile, which includes not only a name and password but also information such as a photograph, skills, the person she reports to, and so on. The SharePoint administrator can set which of these properties should be used within SharePoint and can set each property to be read-only, or to allow users to edit properties. For example, the user's cell phone number would be a property that the user should be able to edit, whereas the Reports To property may be imported from another application or the Active Directory.

This profile information can be searched upon using the MOSS Search Center. You can search for a user by name or by any of the fields. For example, we could search for "Brett Lonsdale" if we knew that person's name, or search for "Turn eyelids inside out" as a skill, which may bring up my name also. The results are shown as regular search results. The hyperlink for each search result points to the user's My Site. This is useful for finding someone in your organization who has a particular skill or reports to a particular person.

The profile information can also be used for audience targeting (targeting list items, links, and web parts to users who appear within a particular audience). Many things in MOSS can be audience targeted, including web parts, list items, and content pages. Many people confuse audience targeting with security permissions. The whole purpose of audience targeting is to not overwhelm users with information, but to provide them content that will be of interest. For example, somebody working out of the New York office probably wouldn't care about sticky toffee pudding being served as a daily special in the London office canteen. So the location property in your user profile can be put to good use here. Whenever the canteen wants to use an announcements list to advertise their daily specials, they can target just the London office. But if a user from the London office emailed a user from the New York office a link to the list item, both users would be able to view the item. The difference is that the daily specials shouldn't be displayed when rolled up to a Content Query Web Part if audience targeting is in place.

Audience targeting and the people search are useful tools in an enterprise organization and, if planned properly, can be very powerful. So where does BDC come into all of this? You may have been thinking that you already store user profile information in enough places. You may have social security numbers, salary information, and bank account information already stored in an accounts system. You may have home address, telephone, and child information stored in the HR system, and then of course you may have some user profile information stored in Active Directory. The Business Data Catalog can pull this information in from these databases for you, and map it to fields in the user's profile. This means you don't have to replicate all of the information from these separate systems to Active Directory. All you have to do is create mappings between the properties in MOSS and the field in the BDC data source. If the fields in a relational database are stored in a "many" side of a relationship, we can map them to a multivalue property in the user profile. For example, the Person and Person Skills fields could still be mapped to SharePoint.

Within this chapter, we'll explore how user profile information is put to good use in audience targeting, how a user can configure his user profile information using My Site, and how the administrator can configure properties that she wants her users to use. We'll then explore how to take information from existing user profiles and import it on a scheduled basis into SharePoint, making your search and audience targeting more powerful.

## 7.1  *Exploring SharePoint user profiles*

It's possible for every user in SharePoint to have a user profile. This profile can be created in one of two ways: by the user creating a My Site, or by the administrator creating a profile for the user. Either way, those profiles are useful, as we've already described.

A user can create a My Site simply by clicking the My Site link in the top right corner of any SharePoint page (MOSS only). As soon as the user's My Site is created, he'll see a web part displayed with a number of actions that he should perform. The top action is to create a profile, as you can see in figure 7.1.

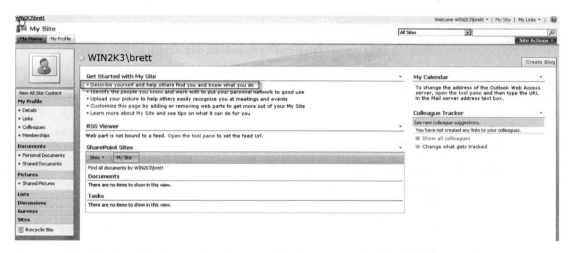

**Figure 7.1   A newly created My Site displaying the Getting Started Web Part. The first action is to set up your profile.**

Once your profile has been configured, you'll also be able to identify people whom you know. (These people must also have a profile set up in SharePoint.) When you complete the properties such as your skills, your recent projects, your phone numbers, and so on, you'll have the opportunity to specify who's allowed to read the property. For example, you may not want everyone knowing your home phone number, but you might not mind your manager having it. So you can specify who can read that property: everyone, your colleagues, members of a particular work group, and so forth. In figure 7.2, you can see a screen dump of these properties being configured.

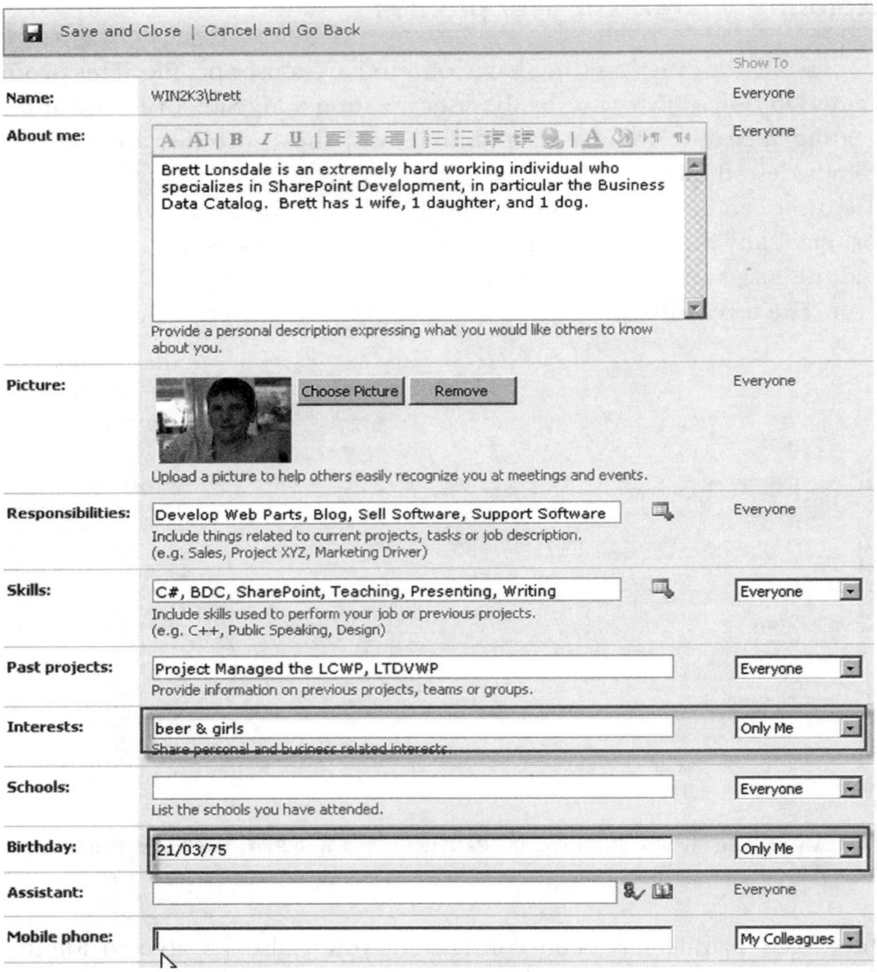

**Figure 7.2  How to set your properties from within your My Site. Most properties can be configured to allow different people to see them. For example, Mobile phone is set to My Colleagues, and I'd better keep my interests to myself!**

### 7.1.1  Identifying colleagues

To identify your colleagues, perform the second action in the web part displayed on your My Site home page. Once you've added a colleague, you can put that colleague into a workgroup. You can create as many workgroups as you like, as shown in figure 7.3.

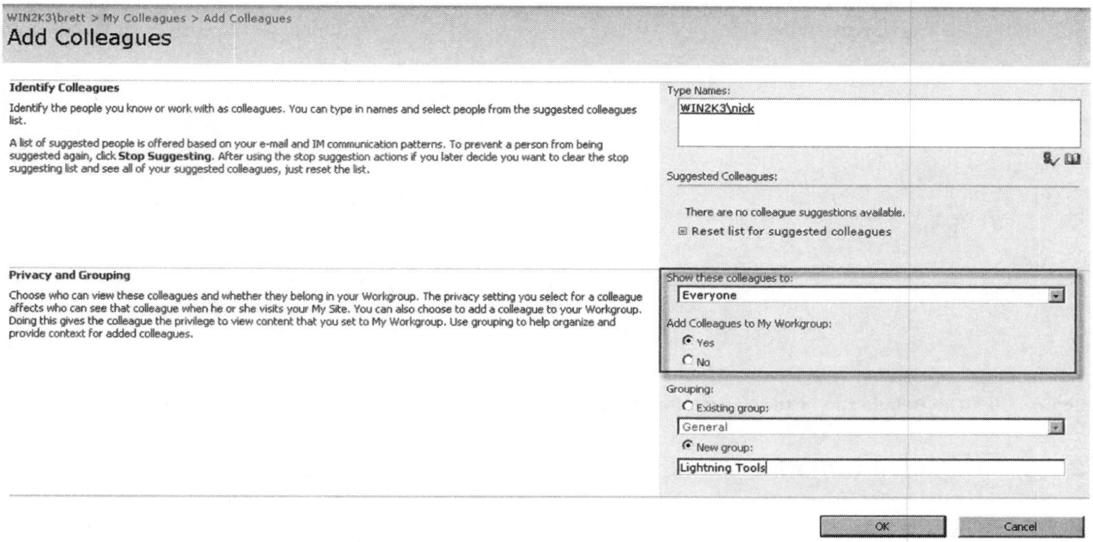

**Figure 7.3   The Add Colleagues page in My Site, and how it can be used to assemble your colleagues in a work group**

### 7.1.2   *Searching user profiles*

Once your users have created a profile, you can use that information within searches and audience targeting. Each property in your profile can be configured by the administrator, and one of the settings is whether the property is indexed. Properties such as Skills, First Name, and Last Name are configured for indexing, meaning that they can be searched from the People tab in the Search Center. Figure 7.4 illustrates the People tab with the search options expanded.

The search results will then be displayed, and you'll be able to see some of the profile data on the Search Results page, including the photo of the user. The hyperlink will allow you to see a limited view of the user's My Site. Searching for a particular skill or responsibility within an organization can be extremely useful, and could also save your company money if you didn't know you had certain skills in-house.

Shared Services Administration: SharedServices1 > Manage Audiences > View Audiences > Audience Rule

**Add Audience Rule: Developers**

Use this page to add a rule for this audience. Learn more about audience rules.

**Operand**

Select **User** to create a rule based on a Windows security group, distribution list, or organizational hierarchy.

Select **Property** and select a property name to create a rule based on a user profile property.

Select one of the following: *
- ○ User
- ⊙ Property
- [Skills                              ▼]

**Operator**

Select an operator for this rule. The list of available operators will change depending on the operand you selected in the previous section.

Operator: *
[=                              ▼]

**Value**

Specify a single value to compare.

Value: *
[c#                                                          ]

[ OK ]    [ Cancel ]

**Figure 7.4    The People tab of the Search Center and how it can be used to search on user profile data**

## 7.1.3    *Audience targeting*

Audience targeting is just as useful. In most organizations, you don't have the time to read every email, let alone every content page or announcement some of your co-workers have made. So the administrators should take the time to set up some useful audiences. These can be based on the properties that make up a profile, or by groups you happen to be a member of. Information workers can then choose the audience(s) that would be the most interested when creating a list item. This doesn't replace permissions, and is only used when list items are aggregated into a Content Query Web Part. If, for example, Nick logged on to a SharePoint page, he'd see all of the aggregated data that's targeted to any audience that he's a member of. Figure 7.5 shows an example of configuring the Content Query Web Part.

You enable audience targeting in the list by modifying the list settings. Users can then target the list item to whichever audience they choose. In figure 7.6, you can see an announcement being targeted to developers.

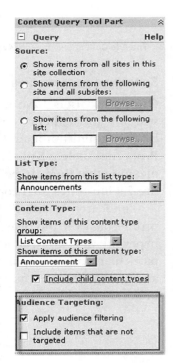

**Figure 7.5    Audience targeting options in the Content Query Web Part**

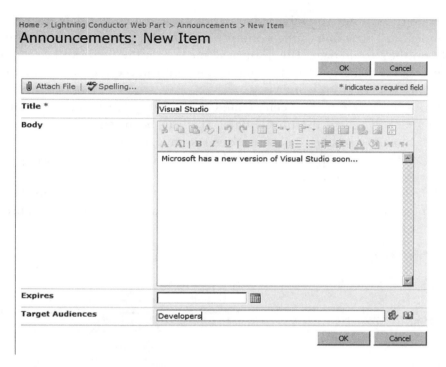

**Figure 7.6   An announcement targeted to an audience named Developers**

So now that we know how the user profiles are used within SharePoint, let's discuss how to configure user profiles using the Business Data Catalog.

## 7.2   Configuring user profiles

One of the first things to do is identify which properties you want to create and have available in your user profiles. For example, you may want Department, Salary, SSN, or even Children's Names. Once you know the properties that you're going to create, you need to establish the data type for each of those properties. The properties are then created by navigating to your Shared Services Provider page, and then to the User Profiles page. A new profile can then be added. You can even give it aliases for other languages. This is useful, for example, with "Cell Phone" or "Teléfono Celular," depending on which is used most in each country.

You then set the data type. This must match closely with the data type that's stored in the back-end database available from the BDC. You can then set whether the field is optional. Does the user have to complete the Profile field? Can he override the setting? You might want to be able to search this data, so it'll need to be indexed. That's one of the options here, but you may not want to display the field on the Profile page. Doing this will mean that the field can be searched on even without being displayed. In figure 7.7, you can see the Add Profile page in the Shared Services Provider.

Once the property has been created, you need to create a connection to the entity that will return the profile data. This can be an entity such as Employee from a human resources database. Your HR database may also have other tables that you want to pull in, which could be a one-to-many relationship such as Employee(1)/Skills(many).

To create the connection to the Business Data Catalog, first you must have created the entity that returns the employee information from your data source. This

Shared Services Administration: SharedServices1 > User Profile and Properties > View Profile Properties > User Profile Property

## Add User Profile Property

Use this page to add a property for user profiles.

* Indicates a required field

**Property Settings**

Specify property settings for this property. The name will be used programmatically for the property by the user profile service, while the display name is the label used when the property is shown. After the property is created the only property setting you can change is the display name.

Name: *
`Salary`
Display Name: *
`Salary`
[ Edit Languages ]
Type:
`float`

**User Description**

Specify a description for this property that will provide instructions or information to users. This description appears on the Edit Details page.

Description:

[ Edit Languages ]

**Policy Settings**

Specify the privacy policy you want applied to this property. Select the Replicate check box if you want the property to display in the user info list for all sites. To replicate properties, the default privacy must be set to Everyone and the User can override check box must not be selected.

Policy Setting:
`Optional`
Default Privacy Setting:
`My Manager`
☐ User can override
☑ Replicable

**Edit Settings**

Specify whether users can change the values for this property in their user profile. Users with the Manage Profile permission can edit any property value for any user.

◉ Allow users to edit values for this property
○ Do not allow users to edit values for this property

**Display Settings**

Specify whether or not the property is displayed in the profile properties section on the My Site profile page, whether the property is displayed on the Edit Details page, and whether changes to the property's values are displayed in the Colleague Tracker web part.

Note: These display settings will obey the user's privacy settings.

☑ Show in the profile properties section of the user's profile page
☑ Show on the Edit Details page
☐ Show changes in the Colleague Tracker web part

**Search Settings**

Aliased properties are treated as equivalent to the user name and account name when searching for items authored by a user, targeting items to a user, or displaying items in the Documents Web Part of the personal site for a user. Alias properties must be public.

Indexed properties are crawled by the search engine and become part of the People search scope schema. Only index a property if it will contain relevant information for people finding or if you want the data displayed in people search results.

☐ Alias
☑ Indexed

**Figure 7.7   The Add Profile page in the Shared Services Provider**

is a regular application definition file and entity as you've created thus far in this book. If you want to include the "many" side of the relationship, make sure that you add both entities with an association between them. Additionally, you'll need to create a filter method on the "many" side of the relationship, even if it has a default value of %. This will ensure that the one-to-many mapping option isn't grayed out, as shown in figure 7.8. Once your ADF is configured correctly, you upload it as usual, then navigate to the Create Connection page, which can be found in your Shared Services Provider under User Profiles and Properties, as shown in figure 7.8.

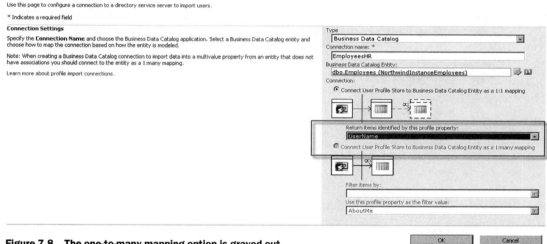

**Figure 7.8   The one-to-many mapping option is grayed out, as there's no filter method on the entity.**

To configure the connection:

1   Launch SharePoint Central Administration.

2   Navigate to your Shared Services Provider.

3   Click User Profiles and Properties.

4   Click View Import Connections.

5   Click Create New Connection.

6   Set the type to be Business Data Catalog.

7   Provide the connection a name, such as Human Resources.

8   Select the entity, for example, Employees.

9   Select either one-to-one mapping or one-to-many mapping. (If you're choosing a one-to-one mapping, you'll need to set the field to the identifier for the profile property—for example, Username. On the other hand, if you're using one-to-many, you need to filter the items and then set the filter value. Your property will need to allow multiple values, which we'll explore in a moment. Here you'll choose which profile property you're passing as the parameter for the filter.)

10  Once you've created the connection, you can start the full import by clicking Start full import on the User Profiles and Properties page, as shown in figure 7.9.

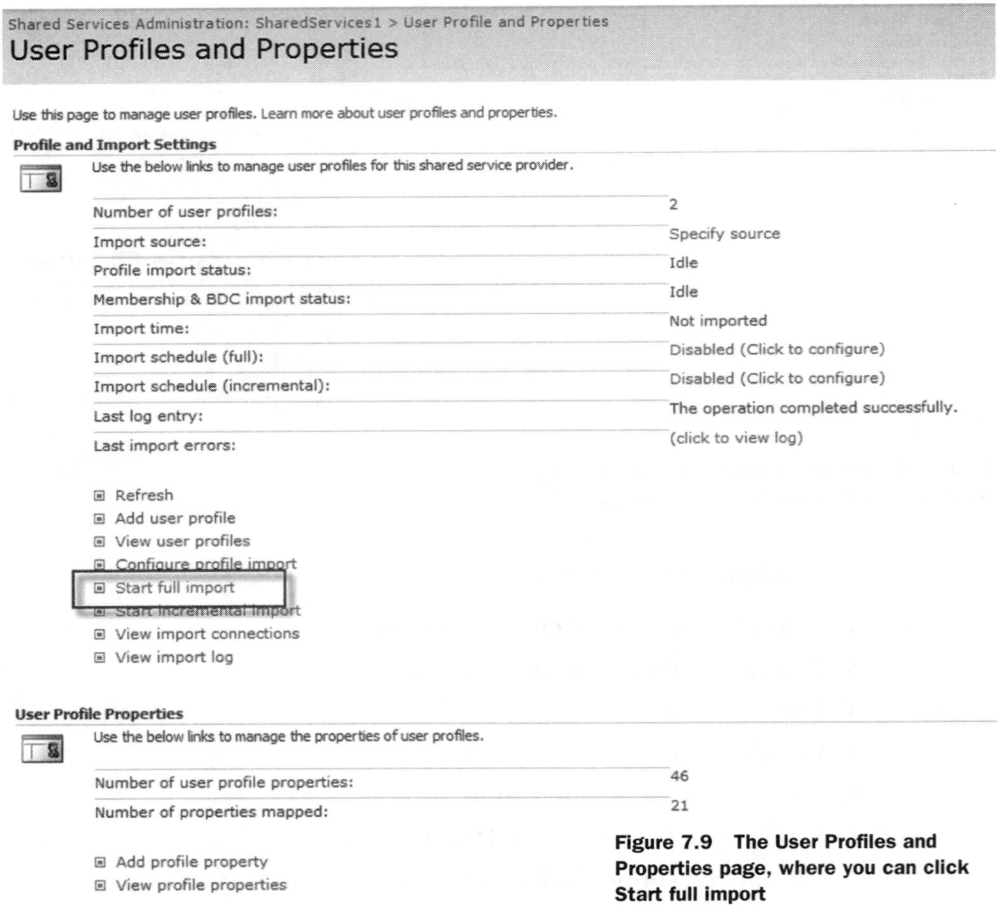

Shared Services Administration: SharedServices1 > User Profile and Properties

## User Profiles and Properties

Use this page to manage user profiles. Learn more about user profiles and properties.

**Profile and Import Settings**

Use the below links to manage user profiles for this shared service provider.

| | |
|---|---|
| Number of user profiles: | 2 |
| Import source: | Specify source |
| Profile import status: | Idle |
| Membership & BDC import status: | Idle |
| Import time: | Not imported |
| Import schedule (full): | Disabled (Click to configure) |
| Import schedule (incremental): | Disabled (Click to configure) |
| Last log entry: | The operation completed successfully. |
| Last import errors: | (click to view log) |

☒ Refresh
☒ Add user profile
☒ View user profiles
☒ Configure profile import
☒ Start full import
☒ Start incremental import
☒ View import connections
☒ View import log

**User Profile Properties**

Use the below links to manage the properties of user profiles.

| | |
|---|---|
| Number of user profile properties: | 46 |
| Number of properties mapped: | 21 |

☒ Add profile property
☒ View profile properties

**Figure 7.9   The User Profiles and Properties page, where you can click Start full import**

Note that, further down the page, you can see how many properties are available and how many properties are mapped. You can map your profile properties by following these steps:

1 From the User Profiles and Properties page, click View Profile Properties.

2 Edit the profile that you wish to map, as shown in figure 7.10.

**Figure 7.10    Edit a profile property.**

3 In the Profile Import Mapping section, choose your data connection, then choose the field from the data source that you wish to map.

4 Finally, reimport your profiles, as shown in figure 7.11.

**Figure 7.11    The Property Mapping page allows configuration of the import field mappings.**

You can also configure the profile import to occur on a scheduled basis. This is useful, as the profile information in your data sources may change regularly. To configure this, you can select Configure Profile Import from the User Profiles and Properties page.

## 7.3    *Audience targeted web parts*

Microsoft Office SharePoint Server 2007 allows you to target a web part at an audience. Using audience targeting, you can hide web parts from certain users. For example, if the currently logged-on user isn't a member of a Sales Person audience, she won't see sales items that are rolled up into a Content Query Web Part. To modify the target audience for the web part, choose Site Actions, Edit Page, click the Edit button in the web part, and choose Modify Shared Properties. You'll then see the Target Audiences property in figure 7.12.

**Figure 7.12   The Target Audiences property of a web part**

Another place in which you can use target audiences is within a content type based on the page content type. These content types are used to create page templates, so that information workers can create content pages. The first thing to do when you create a page layout is create a content type based on page. Note in figure 7.13 that page contains a Site column called Target Audiences.

The Target Audiences field control can be placed on the page inside an Edit Mode Panel control when designing the page layout in SharePoint Designer. This means that an information worker who's creating the content can target the content page to an audience. The person reading the page wouldn't see the Target Audiences field, as it's inside the Edit Mode panel. This is illustrated in figure 7.14.

Home > BDC > Site Settings > Site Content Type Gallery > Site Content Type

**Site Content Type: Products**

**Site Content Type Information**

| | |
|---|---|
| Name: | Products |
| Description: | |
| Parent: | Page |
| Group: | Custom Content Types |

**Settings**

▫ Name, description, and group
▫ Advanced settings
▫ Workflow settings
▫ Delete this site content type
▫ Document Information Panel settings
▫ Information management policy settings
▫ Manage document conversion for this content type

**Columns**

| Name | Type | Status | Source |
|---|---|---|---|
| Name | File | Required | Document |
| Title | Single line of text | Optional | Item |
| Description | Multiple lines of text | Optional | System Page |
| Scheduling Start Date | Publishing Schedule Start Date | Optional | System Page |
| Scheduling End Date | Publishing Schedule End Date | Optional | System Page |
| Contact | Person or Group | Optional | System Page |
| Contact E-Mail Address | Single line of text | Optional | System Page |
| Contact Name | Single line of text | Optional | System Page |
| Contact Picture | Hyperlink or Picture | Optional | System Page |
| Rollup Image | Publishing Image | Optional | System Page |
| Target Audiences | Audience Targeting | Optional | System Page |

**Figure 7.13   The Content Type Creation page with the Target Audiences Site column displayed**

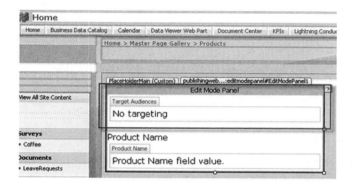

**Figure 7.14 The Target Audiences field in an Edit Mode panel on a page layout within SharePoint Designer**

## 7.4 Summary

This chapter introduced the benefits of using user profiles within MOSS. It explained how users can modify their own profiles using My Site, which in turn allows them to become members of audiences. Audiences are created by administrators within the Shared Services Provider. It's possible to search for people using the People tab within the MOSS Search Center. To provide better audience targeting and searching, user profile properties can be created and mapped to a backend database, which will provide further profile information. This involves creating properties and mapping them to a column within an entity that's returned by the Business Data Catalog. Finally, we saw what type of information can be targeted, such as list items, web parts, and content pages.

In this chapter, we didn't write any code! In the next chapter, we'll explore the BDC Object Model and the `ApplicationRegistry` namespace. This will give us the opportunity to get our hands dirty and learn the types of applications that we can write ourselves and still use the Business Data Catalog.

# The ApplicationRegistry
# namespace

*8*

**This chapter covers**

- Explaining the ApplicationRegistry namespace
- Creating a web service that exposes BDC data from your entity
- Writing a console application to consume the web service

What the Business Data Catalog can do out of the box is extremely powerful. Except for writing the application definition file by hand, it's extremely easy, too. But every company is different, and no matter how hard you try as a software developer, you'll never be able to satisfy every company's requirements. We now know that we can customize the BDC Web Parts with Microsoft Office SharePoint Designer (SPD). But sometimes that just isn't enough. With SPD, our hands are still tied to whatever operation SPD allows us to perform. So when we need real power, we have to turn to Visual Studio.NET. What can we do with BDC data that we can't do with SPD? Well—anything! If you need to manipulate the data and present it in a customized way, Visual Studio.NET will allow you to do it. First, you may need to present your data differently, such as display the data in a chart, export it to another application, make it available through a web service, or use it within an Office-based application. Microsoft provides a BDC API to help you achieve these goals.

The Business Data Catalog has its own runtime object model that allows developers to access data from the Business Data Catalog. Many .NET developers will already have a good handle on how to get at back-end data in a database using ADO.NET or similar, and of course you could achieve the same results using that. But if you're writing ADO.NET code to connect to the data source and get useful data back, you need to have a good understanding of the database schema. You'll also need to know security information and how you can connect to the source. A lot of time is then spent analyzing the data before applying filters or sort criteria so that you can present the data in a useful way. With the Business Data Catalog, this has been done for you in the application definition file. The only real information that you need to know is what LOB system, LOB system instance, and entity you want to connect to. The security information, schema, and so on isn't that relevant. You're simply retrieving business objects.

The Business Data Catalog provides a namespace called `Microsoft.Office.Server.ApplicationRegistry`. Apparently `ApplicationRegistry` was the name given to the Business Data Catalog originally, and then its name was changed. We'll concentrate in this chapter on `ApplicationRegistry.Administration` and `ApplicationRegistry.Runtime` and find out the purpose of these two namespaces. We'll then have some concrete examples of using these namespaces when writing web services and a BDC-centric workflow.

## 8.1   Understanding the ApplicationRegistry namespace

The `Microsoft.SharePoint.Portal.dll` file provides access to the `Microsoft.Office.Server.ApplicationRegistry`. When you add a reference to this DLL, you'll find it listed as Microsoft Office SharePoint Server Component. Figure 8.1 is a screenshot of the Add Reference dialog box, illustrating the DLL that you need to reference in order to obtain access to the BDC Object Model.

Once you've referenced `Microsoft.SharePoint.Portal.dll`, you'll have access to the following namespaces:

- `Microsoft.Office.Server.ApplicationRegistry.Administration`
- `Microsoft.Office.Server.ApplicationRegistry.Administration.UI`
- `Microsoft.Office.Server.ApplicationRegistry.Infrastructure`

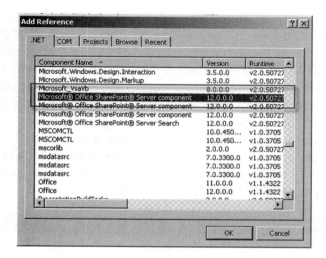

Figure 8.1 The Add Reference dialog box, displaying `Microsoft.SharePoint.Portal.dll`

- `Microsoft.Office.Server.ApplicationRegistry.MetadataModel`
- `Microsoft.Office.Server.ApplicationRegistry.Runtime`
- `Microsoft.Office.Server.ApplicationRegistry.Search`
- `Microsoft.Office.Server.ApplicationRegistry.SystemSpecific.Db`
- `Microsoft.Office.Server.ApplicationRegistry.SystemSpecific.WebService`
- `Microsoft.Office.Server.ApplicationRegistry.WebService`

These namespaces can be confusing, as the classes they contain have similar names, and often you may end up with ambiguous class names within your code. For example, there are `Entity` classes in both `Microsoft.Office.Server.ApplicationRegistry.Administration` and `Microsoft.Office.Server.ApplicationRegistry.MetadataModel`. So an understanding of which namespaces to use for what is important. Let's start off by briefly describing these namespaces. `Search`, `SystemSpecificWebService`, and `WebService` are for internal use only, and have been marked that way in the SDK.

## 8.1.1 *Microsoft.Office.Server.ApplicationRegistry.Administration*

This namespace provides CRUD (Create, Read, Update & Delete) capabilities on the business data objects that are stored within the Shared Services database. If you can cast your mind back to chapter 2, where we created `LobSystems`, `LobSystemInstances`, entities, finder methods, associations, and so on, these are the objects that we're referring to. So you can query them, update them, delete them, and create them via the object model, as well as via the application definition file. We mentioned that there's some ambiguity between some or most of the classes in this namespace, as well as in the `Microsoft.Office.Server.ApplicationRegistry.MetadataModel` namespace. Use the `Metadata-Model` namespace purely to read objects, and not to create, update, or delete. Using the `MetadataModel` namespace offers a faster experience when reading objects, as the objects are cached, whereas they aren't in the `Application-Registry.Administration` namespace.

In listing 8.1, you'll find some code snippets that demonstrate examples from each namespace. We'll then pursue two useful real-world examples, which include creating a WCF (Windows Communication Foundation) web service to return BDC data, and creating a BDC-based Visual Studio workflow.

**Listing 8.1   Creating finder methods in an entity**

```
using System;
using System.Collections.Generic;
using System.Text;
using Microsoft.Office.Server.ApplicationRegistry.Administration;
using Microsoft.Office.Server.ApplicationRegistry.Infrastructure;
using WSSAdmin = Microsoft.SharePoint.Administration;
using OSSAdmin = Microsoft.Office.Server.Administration;

namespace BDCBook
{
    class GetStartedAndCreateSystem
    {
      const string yourSSPName ="EnterYourSSPNameHere";

       static void Main(string[] args)
       {
           SetupBDC();
           CreateFinderMethod();
           Console.WriteLine("Press any key to exit...");
           Console.Read();
       }
       static void SetupBDC()                     ⊲┘ Gets required Shared
         {                                              Services Provider

       SqlSessionProvider.Instance().SetSharedResourceProviderToUse(yourSSPName
       );
       }                                          ⊲┘ Generates new
       static void CreateFinderMethod()               finder method
       {
           LobSystemInstance mySysInstance = null;
           LobSystemInstanceCollection sysInsCollection =
➥ApplicationRegistry.Instance.GetLobSystemInstancesLikeName
➥("NorthwindLOBSystemInstance");
```

```
foreach (LobSystemInstance sysInstance in sysInsCollection)
{
    if (sysInstance.Name == "NorthWindLOBSystemInstance")
    {
        mySysInstance = sysInstance;
        break;
    }
}
EntityCollection entityColl = mySysInstance.LobSystem.Entities;
foreach (Entity entity in entityColl)
{
    if (entity.Name == "ProductModel")
    {
        Method meth = entity.Methods.Create
➡ ("GetProductModels", true, true);
        meth.Properties.Add("RdbCommandText",
➡ "SELECT ProductModelID, Name, CatalogDescription FROM ProductModel
➡ WHERE Name LIKE @Name");
        meth.Properties.Add("RdbCommandType",
    System.Data.CommandType.Text);
```

⬅ **Finder method's Select statement is created**

```
        FilterDescriptor fd =
➡ meth.FilterDescriptors.Create("Name", true,
➡ "Microsoft.Office.Server.ApplicationRegistry.Runtime.WildcardFilter");
        Parameter p1 = meth.Parameters.Create("@Name", true,
➡ Microsoft.Office.Server.ApplicationRegistry.MetadataModel.DirectionType.In,
➡  "Microsoft.Office.Server.ApplicationRegistry.Infrastructure.
➡ DotNetTypeReflector");
```

⬅ **Type descriptors created for each column**

```
        TypeDescriptor td1 =
➡ p1.CreateRootTypeDescriptor("Name", true, "System.String", null,
➡ fd, false);
        Parameter p2 = meth.Parameters.Create("ProductModels",
➡ true, Microsoft.Office.Server.ApplicationRegistry.MetadataModel.
➡ DirectionType.Return, "Microsoft.Office.Server.ApplicationRegistry.
➡ Infrastructure.DotNetTypeReflector");
        IList<Identifier> ids = new
➡ List<Identifier>(entity.Identifiers);
        Identifier id = ids[0];
        TypeDescriptor td2 =
➡ p2.CreateRootTypeDescriptor("ProductModelDataReader", true,
➡  "System.Data.IDataReader, System.Data, Version=2.0.3600.0,
➡  Culture=neutral, PublicKeyToken=b77a5c561934e089", null, null, true);
        TypeDescriptor td21 =
➡ td2.ChildTypeDescriptors.Create("ProductModelDataRecord", true,
➡  "System.Data.IDataRecord, System.Data, Version=2.0.3600.0,
➡  Culture=neutral, PublicKeyToken=b77a5c561934e089",
➡  null, null, false);
        TypeDescriptor td210 =
➡ td21.ChildTypeDescriptors.Create("ProductModelID", true,
➡  "System.Int32", id, null, false);
        TypeDescriptor td211 =
➡ td21.ChildTypeDescriptors.Create("Name", true, "System.String",
```

```
➡ null, null, false);
                    TypeDescriptor td212 =
➡td21.ChildTypeDescriptors.Create("CatalogDescription", true,
➡"System.String", null, null, false);
                    MethodInstance methInst1 =
➡meth.MethodInstances.Create("ProductModelFinder", true, td2,
➡Microsoft.Office.Server.ApplicationRegistry.MetadataModel.
➡MethodInstanceType.Finder);
                    MethodInstance methInst2 =
➡meth.MethodInstances.Create("ProductModelSpecificFinder", true, td2,
➡Microsoft.Office.Server.ApplicationRegistry.MetadataModel.
➡MethodInstanceType.SpecificFinder);
                    IList<MethodInstance> methInstCollection = new
➡List<MethodInstance>(entity.MethodInstances);
                    td1.SetDefaultValue(methInstCollection[0].Id, "%");
                    td1.SetDefaultValue(methInstCollection[1].Id, "%");
                    Console.WriteLine("Created the finder method
➡successfully.");
                    break;
                }
            }
        }
    }
}
```

The code in the listing illustrates how you can use the Administration namespace to create a finder method in an existing entity. In the next section, we'll explore how you can use the Infrastructure namespace to manage connections and security to the data source.

### 8.1.2    *Microsoft.Office.Server.ApplicationRegistry.Infrastructure*

The main role of this namespace is to support other namespaces and provide connection management and security management. Having said that, these classes are available for use in your own code. The runtime object model uses this namespace to create and manage a connection to the data source. SQLSession-Provider and BDCAccessControlLists are among the few classes that you'll find within this namespace. SQLSessionProvider is the only provider present within this namespace. It's there to provide a connection to the Shared Services Provider database where the business data objects reside. The AccessDeniedException class also lives within this namespace and provides Exception messages when a user attempts to access an object that he's not permitted to. Listing 8.2 is a sample code snippet demonstrating how to read AccessControlList information for a LOB system.

**Listing 8.2    How to query the `AccessControlList` for a LobSystem**

```
using System;
using System.Collections.Generic;
using System.Text;
using Microsoft.Office.Server.ApplicationRegistry.Administration;
using Microsoft.Office.Server.ApplicationRegistry.Infrastructure;
using WSSAdmin = Microsoft.SharePoint.Administration;
using OSSAdmin = Microsoft.Office.Server.Administration;

namespace BDCBook
{
    class GetStartedAndCreateSystem
    {
        const string yourSSPName ="EnterYourSSPNameHere";

        static void Main(string[] args)
        {
            SetupBDC();
            GetAccessControlList();
            Console.WriteLine("Press any key to exit...");
            Console.Read();
        }
        static void SetupBDC()
        {

    SqlSessionProvider.Instance().SetSharedResourceProviderToUse(yourSSPName
    );
        }
        public static void GetAccessControlList()
        {
            LobSystemInstance mySysInstance = null;
            LobSystemInstanceCollection sysInsCollection =
ApplicationRegistry.Instance.GetLobSystemInstancesLikeName
("NorthwindLOBSystemInstance");
            foreach (LobSystemInstance sysInstance in sysInsCollection)
            {
                if (sysInstance.Name == "NorthwindLOBSystemInstance")
                {
                    mySysInstance = sysInstance;
                    break;
                }
            }
            LobSystem ls = mySysInstance.LobSystem;        ◁──┐ Retrieves security
            IAccessControlList acl = ls.GetAccessControlList();    information
            foreach (IAccessControlEntry ace in acl)
            {
                Console.WriteLine(ace.IdentityName);
                Console.WriteLine(ace.Rights);
            }
        }
    }
}
```

Now that we've seen how to query the access control list for a LOB system, let's explore how to query other information from the BDC using the `MetaDataModel` namespace.

### 8.1.3    *Microsoft.Office.Server.ApplicationRegistry.MetadataModel*

This namespace provides similar classes to that of the `ApplicationRegistry.Administration` namespace. The main difference is that the `MetadataModel` namespace is read-only and cached. This makes your code exceptionally fast when querying the data, so if you just want to iterate through fields or populate a data table, you're better off using the `MetadataModel` namespace rather than `Administration`.

Through this namespace, you'll find access to classes such as `LobSystem`, `LobSystemInstance`, `Entities`, `Associations`, and so on. An example of the type of thing you'd use this for is to display or query the business objects from the Shared Services Provider database. Listing 8.3 demonstrates this namespace in use.

**Listing 8.3    Querying properties from an entity**

```
using System;
using System.Collections.Generic;
using System.Text;
using System.Data;
using Microsoft.Office.Server.ApplicationRegistry.MetadataModel;
using Microsoft.Office.Server.ApplicationRegistry.Runtime;
using Microsoft.Office.Server.ApplicationRegistry.SystemSpecific;
using Microsoft.Office.Server.ApplicationRegistry.Infrastructure;
using WSSAdmin = Microsoft.SharePoint.Administration;
using OSSAdmin = Microsoft.Office.Server.Administration;

namespace BDCBook
{
    class GetSystemAndEntity
    {
        const string yourSSPName = "EnterYourSSPNameHere";

        static void Main(string[] args)
        {
            SetupBDC();
            DisplayLOBSystemsinBDC();
            GetLOBSystem();
            GetEntity();
            Console.WriteLine("Press any key to exit...");
            Console.Read();
        }
        static void SetupBDC()
        {
```

```
    SqlSessionProvider.Instance().SetSharedResourceProviderToUse(yourSSPName
    );
    }
    static void DisplayLOBSystemsinBDC()
    {
        NamedLobSystemInstanceDictionary sysInstances =
ApplicationRegistry.GetLobSystemInstances();
        Console.WriteLine("Listing system instances...");
        foreach (String name in sysInstances.Keys)
        {
            Console.WriteLine(name);
        }
    }
    static void GetLOBSystem()
    {
        NamedLobSystemInstanceDictionary sysInstances =
ApplicationRegistry.GetLobSystemInstances();
        LobSystemInstance NorthwindLOBSystemInstance =
sysInstances["NorthwindLOBSystemInstance"];
        Console.WriteLine("Getting a system instance and displaying
its ID...");
        LobSystem NorthwindSys =
NorthwindLOBSystemInstance.GetLobSystem();
        Console.WriteLine(NorthwindSys.Name.ToString());
        Console.WriteLine("ID: "+NorthwindSys.Id.ToString());
    }

    static void GetEntity()
    {
        NamedLobSystemInstanceDictionary sysInstances =
ApplicationRegistry.GetLobSystemInstances();
        LobSystemInstance NorthwindLOBSystemInstance =
sysInstances["AdventureWorksSampleInstance"];
        Console.WriteLine("Getting an entity object and displaying
its ID...");
        Entity prodEntity =
NorthwindLOBSystemInstance.GetEntities()["Product"];
        Console.WriteLine(prodEntity.Name.ToString());
        Console.WriteLine("ID: "+prodEntity.Id.ToString());
    }
}
}
```

Displays entity's name as string

Displays entity's ID as string

So far in our examples, we've used the BDC Object Model to read and write BDC objects and metadata into the SSP database. In the next section, we'll explore how to obtain the LOB system data such as customers and products.

### 8.1.4  *Microsoft.Office.Server.ApplicationRegistry.Runtime*

This is the namespace that you'd use to get at the data. This means you don't need to understand in detail how SAP works, or how your tables are structured in the SQL database. Each entity is accessible and you can call methods that allow you to iterate through the data or load the data into a data table. This namespace is used in conjunction with the MetadataModel namespace, allowing you to call the methods that return the data from the entities. Listing 8.4 shows how to iterate through entities and return data. In chapter 9, we'll use this code to create an Ajax-style BDC Web Part.

**Listing 8.4    Executing a finder method using `ApplicationRegistry.Runtime`**

```
using System;
using System.Collections.Generic;
using System.Text;
using System.Data;
using Microsoft.Office.Server.ApplicationRegistry.MetadataModel;
using Microsoft.Office.Server.ApplicationRegistry.Runtime;
using Microsoft.Office.Server.ApplicationRegistry.SystemSpecific;
using Microsoft.Office.Server.ApplicationRegistry.Infrastructure;
using WSSAdmin = Microsoft.SharePoint.Administration;
using OSSAdmin = Microsoft.Office.Server.Administration;

namespace BDCBOOK
{
    class ExecuteFinder
    {
        const string yourSSPName ="EnterYourSSPNameHere";

        static void Main(string[] args)
        {
            SetupBDC();
            FindAll();
            Console.WriteLine("Press any key to exit...");
            Console.Read();
        }
        static void SetupBDC()
        {

    SqlSessionProvider.Instance().SetSharedResourceProviderToUse(yourSSPName
    );
        }
```

Get the Products
entity ◁┘

```
        static void FindAll()
        {
            NamedLobSystemInstanceDictionary sysInstances =
➡ ApplicationRegistry.GetLobSystemInstances();
            LobSystemInstance NorthwindLOBSystemInstance =
```

```
➡sysInstances["AdventureWorksSampleInstance"];
        Entity prodEntity =
➡NorthwindLOBSystemInstance.GetEntities()["Product"];
        FilterCollection fc = prodEntity.GetFinderFilters();
        IEntityInstanceEnumerator prodEntityInstanceEnumerator =
➡prodEntity.FindFiltered(fc, NorthwindLOBSystemInstance);
        while (prodEntityInstanceEnumerator.MoveNext())
        {
            IEntityInstance IE = prodEntityInstanceEnumerator.Current;
            foreach (Field f in prodEntity.GetFinderView().Fields)
                Console.Write(IE[f]);
            Console.WriteLine("");
        }
    }

    }
}
```

> Loop though
> items and write
> to console

The final namespace is SystemSpecific.db. This namespace can be used to provide a list of action URLs on an entity, as well as to iterate through your collection of entities.

### 8.1.5 Microsoft.Office.Server.ApplicationRegistry.SystemSpecific.db

This namespace contains two classes for manipulating database instances. DbEntityInstance represents a specific database entity instance. You can use this class to obtain action URLs, and get associated entities such as Customers > Orders. The other class, DbEntityInstanceEnumerator, allows you to iterate through the collection of entities.

Now that we've explored the namespaces, in the next section we'll put some of the code to good use and expose the business data in a web service. This data can then be used in a wide variety of places, including web, Windows, and Office applications.

## 8.2 Creating a WCF web service to expose BDC data

Once you've configured the Business Data Catalog and can view your data within SharePoint, you may want to expose it using a web service. Exposing LOB system data using a web service is beneficial, and there are a hundred reasons for doing so, such as consuming the data in Office Business Applications (OBA) or Windows applications. As you'll find out in chapter 10, you can use the web service within Microsoft Office to create Office Business Applications that require LOB system data. You may also want to use the data in a corporate website that uses ASP.NET, or even a Windows Forms Application. First of all, we'll create the web service and get the plumbing in place for that before exploring some uses in later chapters.

To create a WCF service project:

1 Open Visual Studio. (In our example, we'll be using Visual Studio 2008.)

2 Choose File, New Project.

3 In the New Project dialog box, click WCF Service Library from the WCF section, as shown in figure 8.2.

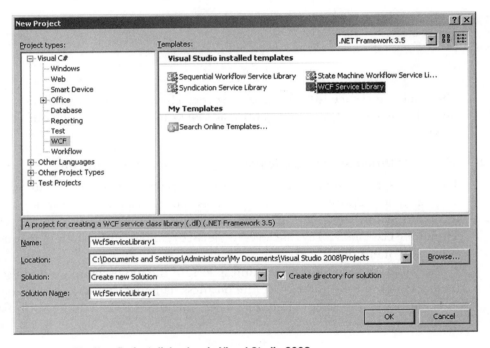

**Figure 8.2   The New Project dialog box in Visual Studio 2008**

4 Our web service will be called `CustomerService`, as it's going to return customer data from the Northwind Customer entity. In the real world, you may decide to create the web service generically so that you can pass the LOB system and entity name to it.

5 Using Solution Explorer, rename `Class1.cs` to `CustomersService.cs`.

6 Right-click References and add references to `Microsoft.Office.Server.dll` and `Microsoft.SharePoint.Portal.dll`.

7 Add the following `Using` statements to the `CustomerService.cs` file:

```
using Microsoft.Office.Server.ApplicationRegistry.MetadataModel;
using Microsoft.Office.Server.ApplicationRegistry.Runtime;
using Microsoft.Office.Server.ApplicationRegistry.SystemSpecific.Db;
using Microsoft.Office.Server.ApplicationRegistry.Infrastructure;
```

**8** Comment out the code and namespace in the `CustomerService.cs` file and add the following namespace:

```
Namespace Customers
```

**9** Add the following data contract to the `CustomerService.cs` file inside the Customers namespace, as shown in listing 8.5.

---

**Listing 8.5   The data contract returning the customer properties**

```
[DataContract]
    public class Customer
    {
        [DataMember]
        public string CustomerID
        {
            get;
            set;
        }
        [DataMember]
        public string CompanyName
        {
            get;
            set;
        }
        [DataMember]
        public string ContactName
        {
            get;
            set;
        }
        [DataMember]
        public string TelephoneNumber
        {
            get;
            set;
        }
    }
```

**10** The service will provide three methods: one that returns a list of customers, one that returns a specific customer, and finally one that returns all customer information in the form of an object array. Add the service contract to the same file, as shown in listing 8.6.

---

**Listing 8.6   The service contract providing the ICustomerService**

```
[ServiceContract]
public interface ICustomersService
{
    [OperationContract]
    List<string> ListCustomers();

    [OperationContract]
    string GetCustomer(string CustomerID);

    [OperationContract]
    List<Customer> GetBusinessData();
}
```

**11**  Implement the ICustomerService service contract by adding the code
shown in listing 8.7.

---

**Listing 8.7   The web service methods that access the BDC API**

```
public class CustomersServiceImpl : ICustomersService
{
    #region ICustomersService Members                      Returns CompanyName
                                                            of each customer
    public List<string> ListCustomers()          ⊲┘
    {
        List<string> Customers = new List<string>();
        SqlSessionProvider.Instance().
⇒SetSharedResourceProviderToUse("SharedServices1");
        NamedLobSystemInstanceDictionary sysInstances =
⇒ApplicationRegistry.GetLobSystemInstances();
        LobSystemInstance instance =
⇒sysInstances["NorthwindInstance2"];
        Entity prodEntity = instance.GetEntities()["dbo.Customers"];
        FilterCollection fc = prodEntity.GetFinderFilters();
        IEntityInstanceEnumerator enumerator =
⇒prodEntity.FindFiltered(fc, instance);
        while (enumerator.MoveNext())
        {
            string CompanyName;
            IEntityInstance entityInstance = enumerator.Current;
            CompanyName = entityInstance["CompanyName"].ToString();
            Customers.Add(CompanyName);
        }

        return Customers;                                    Returns specific
    }                                                        customer based
                                                             on ID
    public string GetCustomer(string CustomerID)     ⊲┘
    {
        string strCustomer;
        NamedLobSystemInstanceDictionary sysInstances =
```

```
➡ApplicationRegistry.GetLobSystemInstances();
        LobSystemInstance instance =
➡ sysInstances["NorthwindLOBSystemInstance2"];
        Entity Entity = instance.GetEntities()["dbo.Customers"];
        DbEntityInstance record =
➡(DbEntityInstance)Entity.FindSpecific(CustomerID, instance);

        //Each value is a separate element
        Field fieldCompanyName =
➡Entity.GetSpecificFinderView().Fields.Find(delegate(Field f)
➡{ return (f.Name == "CustomerID"); });
        strCustomer = fieldCompanyName.ToString();

        return strCustomer;
    }

    public List<Customer> GetBusinessData()
    {
        List<Customer> Customers = new List<Customer>();
        NamedLobSystemInstanceDictionary sysInstances =
➡ApplicationRegistry.GetLobSystemInstances();
        LobSystemInstance instance =
➡sysInstances["NorthwindLOBSystemInstance2"];
        Entity prodEntity = instance.GetEntities()["dbo.Customers"];
        FilterCollection fc = prodEntity.GetFinderFilters();
        IEntityInstanceEnumerator enumerator =
➡prodEntity.FindFiltered(fc, instance);
        while (enumerator.MoveNext())
        {
            Customer C = new Customer();
            IEntityInstance entityInstance = enumerator.Current;
            C.CustomerID = entityInstance["CustomerID"].ToString();
            C.CompanyName = entityInstance["CompanyName"].ToString();
            C.ContactName = entityInstance["ContactName"].ToString();
            C.TelephoneNumber = entityInstance["Phone"].ToString();
            Customers.Add(C);
        }

        return Customers;
    }

    #endregion
}
```

> **Returns columns for each customer**

**12** Add the following code to the `CustomerService.svc` file:

```
<%@ ServiceHost Language="C#" Debug="true"
➡Service="Customers.CustomersServiceImpl"
➡CodeBehind="CustomersService.svc.cs" %>
```

**13** There are four different types of behavior in WCF: service, endpoint, operation, and contract. Edit the `Web.Config` file in the project to add the service behavior that enables metadata publishing, as shown in listing 8.8.

---
**Listing 8.8   Setting the behavior in Web.Config**
---

```
<behavior name="CustomersBehavior">
    <serviceMetadata httpGetEnabled="true"/>
</behavior>
<behavior name="CustomerService.Service1Behavior">
    <!-- To avoid disclosing metadata information, set the value below to
➥false and remove the metadata endpoint above before deployment -->
    <serviceMetadata httpGetEnabled="true"/>
    <!-- To receive exception details in faults for debugging purposes, set
➥the value below to true.  Set to false before deployment to avoid
➥disclosing exception information -->
    <serviceDebug includeExceptionDetailInFaults="false"/>
</behavior>
```

**14** Build the solution by pressing Ctrl + Shift +B.

**15** Navigate to http://localhost/CustomerService/CustomersService.svc? wsdl, as shown in figure 8.3.

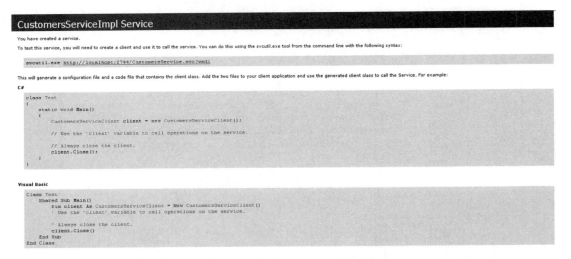

**Figure 8.3   The result of running CustomersService**

To test the web service, add a console application project to your solution.

1 Right-click the CustomersService solution and choose Add Project.

2 Choose the Console Application template.

3 Name the project TestWCFBDC.

4 Right-click Service References and choose Add Service Reference, as shown in figure 8.4.

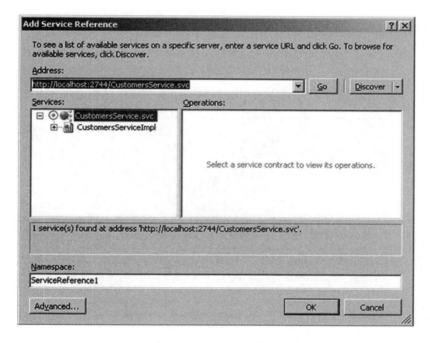

**Figure 8.4 Adding a service reference to CustomersService.svc**

5 Add the following endpoint to the App.Config file, which will set up the binding contract:

```
<client>
            <endpoint address="http://localhost:2744/
CustomersService.svc"
                binding="basicHttpBinding" bindingConfiguration=
➥"BasicHttpBinding_ICustomersService"
                contract="CustomersService.ICustomersService" name=
➥"BasicHttpBinding_ICustomersService" />
        </client>
```

**6**   Add the following method to the Main subprocedure to test the service:

```
static void Main(string[] args)
  {
       CustomersService.CustomersServiceClient proxy = new
➥CustomersService.CustomersServiceClient
➥("BasicHttpBinding_ICustomersService");
       Console.WriteLine("List all Customers");
       string[] customernames = proxy.ListCustomers();
       foreach (string CustomerName in customernames)
       {
            Console.WriteLine("Name: " + CustomerName);
       }
       Console.ReadLine();

  }
```

**7**   Run the console application. The result should look like figure 8.5.

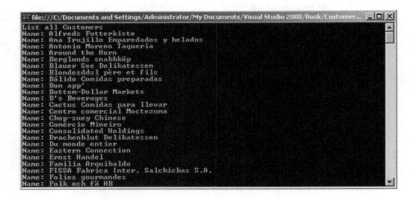

**Figure 8.5   The results of the ListCustomers method**

Web services that expose the line-of-business data from the Business Data Catalog can be useful for Windows applications, web applications, and virtually any other kind of application, making it easier for administrators and developers to consume business data. Later in this book, we'll use this web service to create an Office Business Application that utilizes the Business Data Catalog. Another use of the Business Data Catalog API is to use the object model within a Visual Studio workflow.

## 8.3   *Using the BDC API with a WF workflow*

There are entire books based on the WF (Windows Workflow Foundation), so there's a huge amount of information, perhaps too much to cover in depth within this chapter. This section will focus on the BDC API, but will provide an outline regarding the WF as well. Workflows can be triggered by something changing within a SharePoint list item.

The following example is of a workflow that checks the quantity of products in stock prior to letting someone take an order. If the product isn't in stock, you're prompted to replenish the stocks. This workflow is triggered by an order for a product being placed within a SharePoint custom list. The list is composed of several columns, including a Business Data column that obtains a product ID from a Products table. When an order for a product is made, an information worker will enter the product that she wishes to order along with the quantity. Choosing the product triggers the workflow, which uses the BDC Object Model to check the stock level of that particular product. If the product is in stock, the workflow continues the order process by creating a shipping document, decrementing the stock level, and generating an invoice. If the product doesn't have the required quantity, a SharePoint task item is created in a separate list. The task item requests that we order more of that item from our suppliers. When the task has been completed, the stock level is incremented, and the remainder of the order is placed.

Figure 8.6 is a screenshot of the Visual Studio Workflow Designer, which shows the route the workflow takes.

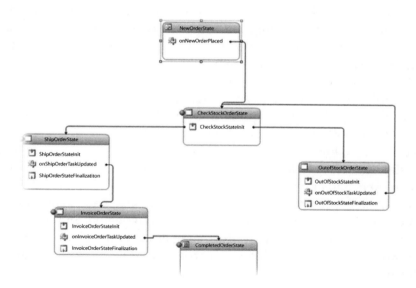

**Figure 8.6   The Visual Studio Workflow Designer**

### 8.3.1  *Types of workflow supported by SharePoint*

Microsoft SharePoint 2007 supports three different types of workflow. Both Windows SharePoint Services (WSS v3) and MOSS 2007 support out-of-the-box workflows. We won't discuss these, as they can't be triggered by the Business Data Catalog. You can also create workflows in Microsoft Office SharePoint Designer. The SPD workflows allow you to create workflows that use the Business Data field type in the conditions. This means that, except for the updates to the stock level, SPD could've been used for this scenario. But while the SPD workflows are powerful, they're difficult to deploy and usually have to be created in the production environment, which is why we decided to use Visual Studio.

Visual Studio provides both Sequential and State Machine workflow templates. The Sequential workflows follow a linear path from start to finish, can include looping and branching, and run from start to finish. The State Machine workflows don't follow a specific path, and activities are triggered by the state of an object changing—for example, the status of an order or a decrease in the number of products available.

#### VISUAL STUDIO WORKFLOWS

Visual Studio provides a visual designer where you can drag workflow activities onto the design surface and set properties. In addition to general activities for WF workflows, you'll find SharePoint-specific workflow activities such as Create Task. This limits the amount of coding that needs to be carried out. The Visual Studio.NET workflow also allows you to use two types of forms. ASPX or InfoPath forms can be created to collect information during the workflow cycle. The forms are used when the workflow is instantiated, and also when you want to check the state of running workflows. The advantage of using Visual Studio workflows is familiarity, whereas the advantage of InfoPath forms is that they'll run within Microsoft Office applications such as Word or Excel.

Once the workflow is complete, like many custom items in SharePoint, you package the workflow as a feature. This provides flexibility in where the workflow can be deployed, and also allows site owners to activate or deactivate the workflow if required. A web solution package (WSP) can also be created, allowing the easy deployment of all the code files from development to staging, and from staging to production. This is a huge benefit when comparing Visual Studio to SharePoint Designer workflows, as SPD workflows are written to the content database and not to the file system.

Of course, the main benefit of using Visual Studio is that you're not limited in what the workflow can do. With a VS.Net workflow, you can go outside the Share-Point environment and gain access to other services or even other applications such as Outlook.

To create a Visual Studio workflow, you can follow these steps:

1  Design and plan the workflow.
2  Author the workflow in Visual Studio.
3  Debug the workflow.
4  Author the feature definition file and elements file.
5  Compile the workflow files into a .NET assembly.
6  Package the workflow as a solution for easy deployment.

These are described in more detail in the following sections.

### DESIGN AND PLAN THE WORKFLOW

While this sounds obvious to developers, it's important that you don't get carried away and design a workflow around the business requirements. Some workflows can be too controlling and rigid, meaning that users aren't provided with any flexibility. You'll end up with the "Computer Says NO!" scenario, which is often bad for business. We like to design our workflows with Visio, where code isn't involved and stakeholders in the workflow can be involved in the process.

### AUTHOR THE WORKFLOW IN VISUAL STUDIO

Authoring the workflow in Visual Studio involves initially dragging activities onto the design surface, as well as setting properties such as the ID of each object and, more importantly, a correlation token. The correlation token is passed through the workflow from activity to activity, keeping track of where the workflow is in the process. Figure 8.7 displays the New Order State Activity. Within the activity is an `OnWorkflowActivated` event object that initializes the correlation token.

Once the workflow activities are in place and the properties are set, you need to write the code to perform the tasks required by the workflow.

The routine shown in listing 8.9 is the start of the workflow. As a new order is placed, the SharePoint object model is used to obtain the column values of the current SharePoint list item.

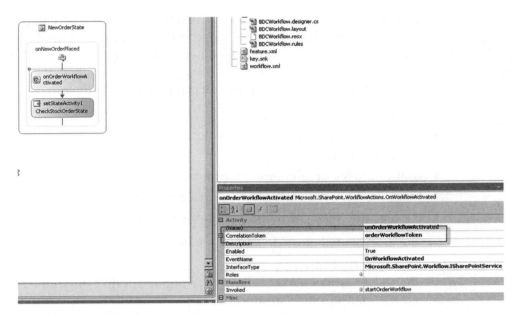

**Figure 8.7    Setting the correlation token**

**Listing 8.9    `startOrderWorkflow` method**

```
private void startOrderWorkflow(object sender, ExternalDataEventArgs e)
    {
        strOrderTitle = workflowProperties.Item["Title"].ToString();

        strCustomerEmailAddress = workflowProperties.Item["Customer:
    EmailAddress"].ToString();

        SPListItem spListItem = workflowProperties.Item;

        BusinessDataField productField =
    (BusinessDataField)spListItem.Fields["Product"];

        string idProductFieldName = string.Format("{0}_ID",
    productField.EntityName);

        string productIDEncoded =
    spListItem.GetFormattedValue(idProductFieldName);

        object[] productID =
    EntityInstanceIdEncoder.DecodeEntityInstanceId(productIDEncoded);

        ProductID = int.Parse(productID[0].ToString());

        BusinessDataField customerField =
    (BusinessDataField)spListItem.Fields["Customer"];
```

```
              string idCustomerFieldName = string.Format("{0}_ID",
➡ customerField.EntityName);

              string customerIDEncoded =
➡ spListItem.GetFormattedValue(idCustomerFieldName);

              object[] customerID =
➡ EntityInstanceIdEncoder.DecodeEntityInstanceId(customerIDEncoded);

         CustomerID = int.Parse(customerID[0].ToString());

              strCustomerTitle = GetEntityColumnValue(customerField,
➡ CustomerID, "Title");

              strCustomerFirstName = GetEntityColumnValue(customerField,
➡ CustomerID, "FirstName");

              strCustomerLastName = GetEntityColumnValue(customerField,
➡CustomerID, "LastName");

              strCustomerCompanyName = GetEntityColumnValue(customerField,
➡CustomerID, "CompanyName");

              strCustomerAddressLine1 = GetEntityColumnValue(customerField,
➡CustomerID, "AddressLine1");

              strCustomerAddressLine2 = GetEntityColumnValue(customerField,
➡ CustomerID, "AddressLine2");

              strCustomerCity = GetEntityColumnValue(customerField,
➡ CustomerID, "City");

              strCustomerStateProvince = GetEntityColumnValue(customerField,
➡ CustomerID, "StateProvince");

              strCustomerCountryRegion = GetEntityColumnValue(customerField,
➡ CustomerID, "CountryRegion");

              strCustomerPostalCode = GetEntityColumnValue(customerField,
➡CustomerID, "PostalCode");

         StringBuilder stringBuilder = new StringBuilder();

              stringBuilder.AppendLine(string.Format("{0} {1} {2}",
➡strCustomerTitle, strCustomerFirstName,strCustomerLastName));
              stringBuilder.AppendLine(",");
              if (strCustomerCompanyName != null)
➡ stringBuilder.AppendLine(strCustomerCompanyName);
              stringBuilder.AppendLine(",");
if (strCustomerAddressLine1 != null)
➡ stringBuilder.AppendLine(strCustomerAddressLine1);
              stringBuilder.AppendLine(",");
              if (strCustomerAddressLine2 != null)
➡ stringBuilder.AppendLine(strCustomerAddressLine2);
➡stringBuilder.AppendLine(",");
              if (strCustomerCity != null)
```

```
⮡ stringBuilder.AppendLine(strCustomerCity);
        stringBuilder.AppendLine(",");
        if (strCustomerStateProvince != null)
⮡ stringBuilder.AppendLine(strCustomerStateProvince);
        stringBuilder.AppendLine(",");
        if (strCustomerCountryRegion != null)
⮡ stringBuilder.AppendLine(strCustomerCountryRegion);
        stringBuilder.AppendLine(",");
        if (strCustomerPostalCode != null)
⮡ stringBuilder.AppendLine(strCustomerPostalCode);

        strCustomerFullAddress = stringBuilder.ToString();
    }
```

This particular workflow uses the Business Data object model to build a data table that's populated by the products stored in the database. This data table is then referenced in situations such as checking stock levels. Listing 8.10 displays the code required to obtain line-of-business data from the database for use as part of the workflow.

**Listing 8.10   Obtaining the LOB system data for the workflow**

```
public DataTable GetEntityDataAsDataTable(BusinessDataField
⮡ businessDataField, int parameter)
    {
        // Get the BDC Instance from the Business Data Field Parameter
        string instance = businessDataField.SystemInstanceName;

        // Get the BDC Entity from the Business Data Field Parameter
        string entity = businessDataField.EntityName;

        // Call method to set the SQL Provider Context
        SetProviderToServerContext();

        // Impersonate the Current Windows user
        WindowsIdentity.GetCurrent().Impersonate();

        NamedLobSystemInstanceDictionary sysInstances =
⮡ ApplicationRegistry.GetLobSystemInstances();

        LobSystemInstance lobSystemInstance = sysInstances[instance];

        // Get desired Entity from the LobSystems Entities
        Entity lobEntity = lobSystemInstance.GetEntities()[entity];

        // Use the Specific Finder to get out Entity Instance
        IEntityInstance entityInstance =
⮡ lobEntity.FindSpecific(parameter, lobSystemInstance);

        return entityInstance.EntityAsFormattedDataTable;
    }
```

The isProductinstock activity reads the property values to cross reference the product number and the number of items in stock, as shown in listing 8.11.

**Listing 8.11 isProductInStock method**

```
private void isProductInStock(object sender, ConditionalEventArgs e)
    {
        // Get the SPList item for the Workflow
        SPListItem spListItem = workflowProperties.Item;

        // Parse the Order Quantity from the List Items Quantity Field
        int orderQuantity =
➥ int.Parse(spListItem.GetFormattedValue("Quantity"));

        // Set the SQL Provider
        SetProviderToServerContext();

        // Impersonate the current windows user
        WindowsIdentity.GetCurrent().Impersonate();

        // Get the Product field from the SPListItem
        BusinessDataField productField =
➥ (BusinessDataField)spListItem.Fields["Product"];

        // Get the Current Stock Level as String from the BDC
        string currentStockLevelAsString =
➥ GetEntityColumnValue(productField, ProductID, "StockLevel");

        // Parser the current Stock Level as Int
        int currentStockLevel = int.Parse(currentStockLevelAsString);
        e.Result = orderQuantity <= currentStockLevel;

        return;
    }
```

**DEBUGGING THE WORKFLOW**

You can easily debug a Visual Studio workflow by setting the SharePoint debugging options. A wizard is triggered by right-clicking the Project file and choosing SharePoint Debug settings. You can then input the name of the workflow as it'll show up in SharePoint, as well as the site you wish to use to perform the debugging, as shown in figure 8.8.

You can then set the SharePoint list or library to test the workflow in, as well as your History list and Task list, as shown in figure 8.9. It's recommended that you always create a new History list and write to it to test the different activities.

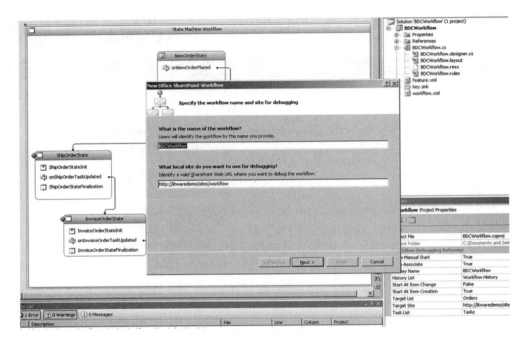

**Figure 8.8   The SharePoint debugging options**

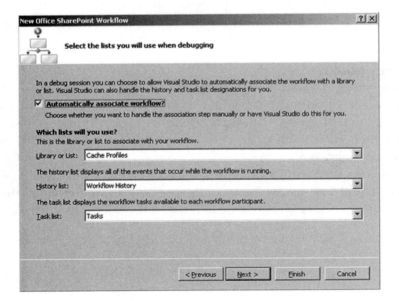

**Figure 8.9   The SharePoint Debug settings**

**AUTHOR THE FEATURE FOR THE WORKFLOW**

The Feature.xml file is used to set properties for a feature, such as the ID, Title, Description, Scope, and so on. Listing 8.12 shows a typical Feature.xml file.

**Listing 8.12   Feature.xml file for the workflow**

```
<Feature  Id="33c4dd00-c4dd-4786-9756-90083aa6338f"
      Title="BDCWorkflow feature"
      Description="My SharePoint Workflow Feature"
      Version="12.0.0.0"
      Scope="Site"
      ReceiverAssembly="Microsoft.Office.Workflow.Feature,
➥ Version=12.0.0.0, Culture=neutral, PublicKeyToken=71e9bce111e9429c"

      ReceiverClass="Microsoft.Office.Workflow.Feature.WorkflowFeatureReceiver
      "
      xmlns="http://schemas.microsoft.com/sharepoint/">
  <ElementManifests>
    <ElementManifest Location="workflow.xml" />
  </ElementManifests>
  <Properties>
    <Property Key="GloballyAvailable" Value="true" />

    <!-- Value for RegisterForms key indicates the path to the forms
➥ relative to feature file location -->
    <!-- if you don't have forms, use *.xsn -->
    <Property Key="RegisterForms" Value="*.xsn" />
  </Properties>
</Feature>
```

The Workflow.xml file is what's described as the elements file. This file describes exactly what the feature intends to do, where to find the assembly file, and which forms to use for the initiation form, status form, and so on. Listing 8.13 shows a typical Workflow.xml file.

**Listing 8.13   Elements.xml file for workflow deployment**

```
<Elements xmlns="http://schemas.microsoft.com/sharepoint/">
  <Workflow
      Name="BDCWorkflow"
      Description="My SharePoint Workflow"
      Id="8f3726f9-a775-4b2c-81b2-5d652e3fbb1c"
      CodeBesideClass="BDCWorkflow.BDCWorkflow"
      CodeBesideAssembly="BDCWorkflow, Version=1.0.0.0, Culture=neutral,
➥ PublicKeyToken=570a2c350488292c">

    <Categories/>
    <MetaData>
      <!-- Tags to specify InfoPath forms for the workflow; delete tags for
➥ forms that you do not have -->
```

```
      <!--<Association_FormURN>[URN FOR ASSOCIATION
➥ FORM]</Association_FormURN>
        <Instantiation_FormURN>[URN FOR INSTANTIATION
➥ FORM]</Instantiation_FormURN>
      <Task0_FormURN>[URN FOR TASK (type 0) FORM]</Task0_FormURN>
      <Task1_FormURN>[URN FOR TASK (type 1) FORM]</Task1_FormURN>-->
      <!-- Modification forms: create a unique guid for each modification
➥ form -->
      <!--<Modification_[UNIQUE GUID]_FormURN>[URN FOR MODIFICATION
➥ FORM]</Modification_[UNIQUE GUID]_FormURN>
      <Modification_[UNIQUE GUID]_Name>[NAME OF MODIFICATION TO BE
➥ DISPLAYED AS A LINK ON WORKFLOW STATUS PAGE</Modification_[UNIQUE
➥ GUID]_Name>
      -->
      <StatusPageUrl>_layouts/WrkStat.aspx</StatusPageUrl>
    </MetaData>
  </Workflow>
</Elements>
```

**PACKAGE THE WORKFLOW INTO A WSP FOR EASY DEPLOYMENT**

Though optional, this part of the process is very important. It means that, as a workflow developer, you can simply provide your administrator with a single WSP file that she can deploy via Stsadm. If for some reason the workflow is retired or causes a problem, it can be easily retracted by the administrator using the command line. We recommend WSP Builder, which is a free tool that will provide you with a DDF (Diamond Directive File) and WSP file.

## 8.4   *Summary*

Within this chapter, we explored each of the Business Data Catalog namespaces. We gave a code example that demonstrated the use of each, and also explained which namespaces are for internal use only. We then gave a working example true to a real-world requirement, which demonstrated using the namespaces to create a WCF web service that exposes data for use in other business-oriented applications such as OBA (Office Business Applications). Finally, we explored how to use the BDC data in a Visual Studio workflow, which allows your workflow to perform SharePoint actions such as create tasks based on conditions set within the back-end LOB system.

In chapter 9, we'll provide another example of using the BDC Object Model, which will involve using a call-back method and BDC to present data in a web part that refreshes automatically.

# Creating a custom
# BDC Web Part

## This chapter covers

- Building a custom BDC Web Part
- Building a basic web part
- Using the ASP.NET Web Part methods
- Packing and deploying the web part

In the previous chapter, we explored the `ApplicationRegistry` namespace and the BDC Object Model. There are several reasons why you'd want to code with the object model, as we explained in the previous chapter. One of those reasons is to create your own custom web parts. Within my company, we've created several web parts, including one that displays address details such as customer, supplier, or employee addresses in a Virtual Earth map. Within this web part, we take the street address and the town, using the object model to access the back-end data, then pass that information to the Virtual Earth web service. Another web part we offer displays data information in a calendar. So we created a Calendar Web Part that takes a start date, end date, and title using the

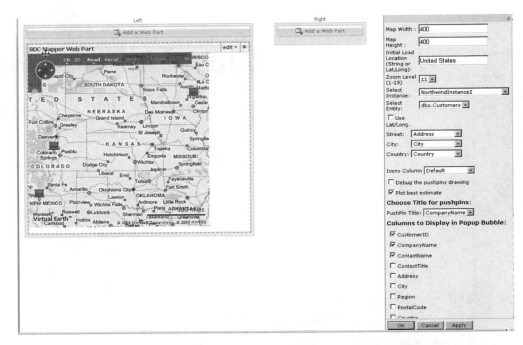

**Figure 9.1   The Lightning Tools BDC Mapper Web Part, which uses business data to pinpoint addresses on a Virtual Earth map. This is done via the BDC Object Model and a custom web part.**

back-end data, and then positions the information in the calendar control. Figure 9.1 shows a screenshot of the Lightning Tools BDC Mapper Web Part and the tool pane that displays how the properties are set. This instance of the web part is used to plot the Northwind customer addresses.

Within this chapter, we'll create our own custom web part that will display the business data in a control. We'll improve on the out-of-the-box Business Data List Web Part by making it an Ajax-style web part. To do that, we're going to use a technique that will allow the data displayed in the grid to refresh every few seconds without requiring the entire page to be refreshed. First, let's describe how to create a basic custom web part.

## 9.1   *Building a basic custom web part*

Tools are available to help you create a custom web part quickly, such as WSP-Builder. But if this is your first attempt at creating a custom web part, it's useful to understand how to create one from scratch. That way, if something goes wrong, you'll know how to fix it.

To create a custom web part, we'll use Visual Studio.NET. It doesn't matter if you use Visual Studio.NET 2005 or Visual Studio.NET 2008. We start off with a Class Library project, and inherit from a `WebPart` class, from which there are now two `WebPart` classes to choose. We'll discuss the pros and cons of both the SharePoint Web Part class and the ASP.NET Web Part class. The namespaces for these web parts are `System.Web.UI.WebControls.WebParts.WebPart` (ASP.NET) and `Micro-soft.SharePoint.WebPartPages.WebPart` (SharePoint, WSS). The `Microsoft.SharePoint.WebPartPages.WebPart` (WSS) class is ideal for backward compatibility with Windows SharePoint Services, version 2.0. The WSS class also offers better web part connection functionality. But if you use the WSS class, your web part will only work in WSS and you won't be able to utilize it in a standard ASP.NET web application. So typically we always use the ASP.NET Web Part class.

There are also some requirements that we have to put in place. In order to access the object model in SharePoint, we'll need to create a custom code access security policy file that permits the web part to access the SharePoint object model. Of course, we could simply put our DLL in the Global Assembly Cache (c:\windows\Assembly). This isn't considered a best practice, however, as the web part would automatically gain full permissions to do everything. Alternatively, we could modify our `Web.Config` file to set the Trust Level to WSS_Medium or Full. WSS_Medium does allow access to the object model, but by changing this setting, you're giving all third-party or custom web parts additional permissions. If we go down the route of creating a custom CAS (code access security) policy, we'll require a strongly named DLL.

Except for coding of course, the last part of creating a custom web part is to create a WSP (web solution package). This is a special kind of CAB file that contains the DLL, the `.webpart` file, and the resource files. When deployed as a solution to SharePoint, the files are all placed where they should be according to a `Manifest.xml` file. The good point of having the web part packaged as a solution is that the policy file, DLL, and resource files can be deployed on each web front-end server without having to manually copy them. They can also be retracted if you have one of those Friday afternoon moments when the web part wasn't quite ready!

Prior to writing any code in a web part or dealing with the WSP, I always prefer to just get the web part created and deployed to the site. That way, I can write my code knowing that, to test it, I only have to build the project and then refresh the page that contains it. Once I end up with a working web part, I then package it up for deployment. To get the web part plumbing taken care of, follow these steps:

1  Start Visual Studio.NET by choosing Start, All Programs, Microsoft Visual Studio 200x, Microsoft Visual Studio 200x.

2   Choose File, New, Project, and select the Class Library project from the Visual C#, Windows section.

3   Name the project `MyBDC.AjaxBDCWebPart`.

4   Expand Properties from the Solution Explorer window, and open the `AssemblyInfo.cs` file and verify that the version number is set to 1.0.0.0. We use a static version instead of a dynamic version, as we have to fully qualify the name of the web part in the `web.config` and `MyBDC.AjaxBDCWeb-Part.webpart` files.

5   Enter the following assembly tag under the existing assembly tags:

```
[assembly: System.Security.AllowPartiallyTrustedCallers()]
```

6   Right-click the project using the Solution Explorer window, and choose Properties.

7   Set the Build Output path to point at the `bin` directory of your web application. If you don't have a `bin` directory, you can create one. This makes it quick to build and refresh when changing your code while still developing. Figure 9.2 is a screenshot showing the Output Path property of the Project properties.

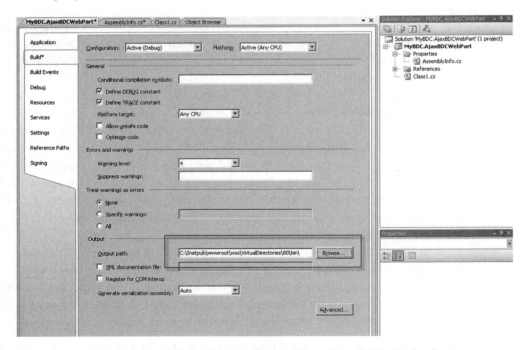

**Figure 9.2   Project properties with the Output path set to the web application's `bin` directory**

8 Sign the web part by clicking the Signing tab of the Project Properties dialog box.

9 Check the Sign the Assembly check box.

10 Choose New from the Choose a strong key file drop-down list box. Give your key file a name such as `BDCBook`, as shown in figure 9.3.

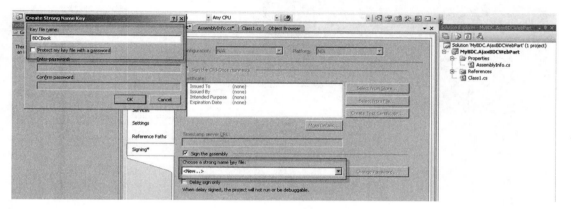

**Figure 9.3   Creating a key file to sign the DLL**

11 Add a reference to `System.Web` file by right-clicking the project and choosing Add Reference. Find `System.Web` in the list and click OK.

12 Rename the `class1.cs` file to `AjaxBDCPart.cs`, and choose Yes to refractor the code when prompted.

13 Open the `AjaxBDCPart.cs` file, and use the `System.Web.UI.WebControls.WebParts` namespace by typing

```
using System.Web.UI.WebControls.WebParts;
```

14 Inherit the Web Part class as shown:

```
public class AjaxBDCPart : System.Web.UI.WebControls.WebParts.WebPart
```

15 Override the `RenderContents` method of the Web Part class by creating the following method:

```
protected override void  RenderContents(System.Web.UI.HtmlTextWriter
➥ writer)
{
    writer.Write("Test Web Part");
}
```

16 Build the Web Part Project by pressing Ctrl + Shift + B.

**17** Obtain the public key token by opening up a Visual Studio.NET command prompt and typing SN -Tp c:\inetpub\wwwroot\wss\virtual directories\ 80\bin\MyBDC\AjaxBDCWebPart.dll, as shown in figure 9.4.

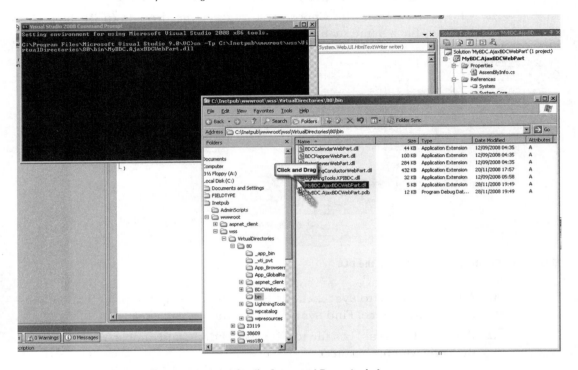

**Figure 9.4   Dragging the DLL into the Visual Studio Command Prompt window**

**NOTE**      We find it easier to drag the DLL from My Computer into the Command Prompt window.

**18** Right-click the Command Prompt window and then choose Mark.

**19** Highlight the public key token and then put it on the clipboard by pressing Enter. (Leave this window open, as later we'll need the public key blob.) Figure 9.5 displays the public key token that needs to be copied.

**20** Edit the `Web.Config` file for your web application and create a `SafeControl` entry such as the following, using your public key token from the clipboard:

```
<SafeControl Assembly="MyBDC.AjaxBDCWebPart, Version=1.0.0.0,
➥Culture=neutral, PublicKeyToken=2b3e278b596a631f"
➥ Namespace="MyBDC.AjaxBDCWebPart" TypeName="*" Safe="True" />
```

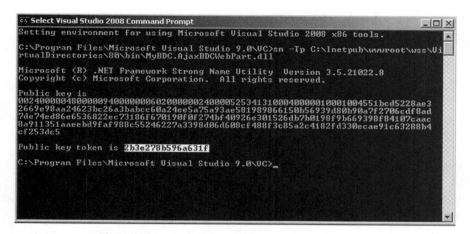

**Figure 9.5   Highlight the public key token**

**21**   Save the `Web.Config` file, then recycle your application pool.

**22**   Navigate to the top-level site of your web application.

**23**   Choose Site Actions, Site Settings, Modify All Site Settings.

**24**   Click the Web Part Gallery link.

**25**   In the Web Part Gallery, click New.

**26**   Select your web part, and then choose Populate Gallery, as shown in figure 9.6.

**27**   Navigate to a SharePoint team site, or create a new SharePoint team site.

**28**   Choose Site Actions, Edit Page.

| | | | |
|---|---|---|---|
| ☐ Microsoft.SharePoint.WebPartPages.MembersWebPart | MembersWebPart | .dwp | Culture=neutral,<br>PublicKeyToken=71e9bce111e9429c |
| ☐ Microsoft.SharePoint.WebPartPages.PageViewerWebPart | PageViewerWebPart | .dwp | Microsoft.SharePoint, Version=12.0.0.0,<br>Culture=neutral,<br>PublicKeyToken=71e9bce111e9429c |
| ☐ Microsoft.SharePoint.WebPartPages.SimpleFormWebPart | SimpleFormWebPart | .dwp | Microsoft.SharePoint, Version=12.0.0.0,<br>Culture=neutral,<br>PublicKeyToken=71e9bce111e9429c |
| ☐ Microsoft.SharePoint.WebPartPages.TitleBarWebPart | TitleBarWebPart | .dwp | Microsoft.SharePoint, Version=12.0.0.0,<br>Culture=neutral,<br>PublicKeyToken=71e9bce111e9429c |
| ☐ Microsoft.SharePoint.WebPartPages.UserDocsWebPart | UserDocsWebPart | .dwp | Microsoft.SharePoint, Version=12.0.0.0,<br>Culture=neutral,<br>PublicKeyToken=71e9bce111e9429c |
| ☐ Microsoft.SharePoint.WebPartPages.UserTasksWebPart | UserTasksWebPart | .dwp | Microsoft.SharePoint, Version=12.0.0.0,<br>Culture=neutral,<br>PublicKeyToken=71e9bce111e9429c |
| ☐ Microsoft.SharePoint.WebPartPages.XmlWebPart | XmlWebPart | .dwp | Microsoft.SharePoint, Version=12.0.0.0,<br>Culture=neutral,<br>PublicKeyToken=71e9bce111e9429c |
| ☑ MyBDC.AjaxBDCWebPart.AjaxBDCPart | AjaxBDCPart | .webpart | MyBDC.AjaxBDCWebPart, Version=1.0.0.0,<br>Culture=neutral,<br>PublicKeyToken=2b3e278b596a631f |

**Figure 9.6   Populating the Web Part Gallery**

**29**  Click Add a Web Part.

**30**  Add your custom web part to the page. The result should look like figure 9.7.

**Figure 9.7    The custom web part with the test code in it**

Now that we've gotten to this point, we can simply add code to our web part, then build it, and refresh the web part page to test the changes. This is always a good practice, as you don't want to be in the situation where you can't even deploy your web part due to a code error. In the next section, we'll add further code to our web part so that it accesses the BDC Object Model and displays data.

## 9.2    *Adding the functional code*

In this section, we'll get our web part to do something more than display some text. We need to reference the Microsoft Office Server DLL so that we have access to the BDC, and then we can design our user interface in code. We'll build a data grid and populate it with BDC data.

**1**  Add a reference to Windows SharePoint Services (`Microsoft.Share-Point.dll`), `System.Drawing`, and Microsoft Office Server Component (`Microsoft.SharePoint.Portal.dll`).

**2**  Make sure that you have the namespaces shown in listing 9.1.

### Listing 9.1    The `using` statements required for your web part

```
using System;
using System.Collections.Generic;
using System.Text;
using System.Web.UI.WebControls.WebParts;
using Microsoft.Office.Server.ApplicationRegistry.MetadataModel;
using Microsoft.Office.Server.ApplicationRegistry.Runtime;
using Microsoft.SharePoint.WebControls;
using System.Web.UI.WebControls;
using System.Data;
```

**3** Create a variable to hold an error message:

```
string errormessage;
```

**4** Create a `BuildTable` method that will iterate the field collection from the entity and then generate a field in a data grid, as shown in listing 9.2.

**Listing 9.2    The `BuildDataTable` method**

```
      private static DataTable BuildDataTable(FieldCollection
fieldCollection)
      {
          DataTable dt = new DataTable();              Create new data
          foreach (Field f in fieldCollection)         table called dt
          {
              DataColumn dc = new DataColumn(f.Name,         Create data
  Type.GetType(f.TypeDescriptor.TypeName));                  column for each
              dt.Columns.Add(dc);                            BDC column
          } return dt;
      }
```

**5** Override the `CreateChildControls()` method to create the `DataTable` and populate it with data from the entity. You can see from listing 9.3 that we're obtaining the `LobSystem`, `LobSystemInstance`, and `Entity` by naming them. The web part could be improved by exposing these as web part properties. Once we have the entity, we execute a filter method and then populate a data table. A separate procedure called `BuildDataTable` allows us to iterate through all of the columns in the entity and create them as columns in the data grid. This could also be improved by creating an admin page that allows the user to set the sort order and choose which columns to display, and also offers grouping options.

**Listing 9.3    The `CreateChildControls` method to create our `GridView`**

```
protected override void CreateChildControls()
      {
          try
          {                                              Obtain LOBSystem
              LobSystem adWorksLobSystem =               and entity
  ApplicationRegistry.GetLobSystems()["NorthwindLOBSystem2"];
              LobSystemInstance myIns =
  adWorksLobSystem.GetLobSystemInstances()["NorthwindInstance2"];
              Entity myEntity = myIns.GetEntities()["dbo.Customers"];
              FilterCollection fc = myEntity.GetFinderFilters();
              IEntityInstanceEnumerator prodEntityInstanceEnumerator =
  myEntity.FindFiltered(fc, myIns);
              // Build a datatable
              DataTable dtResults;
```

```
                   dtResults =
⇒  BuildDataTable(myEntity.GetFinderView().Fields);
                   SPGridView dg;
                dg = new SPGridView();

              dg.DataSource = dtResults.DefaultView;
              while (prodEntityInstanceEnumerator.MoveNext())      ⟵┐
              {                                              Iterate through items
                    IEntityInstance IE =                      and populate grid
⇒  prodEntityInstanceEnumerator.Current;
                    DataRow dr = dtResults.NewRow();
                    BoundField colName = new BoundField();
                    foreach (Field f in myEntity.GetFinderView().Fields)
                    {
                        if (IE[f] != null)
                      {
                            dr[f.Name] = IE[f];
                        }
                  }

                    // Add the Rows to the Data Table
                    dtResults.Rows.Add(dr);              ┐  Set data grid
              }                                       ⟵─┘  properties
              dg.PagerTemplate = null;
              dg.AutoGenerateColumns = true;
              dg.EditRowStyle.BackColor = System.Drawing.Color.LightBlue;
              dg.DataBind();
              this.Controls.Add(dg);
          }
          catch (Exception ex)
          {
              errormessage = ex.Message;
          }
      }
```

All you have to do now is build and refresh to see your data. We're by no means finished, though. First, the web part page will generate error! We have to deal with code access security to get that to work. We'll then see our data, but it won't refresh by itself yet.

### 9.2.1  *The Ajax-style refresh interval*

In order to get the web part to refresh by itself, we could write a web service and use JavaScript to fire the web service similar to Ajax. But my friend Todd Bleeker introduced me to the Callback method, which is a way to embed JavaScript into your code to mimic Ajax. There's no need to write a web service with this method. It seems to work well! First, let's make sure we can continue to test our code by getting around the code access security issue.

1 If you see an error page after rebuilding your project, you'll need to set up a new code access security policy. Before we do that, we can cheat for now so that we can continue developing. We only recommend doing this in your development environment, not in production. We need to edit the `Web.Config` file for the web application and set the Trust Level to Full, as shown:

```
<trust level="Full" originUrl="" />
```

2 Recycle your application pool, then test the web part again.

3 You should now see your data displayed in a data grid. If you open the database that you're connected to and change one of the rows that are displayed, you'll notice that you have to refresh the entire web part page to see your change. If the data updates are critical to your business, you may want them to refresh every few seconds. You may want to see support calls being displayed automatically rather than having to refresh the page.

4 To get started, we'll need to add one more reference. Add a reference to `System.Drawing`.

5 Copy the code that's currently in your `CreateChildControls` method and put it in Notepad for the time being.

6 Add the following `using` statements:

```
using System.IO;
using System.Web.UI;
```

7 Implement the `ICallbackEventHandler` as shown:

```
System.Web.UI.ICallbackEventHandler
```

8 Create a constant that will store the path to an Ajax-style refresh GIF:

```
const string GEARS_GIF = "/_layouts/images/kpiprogressbar.GIF";
```

9 Create a property and variable that will allow the user to set the refresh interval of the web part, as shown in listing 9.4.

**Listing 9.4    The Refresh Rate property for the Ajax-style refresh interval**

```
private int _refresh = 5;

[WebBrowsable(true)
, Personalizable(PersonalizationScope.User)
]
public int Refresh
{
    get { return _refresh; }
    set { _refresh = value; }
}
```

10    Change your `CreateChildControls` method so that it resembles the one in listing 9.5. The `CreateChildControls` method will only be called briefly and will then be overwritten by a call that renders straight after the load event. The purpose that it serves here is to simply display the Ajax-style progress bar.

**Listing 9.5    New `CreateChildControls` method, which renders an image**

```
protected override void CreateChildControls()
{
    try
    {
        Image img = new Image();
        img.ImageUrl = GEARS_GIF;
        this.Controls.Add(img);
    }
    catch (Exception ex)
    {
        errormessage = ex.Message;
    }
}
```

11    We're now going to use the `OnLoad` event to place some JavaScript on the page. You can see how the `ClientScriptManager` is used to register the script. The script generates a unique ID for the web part so that more than one of them can be placed on the page. It also gets the refresh interval from the web part's variable. The script is then loaded into the web part's `innerHTML`. Listing 9.6 is the web part's `OnLoad` event, which has the job of generating the JavaScript functions that in turn get registered into the web part page.

**Listing 9.6    The Ajax-style `OnLoad` event, which fires the JavaScript**

```
protected override void OnLoad(EventArgs e)
{
    System.Web.UI.ClientScriptManager csm = Page.ClientScript;
    StringBuilder js = new StringBuilder();

    //General JavaScript functions that can be added by
➥any Web Part
    string SCRIPT_NAME = "GeneralClientCallbackScript";

    if (!csm.IsClientScriptBlockRegistered(SCRIPT_NAME))
    {
        js.Append("function CallServer(arg, context)")
            .Append("{ \n")
            .Append("  try \n")
            .Append("  { \n")
```

```
                              .Append("     var element =
➡ document.getElementById(context); \n")
                         .Append("     if(element) \n")
                     .Append("     { \n")
                     .Append("        if(arg != 'Initial') \n")
                     .Append("        { \n")
                     //.Append("           element.innerHTML = 'Loading...';
➡ \n")
                     .Append("        } \n")
                 .Append(csm.GetCallbackEventReference(
                              this,
                              "arg",
                              "HandleCallbackResult",
                              "context",
                              true)
                         )
             .Append("     } \n")
             .Append("   } \n")
             .Append("   catch(e){window.status = 'ERROR:' + e.Message}
➡ \n")
             .Append("} \n");

             js.Append("function HandleCallbackResult(arg, context) \n")
               .Append("{ \n")
               .Append("   try \n")
               .Append("   { \n")
               .Append("     var element = \n")
               .Append("        document.getElementById(context); \n")
               .Append("     if(element) \n")
               .Append("     { \n")
               .Append("        element.innerHTML = arg; \n")
               .Append("     } \n")
               .Append("   } \n")
               .Append("   catch(e){window.status = 'ERROR:' + e.Message}
➡ \n")
               .Append("} \n");

             csm.RegisterClientScriptBlock(
                 this.GetType(),
                 SCRIPT_NAME,
                 js.ToString(),
                 true);
         }

         //Clear the string builder
         js.Remove(0, js.Length);

         string refreshSeconds = string.Format("{0:d}", this.Refresh *
➡1000);

         //BootWebPart is needed because functions that run when
         //Body Onload is fired cannot have parameters
         //Invoke CallServer with a call to populate this Web Part's
```

⇒ innerHTML
```
        js.Append("function BootWebPart" + this.ID + "() \n")
          .Append("{ \n")
          .Append("  CallServer('Initial', 'ct100_m_' + '" + this.ID +
⇒ "'); \n")
          .Append("  setInterval( GetTime, " + 1000 + "); \n")
        .Append("} \n");

        js.Append("function GetTime() \n")
        .Append("{ \n")
        .Append("  CallServer('DisplayDataGrid', 'divTime'); \n")
      .Append("} \n");

        //Run BootWebPart when the Page has fully loaded
        js.Append("_spBodyOnLoadFunctionNames.push('BootWebPart" +
⇒ this.ID + "'); \n");

        //Unique JavaScript name for this Web Part script
        SCRIPT_NAME = this.ID + "Script";

      csm.RegisterClientScriptBlock(
          this.GetType(),
          SCRIPT_NAME,
          js.ToString(),
          true);
    }
```

**12**  The `ICallbackEventHandler` members keep track of the `eventArgument` variable, which can be set to `Initial` or `DisplayDataGrid`. The `Initial` call populates the web part initially and fires the `CreateChildControls` method. Then the `DisplayDataGrid` `eventArgument` is passed, creating the `DataGrid`. This is where you place the code that was in the `CreateChild-Controls` method. The callback method in listing 9.7 is fired upon the set interval and displays the data grid periodically without a page refresh.

**Listing 9.7   The callback methods**

```
#region ICallbackEventHandler Members

 //Holds the case of the switch statement requested
 private string _eventArgument = "";

 //Initially called by the client-side JavaScript
 public void RaiseCallbackEvent(string eventArgument)
 {
     //Save aside the function requested
     _eventArgument = eventArgument;
 }
 public string GetCallbackResult()
 {
     StringWriter sWriter = new StringWriter();
```

```
        HtmlTextWriter writer = new HtmlTextWriter(sWriter);
        StringBuilder sb = new StringBuilder();
        Label lbl = null;
        switch (_eventArgument)
        {
            //Called when the page first loads to generate the
User Interface controls
            case "Initial":
                writer = RenderUI(writer);
              break;

            // //Called when the Get Server Time button is clicked
            case "DisplayDataGrid":
                try
                {
                Table tbl;
                tbl = new Table();
                TableRow row = new TableRow();
                TableCell cell = new TableCell();
                LobSystem adWorksLobSystem =
ApplicationRegistry.GetLobSystems()["NorthwindLOBSystem2"];
                LobSystemInstance myIns =
adWorksLobSystem.GetLobSystemInstances()["NorthwindInstance2"];
                Entity myEntity = myIns.GetEntities()["dbo.Customers"];
                FilterCollection fc = myEntity.GetFinderFilters();
                IEntityInstanceEnumerator prodEntityInstanceEnumerator
= myEntity.FindFiltered(fc, myIns);
                // Build a datatable
                DataTable dtResults;
                dtResults =
BuildDataTable(myEntity.GetFinderView().Fields);
                DataGrid dg;
                dg = new DataGrid();
                dg.DataSource = dtResults.DefaultView;
                while (prodEntityInstanceEnumerator.MoveNext())
                {
                    IEntityInstance IE =
prodEntityInstanceEnumerator.Current;
                    DataRow dr = dtResults.NewRow();
                    BoundField colName = new BoundField();
                    foreach (Field f in
myEntity.GetFinderView().Fields)
                    {
                        if (IE[f] != null)
                        {

                            dr[f.Name] = IE[f];
                        }
                    }
                    // Add the Rows to the Data Table
                    dtResults.Rows.Add(dr);
                }
```

```
        dg.AutoGenerateColumns = true;
        dg.DataBind();
        this.Controls.Add(dg);
            dg.RenderControl(writer);
        }
        catch (Exception ex)
        {
            sWriter.Write(ex.Message);
        }
      break;

    //Never called, this is an exception
    default:
        lbl = new Label();
        lbl.Text = "ERROR: Unknown eventArgument";
        lbl.ForeColor = System.Drawing.Color.Red;
        lbl.RenderControl(writer);
        break;
  }

    return sWriter.ToString();
  }
 #endregion
```

**13**  The final part of this code is the `RenderUI` method. The `RenderUI` method generates the `timeSpan` label and stores the `DateTime` so that the web part can fire the appropriate method once the interval has passed. The code is shown in listing 9.8.

**Listing 9.8  The `RenderUI` method writing out the initial HTML**

```
    private HtmlTextWriter RenderUI(HtmlTextWriter writer)
    {
        Panel div = null;
      div = new Panel();

        string dateSpanId = "date" + DateTime.Now.Ticks.ToString();
      string timeSpanId = "divTime";

        Label timeSpan = new Label();
        timeSpan.Attributes.Add("id", timeSpanId);
        Image img = new Image();
        img.ImageUrl = GEARS_GIF;
        this.Controls.Add(img);
        div.Controls.Add(timeSpan);
        div.Controls.Add(img);
        div.RenderControl(writer);
        return writer;
      }
  }
}
```

14  Build the project again, and refresh the web part page.

15  You should see similar results to before, only this time the web part will keep refreshing itself. Modify a record in the database, and this time you won't need to refresh the page. The finished web part should resemble figure 9.8.

**Figure 9.8   The web part while it loads the data. It takes nanoseconds to display the data, so we deliberately delay it to give it the Ajax effect.**

Once the data is displayed, you can test the results by changing the data at the source, and then simply watch the web part refresh itself, as shown in figure 9.9.

So we now have a working Ajax-style web part. We just need to finish it up nicely so that it can be easily deployed by administrators, including setting up a custom code access security policy. In order to achieve that, we need to create a few more files. You're required to have a `.webpart` file. If you have any experience with creating web parts in SharePoint 2003, you may have created a `.dwp` file, which is similar. The `.webpart` file enables SharePoint to locate the web part's DLL, and can also be used to set some of the web part properties. We'll also need to create a solution manifest file. The solution manifest file contains all of the information required to deploy the web part. It requires the public key token and all of the information to create a `SafeControlEntry` in the `Web.Config` file, including the namespace and assembly name. It also requires information about where to put the DLL and any other resource files such as images, XML, JavaScript files, and so forth. One of the features of the solution manifest is to store the information required to create a custom code access security file.

## 9.3    *Creating a code access security file*

We now have a working web part, but we need to change back the Trust Level to keep our operations department happy. Using the solution manifest file, we can get the WSP to create a custom code access security policy file to grant our web part the permissions it requires without having to give every web part Full Trust.

AjaxBDCPart

| CustomerID | CompanyName | ContactName | ContactTitle | Address | City | Region | PostalCode | Country | Phone | Fax |
|---|---|---|---|---|---|---|---|---|---|---|
| ALFKI | Alfreds Futterkiste | Brett | Sales Representative | Obere Str. 57 | Berlin | | 12209 | Germany | 030-0074321 | 030-0076545 |
| ANATR | Ana Trujillo Emparedados y helados | Ana Trujillo | Owner | Avda. de la Constitución 2222 | México D.F. | | 05021 | Mexico | (5) 555-4729 | (5) 555-3745 |
| ANTON | Antonio Moreno Taquería | Antonio Moreno | Owner | Mataderos 2312 | México D.F. | | 05023 | Mexico | (5) 555-3932 | |
| AROUT | Around the Horn | Thomas Hardy | Sales Representative | 120 Hanover Sq. | London | | WA1 1DP | UK | (171) 555-7788 | (171) 555-6750 |
| BERGS | Berglunds snabbköp | Christina Berglund | Order Administrator | Berguvsvägen 8 | Luleå | | S-958 22 | Sweden | 0921-12 34 65 | 0921-12 34 67 |
| BLAUS | Blauer See Delikatessen | Hanna Moos | Sales Representative | Forsterstr. 57 | Mannheim | | 68306 | Germany | 0621-08460 | 0621-08924 |
| BLONP | Blondesddsl père et fils | Frédérique Citeaux | Marketing Manager | 24, place Kléber | Strasbourg | | 67000 | France | 88.60.15.31 | 88.60.15.32 |
| BOLID | Bólido Comidas preparadas | Martín Sommer | Owner | C/ Araquil, 67 | Madrid | | 28023 | Spain | (91) 555 22 82 | (91) 555 91 99 |
| BONAP | Bon app' | Laurence Lebihan | Owner | 12, rue des Bouchers | Marseille | | 13008 | France | 91.24.45.40 | 91.24.45.41 |
| BOTTM | Bottom-Dollar Markets | Elizabeth Lincoln | Accounting Manager | 23 Tsawassen Blvd. | Tsawassen | BC | T2F 8M4 | Canada | (604) 555-4729 | (604) 555-3745 |
| BSBEV | B's Beverages | Victoria Ashworth | Sales Representative | Fauntleroy Circus | London | | EC2 5NT | UK | (171) 555-1212 | |
| CACTU | Cactus Comidas para llevar | Patricio Simpson | Sales Agent | Cerrito 333 | Buenos Aires | | 1010 | Argentina | (1) 135-5555 | (1) 135-4892 |
| CENTC | Centro comercial Moctezuma | Francisco Chang | Marketing Manager | Sierras de Granada 9993 | México D.F. | | 05022 | Mexico | (5) 555-3392 | (5) 555-7293 |
| CHOPS | Chop-suey Chinese | Yang Wang | Owner | Hauptstr. 29 | Bern | | 3012 | Switzerland | 0452-076545 | |
| COMMI | Comércio Mineiro | Pedro Afonso | Sales Associate | Av. dos Lusíadas, 23 | Sao Paulo | SP | 05432-043 | Brazil | (11) 555-7647 | |
| CONSH | Consolidated Holdings | Elizabeth Brown | Sales Representative | Berkeley Gardens 12 Brewery | London | | WX1 6LT | UK | (171) 555-2282 | (171) 555-9199 |
| DRACD | Drachenblut Delikatessen | Sven Ottlieb | Order Administrator | Walserweg 21 | Aachen | | 52066 | Germany | 0241-039123 | 0241-059428 |
| DUMON | Du monde entr | Janine Labrune | Owner | 67, rue des Cinquante Otages | Nantes | | 44000 | France | 40.67.88.88 | 40.67.89.89 |
| EASTC | Eastern Connection | Ann Devon | Sales Agent | 35 King George | London | | WX3 6FW | UK | (171) 555-0297 | (171) 555-3373 |
| ERNSH | Ernst Handel | Roland Mendel | Sales Manager | Kirchgasse 6 | Graz | | 8010 | Austria | 7675-3425 | 7675-3426 |
| FAMIA | Familia Arquibaldo | Aria Cruz | Marketing Assistant | Rua Orós, 92 | Sao Paulo | SP | 05442-030 | Brazil | (11) 555-9857 | |
| | FISSA Fabrica | | | | | | | | | |

**Figure 9.9   The completed custom web part. The highlighted part is the change that was made that didn't require a page refresh.**

1   To create the `.webpart` file, right-click your project and choose Add, New Item. Select the XML file template and name the file `AjaxBDCPart.webpart`, as shown in figure 9.10.

2   Populate the `AjaxBDCPart.webpart` file with the XML shown in listing 9.9.

**Listing 9.9   The .webpart file's XML**

```
<webParts>
  <webPart xmlns="http://schemas.microsoft.com/WebPart/v3">
    <metaData>
      <type name="MyBDC.AjaxBDCWebPart, MyBDC.AjaxBDCWebPart,
    Version=1.0.0.0, Culture=neutral,
➥ PublicKeyToken=[[InsertPublicKeyToken]]" />
      <importErrorMessage>Cannot import this Web Part.</importErrorMessage>
    </metaData>
```

```
        <data>
          <properties>
            <property name="Title" type="string">My BDC Web Partproperty>
            <property name="Description" type="string">My BDC Web Part
➡   Description</property>
            <property name="Group" type="string">My Custom Web Parts</property>
          </properties>
        </data>
      </webPart>
    </webParts>  .
```

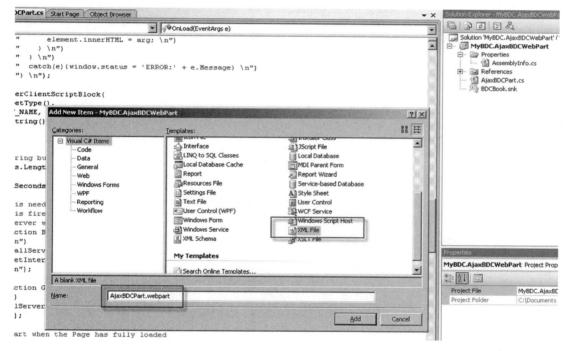

**Figure 9.10  The Visual Studio Add New Item dialog box**

3 In order to create a solution, you'll need a solution manifest file. Add another XML file to your project called `Manifest.xml` and populate it with the XML shown in listing 9.10.

**Listing 9.10  The solution manifest file**

```
<Solution xmlns="http://schemas.microsoft.com/sharepoint/"
          SolutionId="[[Insert Solution ID]]">
  <Assemblies>
```

```
  <Assembly Location="MyBDC.AjaxBDCWebPart.dll"
            DeploymentTarget="WebApplication">
    <SafeControls>
      <SafeControl Namespace="MyBDC.AjaxBDCWebPart"
                   TypeName="*" />
    </SafeControls>
  </Assembly>
</Assemblies>
<CodeAccessSecurity>
  <PolicyItem>
    <PermissionSet
            class="NamedPermissionSet"
            version="1"
            Name="MyCustomPermissionSet">
      <IPermission
            class="System.Web.AspNetHostingPermission, System,
 Version=2.0.0.0, Culture=neutral,
 PublicKeyToken=b77a5c561934e089"
            version="1"
            Level="Minimal"
                      />
      <IPermission
            class="System.Security.Permissions.SecurityPermission,
 mscorlib, Version=2.0.0.0, Culture=neutral,
 PublicKeyToken=b77a5c561934e089"
            version="1"
            Flags="Assertion, Execution, ControlThread,
ControlPrincipal, RemotingConfiguration"
                      />
      <IPermission
class="Microsoft.SharePoint.Security.WebPartPermission,
Microsoft.SharePoint.Security, Version=12.0.0.0,
 Culture=neutral, PublicKeyToken=71e9bce111e9429c"
            version="1"
            Connections="True"
                      />
      <IPermission
   class="Microsoft.SharePoint.Security.SharePointPermission,
 Microsoft.SharePoint.Security, Version=12.0.0.0, Culture=neutral,
 PublicKeyToken=71e9bce111e9429c"
      version="1"
      ObjectModel="True"
                  />
    </PermissionSet>
    <Assemblies>
      <Assembly
        Name = "MyBDC.AjaxBDCWebPart"
        PublicKeyBlob = "[[INSERT PUBLIC KEY BLOB HERE]]"
        Version = "1.0.0.0"></Assembly>
    </Assemblies>
  </PolicyItem>
```

```
</CodeAccessSecurity>
<DwpFiles>
  <DwpFile Location=" AjaxBDCWebPart.webpart" />
</DwpFiles>
</Solution>
```

4 To populate the solution ID for your solution manifest, you'll need to generate a GUID. This can be done using Visual Studio. Choose Tools, Create GUID, select the Registry option, and then choose Copy. You can then paste the solution ID into the Solution ID section of the manifest file.

5 You'll also need to insert your public key blob. This is the larger number that was displayed in the Command Prompt window in step 19 of section 9.1.

6 In order to generate the solution WSP file, you'll need to create a text file with a `.ddf` extension. The file tells a utility called MakeCab what to place inside the special CAB file. It's better than a regular CAB file because the MakeCab utility will also maintain the folder structure of any files. This is particularly useful if you're placing files inside the 12 hive. Add this new text file and insert the text from listing 9.11.

**Listing 9.11  The post-build event**

```
;WSP CAB Generation
.Set DiskDirectory1="c:\wsp"
.Set CabinetNameTemplate=" AjaxBDCWebPart.wsp"

;All file reference should be from the project root

;Files to place into the CAB Root
Manifest.xml
AjaxBDCWebPart.webpart
bin\Debug\ AjaxBDCWebPart.dll
```

7 The last thing to do is create a post-build event. The post-build event will run `MakeCab.exe` for us, calling the DDF file. This saves us having to do it manually each time we make a change to our project. Copy the following code into the post-build event. You can get to the post-build event by choosing Project, Properties.

```
cd "$(ProjectDir)"

MakeCAB /f wsp.ddf
```

8 The final step is to build your project by pressing Ctrl + Shift + B.

9 You should then have an `AjaxBDCWebPart.wsp` file in your c:\wsp folder. This file can be given to an administrator, who will deploy the web part

using SharePoint Central Administration. Follow steps 10-16 to deploy the solution.

10   Open a Command Prompt window and type the following `STSADM.exe` command: `STSADM.exe –o addsolution –f c:\wsp\ AjaxBDCWebPart.wsp`

11   Open SharePoint Central Administration, and click Operations.

12   Click Solution Management from the Global Configuration section.

13   Click your `AjaxBDCWebPart.wsp` solution.

14   Choose Deploy.

15   You should now be able to add the web part in any site collection.

16   If you look at the c:\program file\common files\Microsoft Shared\Web Server Extensions\12\Config folder, you should see that a custom CAS policy file has been created for you, granting your web part the object model permission.

The web part is now complete and can be deployed by operations without their having to modify any files or run `iisreset`. The web part can also be deployed to many web front-end servers all in one go, without having to physically deploy it at every machine like we did in SharePoint 2003.

## 9.4   *Summary*

Within this chapter, we built on the experience of the previous chapter by using the BDC Object Model to create our own custom web part. Creating a custom web part to display the data from the Business Data Catalog is a common thing to do, and can be useful when you need to display your data in different ways. We created an Ajax-style web part that uses a callback event handler so that we can avoid page postbacks, allowing the web part to refresh itself periodically.

Now that we've seen how to create a custom web part, we'll explore another area where we can use the BDC Object Model to create solutions. In the next chapter, we're going to build Office-based applications that use the BDC Object Model. This will involve Excel, Word, and InfoPath.

# Integrating the
# Business Data Catalog
# with Microsoft Office

Office Business Applications (OBA) is a huge topic area that deserves a book in its own right. Steve Fox has done a good job of this already with his book, *Programming Microsoft Office Business Applications*. The website OBACentral.com is also well worth visiting, and includes videos of BDC solutions that you can watch online. But following an introduction to OBA in this chapter, we want to concentrate on where the Business Data Catalog can provide data from your LOB systems and make that data available in your Microsoft Office client applications. We'll look at the development tools available throughout the Microsoft Office suite, and explore in detail the different project templates available to us with VSTO (Visual Studio Tools for Office), including the ability to create custom task panes, ribbons, and documents. We'll then utilize the web service that we created in chapter 8, which will enable us to consume our business data in Office clients for each user whose device is remote from the SharePoint Web Front-End Server.

## 10.1  *An introduction to Office Business Applications (OBA)*

OBA is difficult to describe, as it's a solution that uses parts of the Microsoft Office suite of services, which includes server-side services such as Business Intelligence and workflow, through to client applications such as Microsoft Word 2007. The application can be a collection of services and devices brought together to create an Office-based solution. It's fair to say that most information workers spend a lot of time in Microsoft Outlook, Excel, Word, PowerPoint, and even SharePoint. They also have a collection of devices such as desktop PCs, laptops, and PDAs or smart phones. Using OBA, we can utilize these devices and software that our information workers are already familiar with to help build a solution that saves time and money for your organization.

### The history of Office

Microsoft Office 3.0 was the first version of Microsoft Office for Windows. Back then, there was little or no interoperability between the applications. As Microsoft Office has evolved, we've seen the products work very closely together. SharePoint has now become the hub for all of the Office applications.

I remember teaching my first SharePoint 2003 Power End User class and being blown away by how easy it was to search my portal from within the Research task pane. You could configure the services to allow a SharePoint Portal Server Search, as well as search for translations or thesaurus. Being able to perform a search on portal content from within the Office client was especially useful when you were working on a team-related document, and wanted to quickly search your portal for similar content or a snippet of some kind to reference or incorporate into your own document. Not only could you search for content within documents and lists, but also the network shares and user profiles. Office 2007 has improved upon this by allowing you to create your own task panes and make them look professional using your own custom interface. You could even enhance the interface with Microsoft Expression, providing not only a professional-looking interface, but a striking professional user interface. What's really surprising is that it's so simple to do—even for a non-artist like myself.

### 10.1.1 Overcoming an everyday problem with OBA

OBA isn't just about custom task panes. OBA is a bunch of Office 2007 services, brought together with the aim of cutting down on the number of manual processes that we carry out. Those services include workflow, Business Intelligence, BDC, Excel Services, and so on.

An example of a manual process that OBA could improve upon would be creating a proposal in Word. This is something that I do on a daily basis without any automation. Even though I'm using SharePoint and Office 2007, I still carry out several manual steps that could be made a lot easier and less time-consuming if I adopted an OBA. When I create a proposal, I need to obtain the customer's name and address. I do this by copying the information from a database once I've retrieved the correct customer. Once I have the customer details, I sometimes need to search for the product to find the correct price to quote. This involves another manual step, with room for error because I'm flipping between applications and using copy and paste. Upon saving the document to a SharePoint document library, I take a local copy of the document and attach it to an email, which is then sent to the customer's email address.

This system is a manual process, despite having sophisticated applications at my fingertips. So how can that process be improved upon? First, in Word, we could create a custom task pane that hooks into the Business Data Catalog. This custom task pane will allow us to perform a search on a customer, be it via company name, ZIP code, or whatever column we like, as long as we've set up the ADF correctly with filters on the required columns. After providing a search, summary information about the customer could be displayed, such as the customer's order history or any outstanding invoices. Using content controls, we can then place the BDC data into the Word document in the appropriate location. For example, the Product column in an invoice can be a drop-down list of product names, and then upon choosing the product name, we populate other content controls with the price and availability of that item.

Custom ribbons also help navigate our OBA by providing buttons to display or hide our custom task panes, email the proposal, or trigger a specific workflow. Everything that forms part of the proposal-sending process could be available on our custom ribbon. The nice thing about this solution is that we wouldn't have to Alt+Tab out of Word to obtain information. It would also mean that information workers can carry out simple tasks such as sending a proposal without the need to train that information worker on the LOB system.

What's the situation when the proposal is ready to be sent to the customer? All we'd have to do is save the document to the document library, where a workflow will be triggered. This could be a simple SharePoint Designer workflow or a more complicated Visual Studio workflow that emails the completed document to the customer. Workflow is another part of the Office-based system, as it's incorporated into SharePoint.

Business Intelligence would also be available to this solution, because the proposal is already stored in a document library with metadata associated with it. The customer name, address, proposal amount, and so forth is all available to sort, filter, and create views upon within the document library. If we have MOSS 2007 Enterprise, we can then display that information in the form of KPIs (key performance indicators) on a dashboard page within the Reports Center. This would allow us to predict the sales forecast for the following month and whether we're likely to hit target.

### 10.1.2 *Collaboration of applications*

So really this is what we mean by OBA: we have Office functionality such as Business Intelligence, workflow, communication, collaboration, Business Data Catalog, search, Excel, Word, Outlook, SharePoint Designer, Excel Services, and InfoPath all working together in one solution. The OpenXML file format of Office 2007 has made this possible by allowing us to manipulate and create Office documents more easily through the use of XML and Visual Studio.

There are many different applications and ways in which you can create an OBA. One way is to use InfoPath, SharePoint Designer, and Visual Studio. What we're going to concentrate on here is Visual Studio 2008, and how it can be used to help us build an OBA that integrates our line-of-business data with Word 2007. The diagram in Figure 10.1 displays the many different services at presentation, server, and back-end system level that all contribute to an OBA.

In the next section of this chapter, we'll explore some uses of OBA and BDC that will provide food for thought on how you can build your applications within your own organizations.

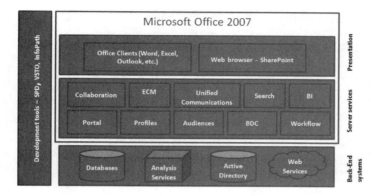

**Figure 10.1** The services within the Microsoft Office system that play a role in OBA, including the tools that can be used to develop within OBA

## 10.2 Where does the Business Data Catalog fit in?

Everything we've been doing with the BDC up to this point is (kind of) already an OBA. Presenting line-of-business data in a dashboard inside SharePoint is an OBA. Using the business data inside the Document Information panel or creating a workflow on BDC metadata is also an OBA. But what we hope to demonstrate here are some real-world uses of line-of-business data within the Office client. Before we start developing, we'll explore some opportunities to use line-of-business data in Outlook, InfoPath, Word, and Excel. InfoPath is also discussed in chapter 11, under the heading of writing back to the line-of-business system.

### 10.2.1 Outlook

Custom form regions in Microsoft Outlook 2007 provide the opportunity to customize the existing forms and also create new forms. An example would be a contact information lookup from your CRM application on the Contacts form. You could even use the customer information from BDC in your email messages. The form regions can replace an entire form or be part of the form. You can also use multiple form regions within one form. Figure 10.2 displays a form region allowing customer and order information to be displayed for a particular customer.

Form regions can be created from within Outlook 2007 or by using Visual Studio 2008. Using Visual Studio 2008, you can create task panes and form regions as add-ins. Form regions are often more beneficial if you have a lot of information, because there's more space available. Task panes are useful for making small panes that blend nicely with out-of-the-box Outlook. Custom ribbons can also be

**Figure 10.2    A custom form region replacing the existing Inspector window. This example is taken from the SDK.**

created for Outlook, as well as command bars. Command bars are still used in some areas of Outlook, as with SharePoint Designer and InfoPath.

## 10.2.2 *Excel*

Microsoft Excel 2007 has the ability to obtain external data from legacy systems without needing the Business Data Catalog. You can connect to data sources directly, such as Microsoft Access, SQL, ODBC, and also data sources that are exposed as a website. Once the data is imported or linked into Excel, it can be manipulated with the usual Excel functionality, such as pivot tables, charts, aggregate functions, and calculations. What's even better is that it can then be displayed in an Excel Web Access Web Part by publishing the workbook to a document library enabled for Excel Services. This allows you to view data in the form of a list, pivot table, or chart via a simple web part on a reporting page that can also be filtered by other Filter Web Parts. The problem with this is that configuring the data source connection has to be carried out by the person who created the workbook. This person doesn't always have a full understanding of the back-end data, especially how to go about connecting to that back-end data. Therefore, through the use of the Business Data Catalog and VSTO, a workbook or workbook template can be created that houses a ListObject content control. This ListObject control is an Excel list, allowing you to bind data to it. The data is usually stored in a data table or data set, and can then be bound to the list within Excel. We can then simply provide our information workers with an Excel Workbook with business data available via the Business Data Catalog. It's recommended that you expose the data to Excel via a web service similar to the one we created in chapter 8. The following is an example of what this can look like and how it can be created.

To begin creating such a solution, you need to start Visual Studio 2008 and create a new project. Under (language of choice), then under Office in the New Project dialog box, you'll see some project templates for Word, Excel, Visio, Project, InfoPath, and Outlook. One of the Excel options is an Excel 2007 Workbook, as illustrated in figure 10.3.

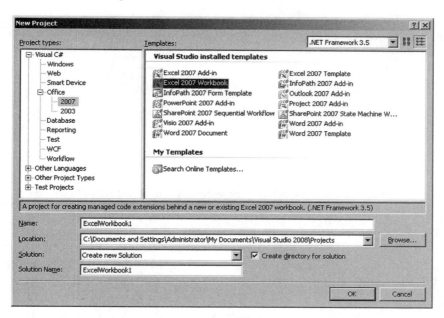

**Figure 10.3   The available project types with Visual Studio 2008 for Microsoft Office 2007**

Once you've created the workbook within Visual Studio 2008, you'll be able to start adding controls and adding some code. Ideally, you'll reference your web service that returns the data from your entity, and then instantiate the web service and use the results to populate the ListObject control within the workbook. Figure 10.4 displays the Excel controls within Visual Studio 2008, with the ListObject added to the workbook sheet. The ListObject is then bound to the BDC data returned by the web service.

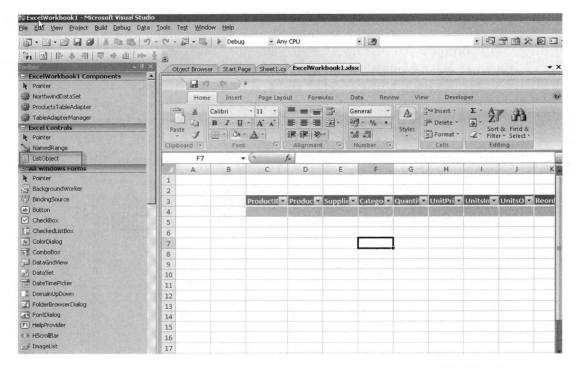

**Figure 10.4    The ListObject control in an Excel Workbook Document project type within Visual Studio**

When you press F5 to run your application, Excel is launched and you can see that the data is retrieved at runtime. We ran the code to bind the ListControl in the `ThisWorkbook_startup` event. Figure 10.5 shows the result from running the OBA. The business data is retrieved and displayed in the list. We then configured a chart on the data, which will be used within an Excel Web Access Web Part. Figure 10.5 illustrates the result of using the list object with the Business Data Catalog.

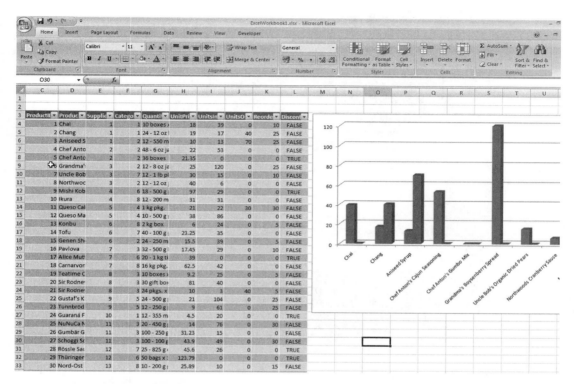

**Figure 10.5    The runtime of the Excel document**

Once you have the BDC data within the Excel Workbook and you've manipulated it, you can publish the workbook to Excel Services. The advantage of doing so is that any named object within the sheet can be displayed within the Excel Web Access Web Part. To publish the workbook, click the Office button and then choose Publish, Excel Services, as shown in figure 10.6.

When you're publishing the workbook, you can either publish everything or publish specific objects. In figure 10.7, you can see that we're publishing both the list and the chart. These objects can then be displayed selectively via Filter Web Parts in a SharePoint dashboard page. Figure 10.7 demonstrates how to choose which options to include.

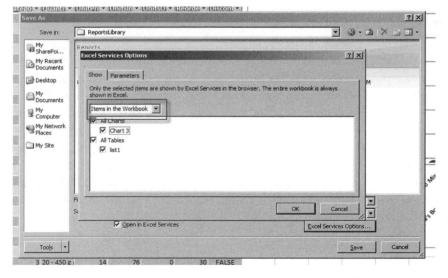

**Figure 10.6   The Publish to Excel Services option in Microsoft Excel 2007**

**Figure 10.7   Excel Services options, set to publish only certain items within the workbook**

Once the workbook has been published, you can set up the Excel Web Access Web Part in a dashboard to display either of the two objects. As you can see, the Excel Web Access Web Part has been configured to display the list1 object. The toolbar in the web part gives you the ability to flip back and forth from displaying the list or the chart. Of course, it's possible to display more than one web part so that both objects are displayed at the same time on the dashboard, or I could add a Filter Web Part that would allow the user to choose. Figure 10.8 illustrates the Excel Web Access Web Part in use on a dashboard page.

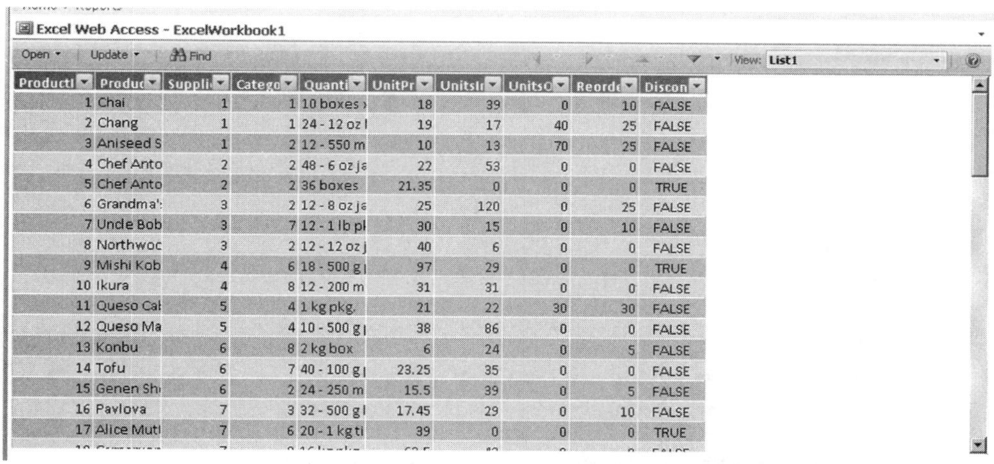


| ProductI | Produc | Suppli | Catego | Quanti | UnitPr | UnitsI | UnitsO | Reord | Discon |
|---|---|---|---|---|---|---|---|---|---|
| 1 | Chai | 1 | 1 | 10 boxes | 18 | 39 | 0 | 10 | FALSE |
| 2 | Chang | 1 | 1 | 24 - 12 oz | 19 | 17 | 40 | 25 | FALSE |
| 3 | Aniseed S | 1 | 2 | 12 - 550 m | 10 | 13 | 70 | 25 | FALSE |
| 4 | Chef Anto | 2 | 2 | 48 - 6 oz ja | 22 | 53 | 0 | 0 | FALSE |
| 5 | Chef Anto | 2 | 2 | 36 boxes | 21.35 | 0 | 0 | 0 | TRUE |
| 6 | Grandma' | 3 | 2 | 12 - 8 oz ja | 25 | 120 | 0 | 25 | FALSE |
| 7 | Uncle Bob | 3 | 7 | 12 - 1 lb pl | 30 | 15 | 0 | 10 | FALSE |
| 8 | Northwoc | 3 | 2 | 12 - 12 oz j | 40 | 6 | 0 | 0 | FALSE |
| 9 | Mishi Kob | 4 | 6 | 18 - 500 g | 97 | 29 | 0 | 0 | TRUE |
| 10 | Ikura | 4 | 8 | 12 - 200 m | 31 | 31 | 0 | 0 | FALSE |
| 11 | Queso Cal | 5 | 4 | 1 kg pkg. | 21 | 22 | 30 | 30 | FALSE |
| 12 | Queso Ma | 5 | 4 | 10 - 500 g | 38 | 86 | 0 | 0 | FALSE |
| 13 | Konbu | 6 | 8 | 2 kg box | 6 | 24 | 0 | 5 | FALSE |
| 14 | Tofu | 6 | 7 | 40 - 100 g | 23.25 | 35 | 0 | 0 | FALSE |
| 15 | Genen Sh | 6 | 2 | 24 - 250 m | 15.5 | 39 | 0 | 5 | FALSE |
| 16 | Pavlova | 7 | 3 | 32 - 500 g | 17.45 | 29 | 0 | 10 | FALSE |
| 17 | Alice Mut | 7 | 6 | 20 - 1 kg ti | 39 | 0 | 0 | 0 | TRUE |

**Figure 10.8 The configured Excel Web Access Web Part displaying the list of BDC data from the workbook**

Now that we have the workbook published to a document library in SharePoint, I can configure some key performance indicators on the data within the workbook. Within the Reports Center in MOSS, you'll already have a KPI list created called Sample KPIs. This KPI list gives you the option to create KPIs on Excel Workbooks, SharePoint lists, SQL analysis services, or on manually entered data. We've configured it to look at our published workbook, and have set up a KPI to warn us if the stock level falls below the reorder level. Figure 10.9 demonstrates that you can then create KPIs on the published workbook.

**Sample KPIs: New Item**

Home > Reports > Sample KPIs > New Item

**Name and Description**
Enter the name and description of the indicator.

The description explains the purpose or goal of the indicator.

Name
Product Stock

Description

**Comments**
Comments help explain the current value or status of the indicator.

Comments

**Indicator Value**
Select the workbook that contains the information for the indicator value.

Select the cell in the workbook that contains the indicator value.

The cell address can be any valid Excel cell address for the selected workbook such as Sheet1!$A$1 or the name of a cell such as 'Total'.

Workbook URL
/Reports/ReportsLibrary/ExcelWorkbook1.;

Examples:
http://portal/reports/workbook.xlsx
or   /reports/workbook.xlsx

Cell Address for Indicator Value
Sheet1!H73

Example: Sheet1!A1 or Total

**Status Icon**
The status icon rules determine which icon to display to represent the status of the indicator.

Values can be either numbers, or valid Excel workbook cell addresses such as: Sheet1!$A$1 or Sheet1!A1.

For some indicators, such as 'The percentage of tasks completed', better values are usually higher.

For other indicators, such as 'The number of active tasks', better values are usually lower.

Status Icon Rules:
Better values are  higher

Display ⬤ when has met or exceeded goal    18

Display △ when has met or exceeded warning    16

Display ◆ otherwise

**Figure 10.9   The KPI configuration page in the Sample KPIs list**

Once that list item has been created in the sample KPIs list, the KPI will automatically display in the Sample KPIs Web Part on the dashboard page. Of course, it's possible to configure your own KPI Web Part rather than reusing the Sample KPI Web Part, as shown in figure 10.10.

We hope this has given you some idea of how BDC, Excel, Excel Services, and Business Intelligence can work together to create an OBA with your line-of-business data using Excel. Next, we'll look at Word and will create a custom task pane to display business data, a custom ribbon, and a Word document using content controls.

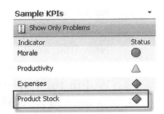

**Figure 10.10   The Sample KPI Web Part showing the Product Stock KPI that was configured in the KPI list**

### 10.2.3 *Word*

There are many ways to use the Business Data Catalog with Word. Through the use of content controls, we can select line-of-business data within documents such as invoices or proposals. What we're going to achieve initially in this demonstration is similar to a mail merge. The document is more interactive, allowing you to actually select data from inside the document itself. So every time you create a proposal or an invoice, you can choose the customer that will receive the document, and your code fills in the other details such as the customer's address. Note that the Customer section in figure 10.11 is just text copied and pasted from a CRM application. This takes a lot of time to flip between applications, find the right customer, and then copy and paste the address.

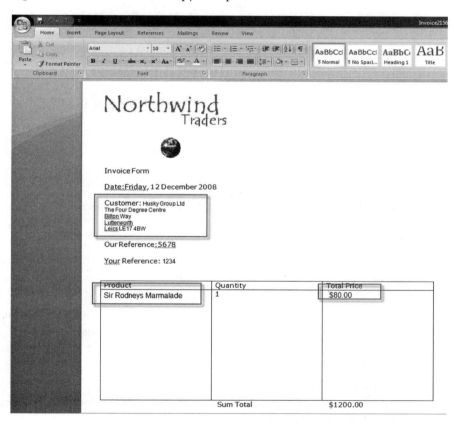

**Figure 10.11   The problem in Word with completing the address details**

So rather than using copy and paste, we decided to use the Business Data Catalog to allow us to select our customer from the CRM application. To do this:

1   Start Visual Studio 2008.

2   Choose Visual C#, Office, and then Word Document from the New Project dialog box, as shown in figure 10.12.

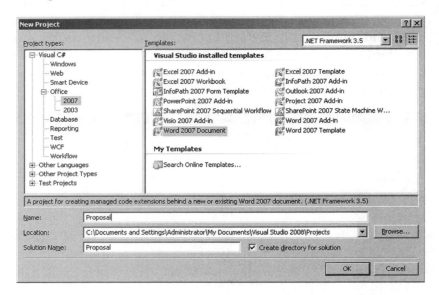

**Figure 10.12   The New Project dialog box with Word Document selected**

3   Name the project and click OK.

4   On the next dialog box, you can either choose to create a brand new document or open an existing document. In our case, we opened an existing invoice document.

5   The document then displays in Visual Studio 2008. Click the Toolbox icon to display the tools if they're not already showing. Then add a `DropDownListContentControl` next to the Customer: text in the Word document, as shown in figure 10.13.

6   Immediately below the `DropDownListContentControl`, add a `RichText-ContentControl` for the address details. You could do the same thing for the product if you wanted to.

7   Add a web reference to your web service that returns the entity data to your Visual Studio project. This can be done by right-clicking References, and

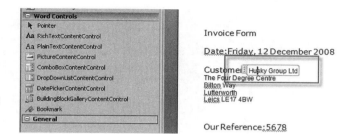

**Figure 10.13 The toolbox of controls available in Visual Studio 2008**

then choosing Service Reference. On the Advanced tab of the Service Reference dialog box, you can choose to add a .NET Framework 2.0 web reference if you prefer.

**8** Double-click your `DropDownListContentControl` to access the code window. Add the code to populate the `DropDownListContentControl` with data returned from a web method to the `ThisAddIn_Startup` event, so that your control is populated with choices upon creating the document.

**9** Add code to the `DropDownListContentControl_Exiting` event to populate the `RichTextBoxContentControl` with the remainder of the address upon selection of a customer. The code in listing 10.1 makes a call to the WCF web service to populate the `DropDownList` control.

**Listing 10.1** `DropDownListContentControl` **web service call**

```
    private void dropDownListContentControl1_Entering(object sender,
➥ Microsoft.Office.Tools.Word.ContentControlEnteringEventArgs e)
    {
        CustomerService.CustomersServiceClient proxy = new
➥CustomerService.CustomersServiceClient
➥("BasicHttpBinding_ICustomersService");
        string[] customernames = proxy.ListCustomers();

        int x = 1;
        foreach (string CustomerName in customernames)
        {
            x += 1;
            dropDownListContentControl1.DropDownListEntries.Add
➥ (CustomerName.ToString(), CustomerName.ToString(), x);
        }
    }
```

**10** Test the document by pressing F5 on your keyboard. The result should look like figure 10.14.

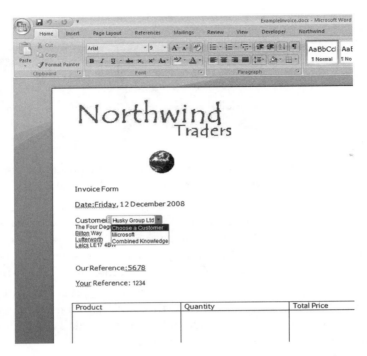

**Figure 10.14   The result of customizing the content controls to allow a customer to be chosen from the `DropDownListContentControl`**

In addition to creating content controls, you can create custom task panes. Figure 10.15 shows an example of the kind of task pane that would be useful to sales representatives when sending out quotes. Users can look up customers easily to find out information about them.

1   To create a custom task pane, launch Visual Studio 2008.

2   From the New Project dialog box, select Word 2007 Add-In from the C# Office section.

3   Add the web reference to your BDC web service as we did in the previous exercise.

4   Right-click your project and add a `UserControl`.

5   Design your task pane interface on the `UserControl`, as shown in figure 10.16.

**Figure 10.15   A custom task pane showing useful data about a customer from the LOB system**

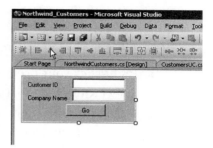

**Figure 10.16   Designing the custom UserControl**

6   To populate the controls, you need to call the method that exposes your specific finder from your web service. Pass through the Customer ID, and then assign the company name to the `CompanyName.txt` field. Soon, we'll use a similar piece of code to create the ribbon.

7   Open the `.cs` file for your add-in class.

8   In the Startup event for the add-in class, add the code from listing 10.2 to instantiate the `UserControl`. Position it correctly within Word by setting the dimension properties of the task pane, as shown in the listing.

**Listing 10.2   The add-in startup event**

```csharp
private void ThisAddIn_Startup(object sender, System.EventArgs e)
{
    CUC = new CustomersUC();
    myCustomTaskPane = this.CustomTaskPanes.Add(CUC,
        "New Task Pane");

    myCustomTaskPane.DockPosition =
        Office.MsoCTPDockPosition.msoCTPDockPositionFloating;
    myCustomTaskPane.Height = 500;
    myCustomTaskPane.Width = 500;

    myCustomTaskPane.DockPosition =
        Office.MsoCTPDockPosition.msoCTPDockPositionRight;
    myCustomTaskPane.Width = 300;

    myCustomTaskPane.Visible = true;

}
```

9   Press F5 to test your solution.

You should now be able to search for customers using the custom task pane, which is loaded during the startup of the document. Next, we'll create a custom ribbon that uses an alternate method to look up customer details.

1  Right-click your project and choose Add, New Item.

2  Select Ribbon (Visual Designer).

3  From the Office Ribbon Toolbox controls, drag a toggle button into the first group on your ribbon.

4  In the Properties pane, set an image for your button, along with a tooltip and a label. The label should say "Display Customers."

5  Double-click the button to open the Code view.

6  Add the code to the button, as shown in listing 10.3.

---

**Listing 10.3   Customer information lookup ribbon button**

```
CustomerService.CustomersServiceClient proxy = new
CustomerService.CustomersServiceClient
("BasicHttpBinding_ICustomersService");
        string[] customernames = proxy.ListCustomers();

        gallery1.Items.Clear();

        RibbonDropDownItem item = new RibbonDropDownItem();
          foreach (string CustomerName in customernames)
        {
            string customeraddress =
proxy.GetCustomer(CustomerName).ToString();
            RibbonDropDownItem dditem = new RibbonDropDownItem();

            dditem.Label = CustomerName.ToString();
            dditem.SuperTip = customeraddress.ToString();

            gallery1.Items.Add(dditem);
        }
```

7  Press F5 to test the solution.

8  The finished ribbon should look like figure 10.17 in Word.

Once you've finished your custom document with the task pane, ribbon, and content controls, you'll want to publish the document so that it can be used within a SharePoint content type. The first thing you'll need to do is set up the document's Publish location. This can be done in the Project properties and is usually set to a file share, as shown in figure 10.18.

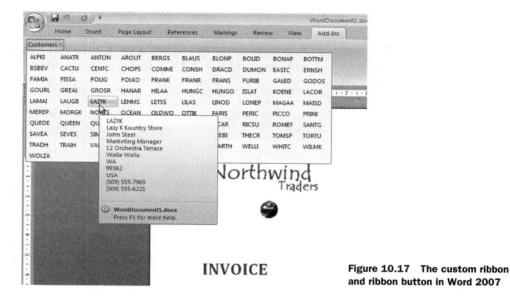

**Figure 10.17  The custom ribbon and ribbon button in Word 2007**

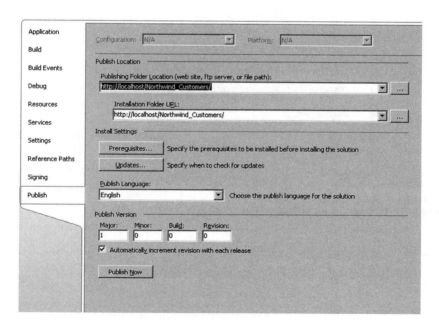

**Figure 10.18  The Publish settings in the Project properties**

You'll also need to configure the Trust settings. The Trust is configured in Word Options. To set this, you need to trust the location where the document is stored. Click the Office button, then Word Options. Under the Trust Center, click the Trust Settings button. You can then add the Publish location as a trusted location, as shown in figure 10.19.

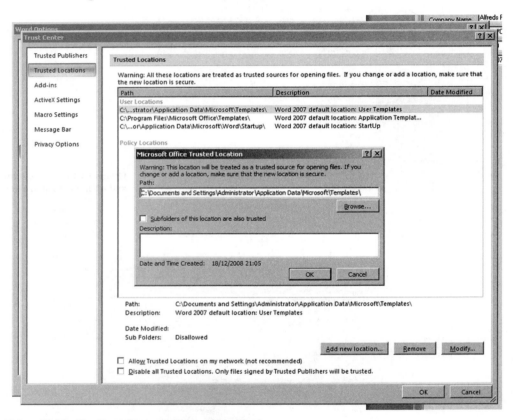

Figure 10.19   The Trust Center settings within Word

Finally, you can upload this document as a template within your content types. To create a content type:

1   Choose Site Actions, Site Settings from your team site.

2   Choose Site Content Types from the Galleries section.

3   Click Create to create a new content type.

4    Give the content type a name such as `Proposal`.

5    Inherit from `Document`, which is in the Documents group.

6    Click Advanced Settings.

7    Choose Upload a New Document Template and browse to the share where your document is published.

8    Add the content type to the document library where users will create invoices.

You've now successfully created an OBA using Visual Studio.NET 2008, Word 2007, and SharePoint 2007. Combining these products with the Business Data Catalog provides some powerful solutions.

## 10.3   Summary

Within this chapter, we took a brief look at Office Business Applications. Having written this chapter, we're inspired to write a whole book on Office Business Applications and the Business Data Catalog. There are so many solutions that could be created! We utilized the web service that we developed in chapter 9 of this book within OBA. We explored OBA solutions within both Excel and Word. We looked in detail at how to create custom task panes, custom ribbons, and content controls. We discussed mixing OBA and BDC, and also how information could then be used with other services such as Excel Services. Given more time and more pages, we could've also explored InfoPath and how that can be used in an OBA.

In the next chapter, we'll explore how to use InfoPath and Visual Studio.NET code to write back to the LOB system. BDC Meta Man can be used to generate Insert and Update Web Parts. In chapter 11, we'll explore exactly how this is achieved.

# *Writing back to the line-of-business system*

11

**This chapter covers**

- Writing back to the BDC
- Creating custom web parts for write back
- Using InfoPath forms for write back

You may be a little confused at the title of this chapter, or possibly think that we're off our rockers, because Microsoft markets the Business Data Catalog in Microsoft Office SharePoint Server (MOSS) 2007 Enterprise as "read only" and this chapter is all about writing back to the LOB system. The Business Data Catalog does support read/write, both in the object model and in the application definition file. It's the web parts that don't support write back or updates. There are mixed reviews about writing back to the LOB system, which may be why Microsoft didn't allow the out-of-the-box web parts to read and write. In the back-end databases, you'll find validation, and referential integrity, which won't be present in the web parts. Therefore, when you write custom code that does write back, you'll need to make sure that all of the validation rules are met! Most business applications implement lots of validation on the data prior to submitting it to the back-end database. Some validation is carried out at database level, and some is done at presentation level. Take Microsoft Dynamics CRM, for example: in the UI, there are checks for valid phone numbers and ZIP codes before a round trip is made to the database.

In this chapter, we'll explore two methods of writing back to the line-of-business system. One is to use InfoPath, and the other is to use Visual Studio.NET code to generate two web parts.

## 11.1   An introduction to writing back to the BDC

Within the application definition file, in addition to creating methods that allow you to select items from the database, you can also create `GenericInvoker` methods that allow updates and inserts. `GenericInvoker` methods are used to edit an entity or update/insert a value into an entity. Listing 11.1 demonstrates how to create the `Insert` method using the `GenericInvoker`. Using BDC Meta Man (even the Developer free edition), you can generate these methods. You'll just need to specify which columns from your entity to include in the `Insert` method. The `Insert` method uses parameters for each column that will be inserted.

> **Listing 11.1   A `GenericInvoker` `Insert` method in the application definition file**

```
<Method Name="insertdbo.Orders">          ◁┤  Insert method using SQL
        <Properties>                           Insert statement
          <Property Name="RdbCommandText" Type="System.String">Insert
➥ into dbo.Orders([OrderID],[CustomerID],[EmployeeID],[OrderDate],
➥ [RequiredDate],[ShippedDate],[ShipVia],[Freight],[ShipName],
➥ [ShipAddress],[ShipCity],[ShipRegion],[ShipPostalCode],
➥ [ShipCountry]) Values(@OrderID,@CustomerID,@EmployeeID,@OrderDate,
➥@RequiredDate,@ShippedDate,@ShipVia,@Freight,@ShipName,
➥@ShipAddress,@ShipCity,@ShipRegion,@ShipPostalCode,@ShipCountry);
➥select SomethingToReturn = @@Identity</Property>
          <Property Name="RdbCommandType" Type="System.String">Text
➥</Property>
        </Properties>                       Input parameters
        <Parameters>                        accept new values
          <Parameter Direction="In" Name="@OrderID">          ◁┘
            <TypeDescriptor TypeName="System.Int32" Name="OrderID" />
          </Parameter>
          <Parameter Direction="In" Name="@CustomerID">
            <TypeDescriptor TypeName="System.String" Name="CustomerID" />
          </Parameter>
          <Parameter Direction="In" Name="@EmployeeID">
            <TypeDescriptor TypeName="System.Int32" Name="EmployeeID" />
          </Parameter>
```

```
        <Parameter Direction="In" Name="@OrderDate">
         <TypeDescriptor TypeName="System.DateTime" Name="OrderDate" />
        </Parameter>
        <Parameter Direction="In" Name="@RequiredDate">
          <TypeDescriptor TypeName="System.DateTime"
➡Name="RequiredDate" />
        </Parameter>
        <Parameter Direction="In" Name="@ShippedDate">
          <TypeDescriptor TypeName="System.DateTime"
➡Name="ShippedDate" />
        </Parameter>
        <Parameter Direction="In" Name="@ShipVia">
          <TypeDescriptor TypeName="System.Int32" Name="ShipVia" />
        </Parameter>
        <Parameter Direction="In" Name="@Freight">
          <TypeDescriptor TypeName="System.Decimal" Name="Freight" />
        </Parameter>
        <Parameter Direction="In" Name="@ShipName">
          <TypeDescriptor TypeName="System.String" Name="ShipName" />
        </Parameter>
        <Parameter Direction="In" Name="@ShipAddress">
          <TypeDescriptor TypeName="System.String"
➡Name="ShipAddress" />
        </Parameter>
        <Parameter Direction="In" Name="@ShipCity">
          <TypeDescriptor TypeName="System.String" Name="ShipCity" />
        </Parameter>
        <Parameter Direction="In" Name="@ShipRegion">
          <TypeDescriptor TypeName="System.String" Name="ShipRegion" />
        </Parameter>
        <Parameter Direction="In" Name="@ShipPostalCode">
          <TypeDescriptor
➡TypeName="System.String" Name="ShipPostalCode" />
        </Parameter>
        <Parameter Direction="In" Name="@ShipCountry">
          <TypeDescriptor TypeName="System.String"
➡Name="ShipCountry" />
        </Parameter>
        <Parameter Direction="Return" Name="dbo.Orders">
          <TypeDescriptor
➡TypeName="System.String" Name="SomethingToReturn" />
        </Parameter>
      </Parameters>
      <MethodInstances>                    ┐ Method instance as
                                        ⟵┘ described in chapter 2
        <MethodInstance Name="dbo.OrdersInserter"
➡Type="GenericInvoker" ReturnParameterName="dbo.Orders" />
      </MethodInstances>
    </Method>
```

Listing 11.1 is an XML example of an `Insert` method using a `GenericInvoker` method. In listing 11.2, you can see how the same application definition file will allow you to use a `GenericInvoker` to create the `Update` statements.

> **Listing 11.2   A `GenericInvoker` `Update` method in the application definition file**

```
- <Method Name="updatedbo.Orders">              ◁┤ Update statement uses identifier
- <Properties>                                      │ to locate record to update
  <Property Name="RdbCommandText" Type="System.String">Update dbo.Orders
➥SET [CustomerID]=@CustomerID,[EmployeeID]=@EmployeeID,[OrderDate]=
➥@OrderDate,[RequiredDate]=@RequiredDate,[ShippedDate]=@ShippedDate,
➥[ShipVia]=@ShipVia,[Freight]=@Freight,[ShipName]=@ShipName,
➥[ShipAddress]=@ShipAddress,[ShipCity]=@ShipCity,[ShipRegion]=
➥@ShipRegion,[ShipPostalCode]=@ShipPostalCode,[ShipCountry]=@ShipCountry
➥WHERE([OrderID]=@OrderID);select SomethingToReturn =
➥@@Identity</Property>
  <Property Name="RdbCommandType"
➥Type="System.String">Text</Property>       ◁┤ Input parameters to
  </Properties>                                 │ accept new values
- <Parameters>
- <Parameter Direction="In" Name="@OrderID">
  <TypeDescriptor TypeName="System.Int32" Name="OrderID" />
  </Parameter>
- <Parameter Direction="In" Name="@CustomerID">
  <TypeDescriptor TypeName="System.String" Name="CustomerID" />
  </Parameter>
- <Parameter Direction="In" Name="@EmployeeID">
  <TypeDescriptor TypeName="System.Int32" Name="EmployeeID" />
  </Parameter>
…Trimmed code as it is repetitive.
- <Parameter Direction="Return" Name="dbo.Orders">
  <TypeDescriptor TypeName="System.String" Name="SomethingToReturn" />
  </Parameter>
  </Parameters>
- <MethodInstances>
  <MethodInstance Name="dbo.OrdersUpdater" Type="GenericInvoker"
➥ReturnParameterName="dbo.Orders" />
  </MethodInstances>
  </Method>
```

Now that the application definition file will allow us to insert and update using these two methods, we can create our two web parts that will allow us to invoke the `Update` and `Insert` methods in the entity.

## 11.2   *Creating custom web parts to update LOB data*

Using the BDC Object Model, as discussed in chapter 8, it's possible to execute these `GenericInvoker` methods using the `Entity.Execute()` method. First, you'll need to build an interface for your custom web part. (To learn more about creating web parts, refer to chapter 9.) The web part should have a control for each item you want to insert into the database—for example, a TextBox control for the Customer Name column. You can create validation methods on the TextBox control to ensure that you're only going to accept legitimate data and that the column can't allow nulls. Once the interface has been created, an object is created that reads the values from your controls into an array. The array can then be passed to the Entity.Execute() method along with the method instance name, the LOB system instance name, and the object array containing the parameter values, as shown in listing 11.3.

**Listing 11.3  Calling Entity.Execute()**

```
void btnNew_Click(object sender, EventArgs e)
{
    lblError.Text = "";                               Assign values from
                                                      TextBox controls to
    object[] parameters = new object[14];    ◁┘      parameters
    parameters[0] = txtOrderID.Text;
    parameters[1] = txtCustomerID.Text;
    parameters[2] = txtEmployeeID.Text;
    parameters[3] = txtOrderDate.Text;
    parameters[4] = txtRequiredDate.Text;
    parameters[5] = txtShippedDate.Text;
    parameters[6] = txtShipVia.Text;
    parameters[7] = txtFreight.Text;
    parameters[8] = txtShipName.Text;
    parameters[9] = txtShipAddress.Text;
    parameters[10] = txtShipCity.Text;
    parameters[11] = txtShipRegion.Text;
    parameters[12] = txtShipPostalCode.Text;
    parameters[13] = txtShipCountry.Text;

    try                 Call GenericInvoker
    {          ◁┘
        BdcHelpers.ExecuteGenericInvoker(lobSystemInstance,
entityName, "dbo.OrdersInserter", parameters);
    }
    catch (Exception exception)
    {
        lblError.Text = exception.ToString();
    }
}
```

A helper class is used to query the LOBSystemInstances and obtain the required instance and entity that were passed to it, along with the object array containing the parameters. The Entity.Execute() method is then called, which performs the insert, as shown in listing 11.4.

**Listing 11.4   The helper class and the firing of the `Entity.Execute()` method**

```
        public static void ExecuteGenericInvoker(string lobSystemInstance,
➡string entityName, string methodInstance, object[] parameters)
        {
            NamedLobSystemInstanceDictionary instances =
➡ApplicationRegistry.GetLobSystemInstances();
            LobSystemInstance instance = instances[lobSystemInstance];
            Entity entity = instance.GetEntities()[entityName];

            MethodInstance methInst =
➡entity.GetMethodInstances()[methodInstance];

            entity.Execute(methInst, instance, ref parameters);
        }
```

A similar example is used to update records in the database. This time, you need to obtain the record that's going to receive the updates by using the specific finder. (Specific finders are explained in chapter 2.) After creating the user interface for the web part that contains controls for each column to accept an update, we need to populate the controls with the value for the record to be updated so that the current values are shown to the user. Listing 11.5 displays the code that's called from the `CreateChildControls()` method of the web part after the controls are created. The code finds the row using the specific finder method. In our example, the identifier is passed to the web part using a URL parameter, which can be fired using a custom action, as shown in listing 11.5.

**Listing 11.5   The `OrderID` property obtains the identifier from the page URL parameter**

```
private string OrderID
        { get { return Page.Request.QueryString["OrderID"].ToString(); } }
```

Listing 11.6 is the `loaddboOrders` method, which uses the identifier along with the specific finder method to populate the textbox controls, allowing the data to be changed in the web part's user interface.

**Listing 11.6   The `loaddboOrders` method called from `CreateChildControls`**

```
    private void loaddboOrders()
        {
            // add the identifiers...
            object[] identifiers = new object[1];
            identifiers[0] = Convert.ToInt32(OrderID);

            IEntityInstance ie = null;
            try
            {
```

```
                  ie = BdcHelpers.GetSpecificRecord(lobSystemInstance,
➥entityName, identifiers);
              }
              catch (Exception exception)
              {
                  lblError.Text = exception.ToString();
          }

          lblDisplayOrderID.Text = ie["OrderID"].ToString();
          if (ie["ShipName"] != null)
              txtShipName.Text = ie["ShipName"].ToString();
          if (ie["ShipAddress"] != null)
              txtShipAddress.Text = ie["ShipAddress"].ToString();
          if (ie["ShipCity"] != null)
              txtShipCity.Text = ie["ShipCity"].ToString();
          if (ie["ShipRegion"] != null)
              txtShipRegion.Text = ie["ShipRegion"].ToString();
          if (ie["ShipPostalCode"] != null)
              txtShipPostalCode.Text = ie["ShipPostalCode"].ToString();
          if (ie["ShipCountry"] != null)
            txtShipCountry.Text = ie["ShipCountry"].ToString();

      }
```

The helper class also contains a `GetSpecificRecord` method, allowing the specific finder to be called via the `Entity.FindSpecific()` method, as shown in listing 11.7.

**Listing 11.7  The object model code to find a specific record**

```
public static IEntityInstance GetSpecificRecord(string lobSystemInstance,
➥string entityName, object []identifiers)
      {
          NamedLobSystemInstanceDictionary sysInstances =
➥ApplicationRegistry.GetLobSystemInstances();
          LobSystemInstance instance = sysInstances[lobSystemInstance];
          Entity entity = instance.GetEntities()[entityName];

          IEntityInstance ie = entity.FindSpecific(identifiers,
➥instance);

          return ie;
      }
```

Once the user has updated the values in the web part, the user clicks an Update button, which once again calls the `Entity.Execute()` method, passing an object array with the existing and updated values back to the database. Listing 11.8 shows the call to the helper class, passing the method instance name, LOB system instance name, and parameters.

**Listing 11.8   Executing the generic invoker**

```
void btnUpdate_Click(object sender, EventArgs e)
{
    object[] parameters = new object[7];
    parameters[0] = lblDisplayOrderID.Text;
    parameters[1] = txtShipName.Text;
    parameters[2] = txtShipAddress.Text;
    parameters[3] = txtShipCity.Text;
    parameters[4] = txtShipRegion.Text;
    parameters[5] = txtShipPostalCode.Text;
   parameters[6] = txtShipCountry.Text;

    try
    {
        BdcHelpers.ExecuteGenericInvoker(lobSystemInstance,
➥entityName, "dbo.OrdersUpdater", parameters);
    }
    catch (Exception exception)
    {
        lblError.Text = exception.ToString();
    }
}
```

We now have two web parts that will allow us to insert and update data. Next, we have to wire up the Update Web Part by adding it to a web part page, then creating a custom action to take us to the page displaying the record that we wish to edit. This is achieved by using a parameter to pass the identifier as a query parameter to the web part, similar to the View Profile action.

### 11.2.1   *Wiring up the web parts*

As mentioned previously, the Update Web Part is able to obtain the identifier for the specific finder method using a URL parameter. For this solution to work, we need to be able to send the identifier to the web part somehow using the URL. You can achieve this by creating a custom action. The action can then be displayed in the Title column's drop-down list of actions, along with View Profile and any other actions in the Business Data List Web Part or on the Business Data field type. Figure 11.1 displays the custom action Update Orders in the Title field for the entity.

To create the custom action, you first of all need the URL of the web part page that will contain the custom Update Web Part. Then, create your custom action URL using a parameter such as ?orderid={0} at the end of the URL. You can then specify which column will be passed to the URL. Listing 11.9 is an XML sample from the application definition file showing how to create the custom action.

**dbo.Orders List**

| OrderID | CustomerID | EmployeeID | OrderDate | RequiredDate | ShippedDate | ShipVia | ShipName |
|---------|-----------|-----------|-----------|--------------|-------------|---------|----------|
| 10643 | ALFKI | 6 | 8/25/1997 12:00:00 AM | 9/22/1997 12:00:00 AM | 9/2/1997 12:00:00 AM | 1 | Alfreds Futterkiste |
| 10692 | ALFKI | 4 | 10/3/1997 12:00:00 AM | 10/31/1997 12:00:00 AM | 10/13/1997 12:00:00 AM | 2 | Alfred's Futterkiste |
| 10702 | ALFKI ▾ | 4 | 10/13/1997 12:00:00 AM | 11/24/1997 12:00:00 AM | 10/21/1997 12:00:00 AM | 1 | Alfred's Futterkiste |
| 10835 | Update Orders | | 1/15/1998 12:00:00 AM | 2/12/1998 12:00:00 AM | 1/21/1998 12:00:00 AM | 3 | Alfred's Futterkiste |
| 10952 | View Profile | 1 | 3/16/1998 12:00:00 AM | 4/27/1998 12:00:00 AM | 3/24/1998 12:00:00 AM | 1 | Alfred's Futterkiste |
| 11011 | ALFKI | 3 | 4/9/1998 12:00:00 AM | 5/7/1998 12:00:00 AM | 4/13/1998 12:00:00 AM | 1 | Alfred's Futterkiste |
| 10308 | ANATR | 7 | 9/18/1996 12:00:00 AM | 10/16/1996 12:00:00 AM | 9/24/1996 12:00:00 AM | 3 | Ana Trujillo Emparedados y helados |
| 10625 | ANATR | 3 | 8/8/1997 12:00:00 AM | 9/5/1997 12:00:00 AM | 8/14/1997 12:00:00 AM | 1 | Ana Trujillo Emparedados y ... |

**Figure 11.1   The Update Orders action in the Title field on the Orders entity**

**Listing 11.9   The custom action created in the application definition file**

```
<Actions>
- <Action Name="Update Orders" Position="1" IsOpenedInNewWindow="false"
➥ Url="http://win2k3/pages/updateorders.aspx?OrderID={0}"
➥ ImageUrl="">
- <ActionParameters>
  <ActionParameter Name="OrderID" Index="0" />
  </ActionParameters>
  </Action>
  </Actions>
```

Upon clicking the custom action, you can see that the URL for the web part page is fired and the OrderID for the current record is sent to the web part page, as shown in figure 11.2.

**Figure 11.2   The URL of the web part page**

The custom action will fire when it's selected, and will then take you to your new web part page and display the web part ready for editing. See figure 11.3.

You should now be able to read and write back to the LOB system via these custom web parts. It's possible to do all of this without writing any code by using our product, BDC Meta Man.

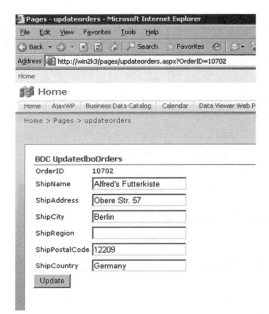

**Figure 11.3    The Update Web Part for OrderID 10702, which was passed via the URL parameter**

### 11.2.2 Configuring the web parts with BDC Meta Man

BDC Meta Man can be used to generate these web parts and the application definition file markup for you, allowing you to generate these web parts in minutes. The code is also available so that you can customize the field validation. To generate the write-back web parts, follow these steps:

1   Download the Developer Edition of BDC Meta Man from http://www.lightningtools.com.

2   Install the application if you haven't already.

3   Launch BDC Meta Man.

4   Click the Connect to Data Source option.

5   Choose SQL Server.

6   Type the server name and configure the authentication options, then click Connect.

7   Expand the Northwind database.

8   Drag the Customers table onto the design surface, as shown in figure 11.4.

9   Right-click the `dbo.Customers` table (entity) and choose Edit Entity.

10   Click the Write Back tab on the Entity Properties dialog box.

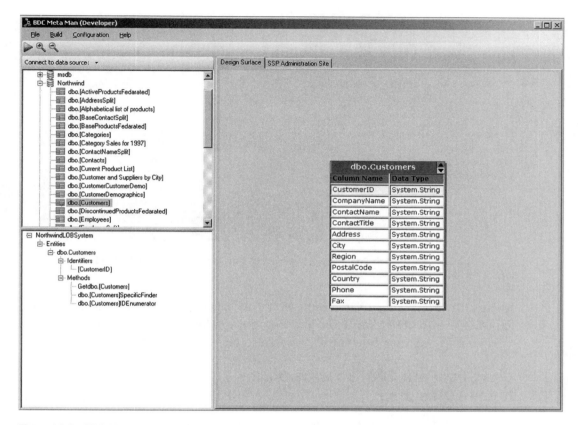

**Figure 11.4 BDC Meta Man (Developer) with the Customers table added to the design surface**

11   Tick the check box to enable the Write Back Web Parts.

12   Choose which columns to add for the `Insert` and `Update` methods, as shown in figure 11.5.

13   Click Save.

14   From the main menu in BDC Meta Man, choose Configuration, Settings.

15   Type a folder path for your generated web parts.

16   Type a namespace that you want your project to have.

17   Click Save.

18   Click the green icon on the toolbar in BDC Meta Man to generate the application definition file and the Visual Studio project for the two web parts.

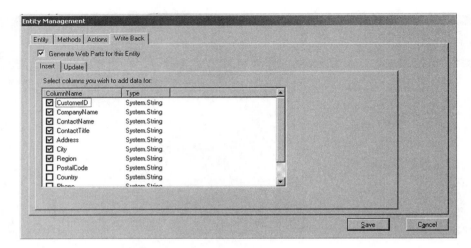

**Figure 11.5   The Edit Entity dialog box enables the fields to be chosen for the Insert and Update methods.**

Using BDC Meta Man to generate your web parts gives you a great head start, allowing you to concentrate on building the validation for your controls. In the next section, we'll see how InfoPath can also be used as a write-back tool.

## 11.3   Using InfoPath 2007 to write back to the LOB system

It took a while to think about where to put this section, as it belongs both in this chapter and in the chapter on OBA. But the OBA chapter was already quite lengthy, so we decided that putting it here would be fine.

InfoPath is a great tool for turning paper-based forms into electronic forms. It's perfect for vacation request forms, proposals, and so on. InfoPath collects its data in an XML file, which makes it perfect for interfacing with other applications. It also allows you to update a database either directly or via web services. Combine that with forms services and we have a perfect solution for collecting information via SharePoint and utilizing BDC to read from and populate our LOB systems. Creating an InfoPath form from a web service allows us to design the form based on the parameters within the web method. We're going to base our example on a product sale InfoPath form. The first thing we'd need to do is create a web service and web method called `sales.asmx` that use the BDC to submit sales information. The web method would be similar to the code for the web part we created earlier, where you create an object for the information you want to create in the database

(for example, a customer) and then your web method would execute the
`Entity.Execute()` method, as shown in listing 11.10.

**Listing 11.10**  **AddSale web method calls `ExecuteGenericInvoker` method**

```
[WebMethod]
public void AddSale(Sale sale)
{
    object[] parameters = new object[7];
    parameters[1] = sp.ProductId;
    parameters[2] = sp.Quantity;
    parameters[3] = sp.SalePrice;
    parameters[4] = insertSale.SaleId;
    try
        {
          BdcHelpers.ExecuteGenericInvoker(lobSystemInstance, entityName,
    "dbo.AddSale", parameters);
        }
    catch (Exception exception)
        {
            //Display Error
        }
    }
```

These properties are described in the helper class, as shown in listing 11.11.

**Listing 11.11**  **A sale helper class describes the sale properties**

```
public class Sale
    {
        int saleId;

        [XmlIgnore]
        public int SaleId
        {
            get { return saleId; }
            set { saleId = value; }
        }

        int salesPersonId;

        public int SalesPersonId
        {
            get { return salesPersonId; }
            set { salesPersonId = value; }
        }

        int customerId;

        public int CustomerId
        {
            get { return customerId; }
```

```
        set { customerId = value; }
    }

    DateTime saleDate;

    public DateTime SaleDate
    {
        get { return saleDate; }
        set { saleDate = value; }
    }

    List<SaleProduct> products = new List<SaleProduct>();

    public List<SaleProduct> Products
    {
        get { return products; }
        set { products = value; }
    }
}
```

Once you've configured your web service, you'll need to create a virtual directory within your web application in IIS. The virtual directory is created by using IIS, expanding the website, and choosing Create Virtual Directory from the context menu of the website. Once that has been created, you can launch InfoPath and begin to design your form.

1 Upon opening InfoPath from the Getting Started page, click Design a Form Template. Make sure you check the Enable browser-compatible features only check box, and choose the Web Service template, as shown in figure 11.6.

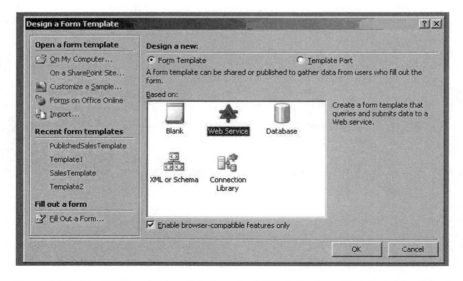

**Figure 11.6  The Web Service template from the InfoPath Design a Form Template dialog box**

2   Specify how the form works with the web service. For now, we only want to think about submitting data to our web services, so just select the Submit data option, as shown in figure 11.7.

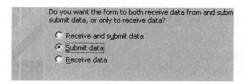

**Figure 11.7  Choose Submit data for the web service option in the wizard.**

3   Enter the URL of our web service, as shown in figure 11.8. The URL will depend on your web service.

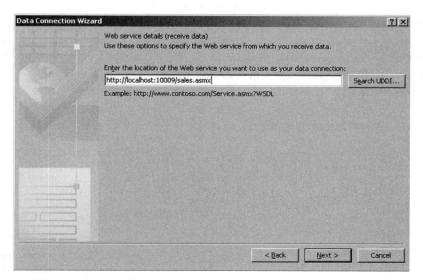

**Figure 11.8   Enter the web service URL.**

4   Select the web service method you want to submit data to. You can see our example in figure 11.9.

**Figure 11.9   The AddSale web method from the web service**

5   Give the data connection a useful name, such as `Submit Sale`.

Once InfoPath has finished loading, you'll notice that you get a blank form with a title area and some controls. In the Design Tasks panel, you should be able to see the Data Source panel. InfoPath has used the WSDL (Web Services Description Language) file of the web service to go through and work out what objects need to be passed to the AddSale method to successfully call it. Drill down the tree starting at myFields > dataFields >tns:AddSale > sale.

If you drill down further, you'll see each individual property that makes up a sale, including the Products array, which itself is made up of SaleProduct properties. This is shown in figure 11.10.

We can drag and drop the required fields from the Data Connections Design Task onto our design surface, and depending on which level we've pulled objects from, it'll create the necessary fields for us on the InfoPath form. We want to drag the sale object over and drop it into the Fields area. When we let go of the cursor in the Fields section, we get a number of options for how we want to create and display these controls, as shown in figure 11.11.

Figure 11.10   The Design Tasks pane, which has exposed the properties based upon the web method's properties

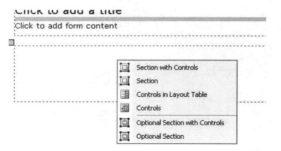

Figure 11.11   The options available when you drag an object from the Design Tasks pane onto the form

You should choose Section with Controls from the context menu. Once you do, you'll be happy to see all our controls nicely laid out. A repeating table is also created for our SalesProducts. If you click the Preview button on the toolbar now, you'll see that you get a nice calendar control for entering dates, and you can add multiple SalesProduct rows to the table for each product sold. You won't be able to submit the form yet, because of the Trust setting under the Form options. We'll address this setting later in the chapter.

As with the Document Information panel within Office 2007, when you use the Business Data column, your information workers will be required to key in the identifier. Changing the control for the Identifier column is simply a case of right-clicking it and choosing Convert to Drop-Down List. We can then configure the drop-down list to read from the database again. To configure the connection, navigate back to the Data Source design pane, and toward the bottom, click Manage Data Connections, as shown in figure 11.12.

**Figure 11.12    The Manage Data Connections option**

Choose the option to receive data and enter the URL for the appropriate web method that returns the list of identifiers, as shown in figure 11.13.

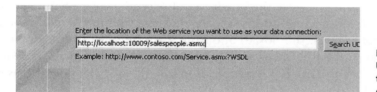

**Figure 11.13    Enter the URL of the web method that returns data for the drop-down list.**

In our example, we select GetSalesPeople as the operation, and click Next. On the next form, click Store a copy of the data in the form template. On the final form of this wizard, make sure the Automatically retrieve data when form is opened check box is checked. Then click Finish, as shown in figure 11.14.

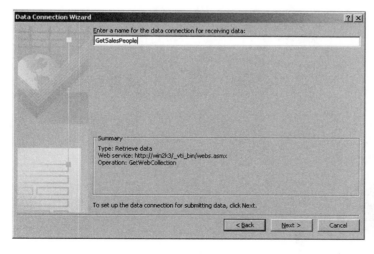

**Figure 11.14    Provide the connection a meaningful name for later use.**

Click Finish to close the Data Connections form. Once that's closed, if you go back to the Data Source Design Tasks pane, you'll see that, in the Data source drop-down, we have a secondary data source. This is shown in figure 11.15.

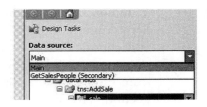

Before we edit our text boxes on our form, we want to change the compatibility settings so we're sure our InfoPath forms can be used with browsers and mobile devices.

**Figure 11.15  Our secondary data source for use in controls such as drop-down lists**

1  To enable the form to be used on mobile devices, choose Tools, Form Options, and then check the box for Enable rendering on a mobile device.

  While in the Form Options screen, click the Compatibility option at the bottom left. Check the box to allow the Form template to be opened in a browser or InfoPath. Check the Design a form template that can be used in a browser or InfoPath box and enter the URL of your MOSS server, as shown in figure 11.16.

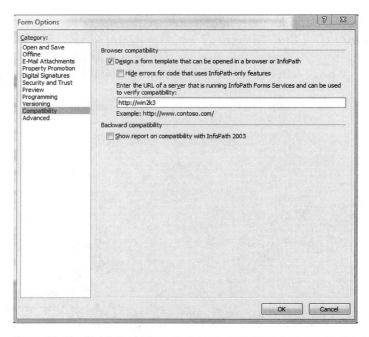

**Figure 11.16  The Form Options dialog box containing the compatibility settings**

2  Locate the `SalesPersonId` text box on your form design and right-click it. From the context menu, select Change To, Drop-Down List Box, as shown in figure 11.17.

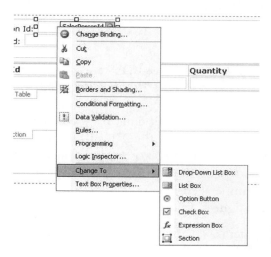

**Figure 11.17  Converting the text box to a drop-down list**

Once it's changed on your form, double-click the drop-down list box to bring up the controls properties. On the Data tab, in the List Box entries section, select Look up value from an external data source. The form view will now change slightly. GetSalesPeople will be the data source selected for you, as it's the only one we've added so far. Click the button next to the Entries text box so we can select our group of data, as shown in figure 11.18.

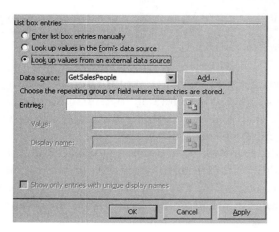

**Figure 11.18  The lookup options for the drop-down list**

Set the options so that the Value column is set as the identifier, but the Display column is set as the display name. In figure 11.19, the display name is `Name`.

Figure 11.19  **Configuring the drop-down list display options**

We can almost preview our form and submit data. If we try to now, though, we'll get an error about our data source being offline. That's because our form is currently set at a security level where it can't access data outside of the form. To change this setting, we need to go to Tools, Form Options, Security and Trust and uncheck Automatically determine security level. Then select the Full Trust radio button. See how to set this in figure 11.20.

**NOTE**  This is a development scenario showing the power of InfoPath 2007 and web services. Think carefully before giving a form Full Trust in a live environment.

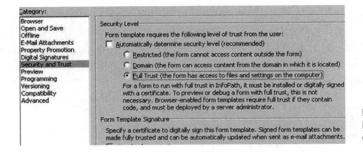

Figure 11.20  **Selecting the Full Trust option in the Form Options dialog box**

Once we've selected that and clicked OK, we can select the Preview button on the main toolbar. You should now be able to select a sales person and enter the data into the InfoPath form for the sale. Click the Submit button to ensure that the sales information has been submitted to the LOB system.

The final stage is to make the InfoPath form available to SharePoint users. To achieve this, we simply publish the InfoPath form using the Publish option under the Office button in the top left corner of the page. You'll have several options. We need to publish the form to an InfoPath form library. For some reason this is labeled Document Library within the wizard. Follow the options to create a new document library within your team site. The form will then be available within the team site when the user clicks the New button. You'll notice that, if you have the InfoPath client installed, InfoPath will be used to complete the form. If the Info-Path client isn't installed, the browser will be used, as form services is running in your environment. If you want to force the browser to be used (useful for testing purposes), this can be achieved by setting the Browser Enable option under Advanced in the Form Library settings.

## 11.4  Summary

In this final chapter, we explored two options for using the Business Data Catalog. With a GenericInvoker, we can not only read BDC data but also update, insert, and delete data in the LOB system. We explored how both the application definition file and the object model support this process. We saw how—by using Visual Studio, custom actions, and BDC—we could write back to the LOB system. This involved changes to the ADF as well as writing code. BDC Meta Man will even write the code for you.

Another method of writing back to the data source via BDC is to use InfoPath 2007. Via a web service, we were able to generate a form and configure it to write back to the LOB system. Microsoft doesn't officially support this, so please keep in mind that this process may or may not be supported in the next release of Share-Point.

By now, we hope you have a good grasp of the Business Data Catalog and its possibilities. This book has three appendixes that will tell you more about specific data sources such as web services, Oracle, and SAP.

# Connecting to SAP with the BDC

Probably the best way to understand a system that's in place is to work backward from the end to the beginning. Understanding what's in place and the purpose of each layer will help you in the forward planning of the system that you want to implement. We'll use two examples to convey both the use of the data and the technical implementation. The two entities we'll use are suppliers and customers. In this example, SAP data is available via SharePoint Search and also, in the case of the supplier data, ends up populating a SharePoint custom list. Note that there's an overlap between the supplier and customer data.

In the following paragraphs, we'll look at the data in SAP, look at it in Share-Point, and review what artifacts have to be in place to support surfacing the data into SharePoint via the BDC. As such, the first stop will be to review getting to the customer data in SAP via the traditional GUI.

## A.1    *The benefits of using the BDC to expose SAP data*

Often people need to work in different applications and/or portals. Imagine working in SharePoint Portal or Microsoft Excel, and in order to get a piece of information from SAP, you need to open the GUI and go through the SAP user interface. This would be time-consuming, as well as distracting, even for somebody who understands SAP, so being able to display SAP data in SharePoint is useful. To get to the screen shown in figure A.1, you'd need to open SAP, provide your credentials, and then navigate to the appropriate module.

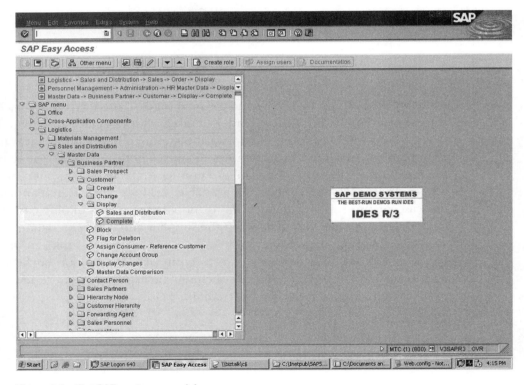

**Figure A.1    The SAP customer module**

You'd then need to locate the correct customer by performing a find, as shown in figure A.2.

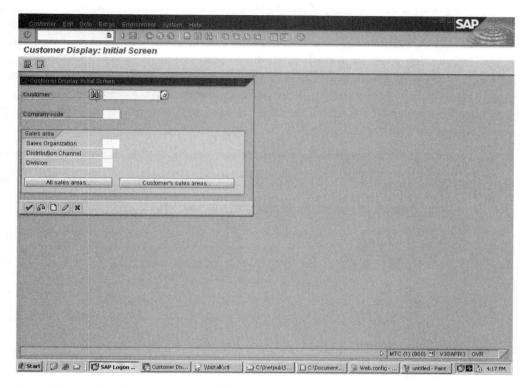

**Figure A.2   The Find Customer screen in SAP**

After going through those steps, you'd just be at the point where you could copy the data to paste it into the application you're working in so that you could continue with the task at hand. To exacerbate the problem, if you then needed related information, there'd be another set of actions. If you had to repeat these for each unit of work, it would become tedious. Worse yet, there's a real possibility of missing some important related information, because there's no out-of-the-box unification or federation between the data in the custom set of applications and the data that's stored within the back-end system (in this case SAP). Having walked through the GUI screens, let's look at viewing that same data from within Share-Point, starting with figure A.3.

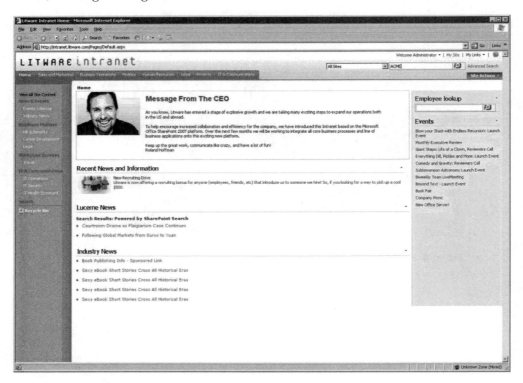

**Figure A.3    A sample SharePoint page that will be used to display SAP data**

From the home page, you can open the Search Center and perform a search on SAP data using the BDC Index Service. An example of SAP search is shown in figure A.4. This would be far less time-consuming than having to navigate SAP.

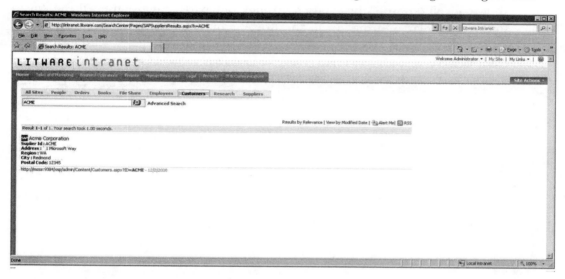

**Figure A.4   The search results displaying SAP data**

You might take the next step of spending a long time navigating SAP, or it's entirely possible that the information you're looking for is provided within the search result. In addition to the data being available via search and accessed as shown, it could possibly be exposed through web parts that give users the ability to find and display information in the BDC. Figure A.5 shows two connected web parts—the Business Data List and Business Data Item Web Parts—displaying data from SAP.

**Figure A.5    Out-of-the-box MOSS BDC Web Parts displaying SAP data**

The Business Data List Web Part on the left shows the list of available selections (which may be filtered based on the implementation of the service that's providing the data). When the user chooses a person, the web part on the right picks up the selection from the left and then displays further details in its view. These are trivial examples, but you can imagine a more complex scenario for accessing back-end data via search, displaying the results, and retrieving and displaying details of a single row.

If the BDC data were used to build a list and provide the data to other applications via a SharePoint list, you could create a custom list that uses fields from entities defined in the BDC to populate the columns of the list. The end result might look like figure A.6.

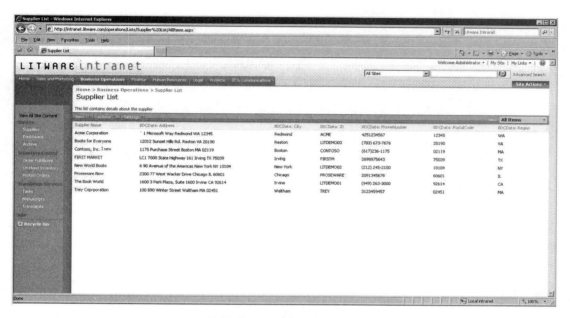

**Figure A.6    The Business Data column being used with BDC data from SAP**

Whereas the data in a list has some size limitations in the current version of SharePoint, it does serve as a good way to make data visible and consumable by more out-of-the-box web parts. It also provides a sort of data cache in front of the backend system. Thus in many instances, such an implementation could be not only a viable but also a good solution. The point is that, once the data has been exposed and is available within SharePoint, a lot more can be done with it across any number of applications that live outside of SAP.

To make this possible, a number of things must be set up. In order for Share-Point to be able to access the data, it must first know about the data. Therefore, an application must be defined within the BDC, and that application's entities must be visible. In figure A.7, you see the applications that have been defined for our BDC instance.

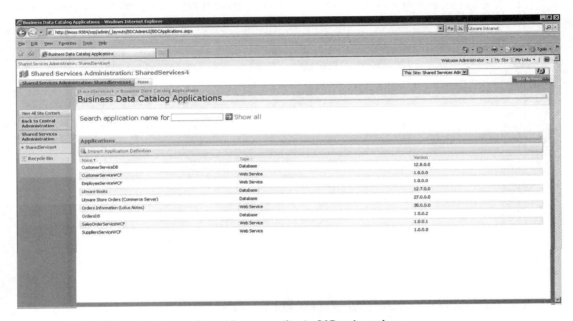

**Figure A.7   The BDC application configured for connection to SAP web services**

If the CustomerServiceWCF item were chosen and subsequently the Customers entity were selected, you'd see the configured information for the Customers entity. Figure A.8 includes items such as the fields that make up the entity, the relationships that it might have with another entity, the actions and URLs that have been defined for it, and finally the available filters that have been defined for it.

Now that we've seen what can be achieved, let's see what's involved in connecting to SAP via the Business Data Catalog.

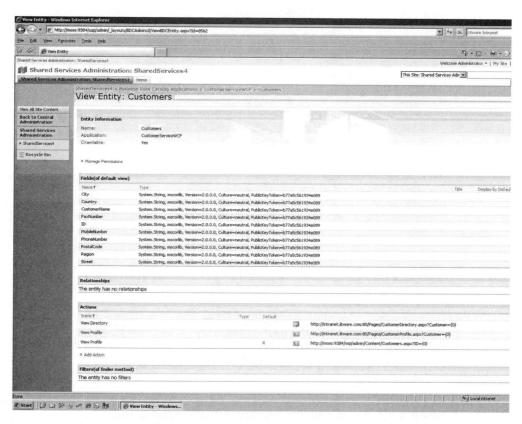

**Figure A.8   The fields and actions for the Customers (SAP) table**

## A.2   *How to connect the BDC to SAP*

The connection information to connect to SAP is all created in the ADF for the application that describes the data source and its entities, and in this case, the web service endpoints by which data is retrieved. Listing A.1 is a snippet from the SupplierServiceWCF ADF, in which you can see the entity definition and the link to the service for it.

**Listing A.1   Code for the LobSystem and URL from which to fetch the WSDL**

```
- <LobSystem xmlns:xsi="http://www.w3.org/2001/XMLSchema-instance"
➥xsi:schemaLocation="http://schemas.microsoft.com/office/2006/03/
➥ BusinessDataCatalog BDCMetadata.xsd" Type="WebService"
➥Version="1.0.0.0"          Name="SuppliersServiceWCF"
➥xmlns="http://schemas.microsoft.com/office/2006/03/
➥BusinessDataCatalog">                          ADF to connect to
- <Properties>                             ⟵  SAP via web service
  <Property Name="WsdlFetchUrl" Type="System.String">http://
    sql2008.litware.com/sapservice/Supplier/
➥ SupplierService.svc</Property>
  <Property Name="WebServiceProxyNamespace" Type="System.String">
➥ BDC</Property>
  </Properties>
- <LobSystemInstances>
- <LobSystemInstance Name="SuppliersServiceWCF">
- <Properties>
  <Property Name="LobSystemName" Type="System.String">SuppliersServiceWCF
➥</Property>
  <Property Name="WebServiceAuthenticationMode"
➥Type="Microsoft.Office.Server.ApplicationRegistry.SystemSpecific.
➥ WebService.HttpAuthenticationMode">PassThrough</Property>
  </Properties>
  </LobSystemInstance>
  </LobSystemInstances>
```

The code is the part of the application definition file that defines how to connect to the data source, including the URL for the web service and the authentication settings. Listing A.2 is the entity definition, including the finder and IDEnumerator methods.

**Listing A.2   Definition for the entity and its finder, identifier, and enumerator methods**

```
<Entity EstimatedInstanceCount="10000" Name="Suppliers">
- <Properties>
  <Property Name="DefaultAction" Type="System.String">View          Profile
➥</Property>                  ⟵  View Profile
  </Properties>                    action
- <Identifiers>
```

```
  <Identifier TypeName="System.String" Name="SupplierID" />
  </Identifiers>
- <Methods>
- <Method Name="GetSuppliers">
- <Parameters>
+ <Parameter Direction="Return" Name="Return">
- <TypeDescriptor TypeName="BDC.Supplier[],SuppliersServiceWCF"
➥IsCollection="true" Name="Return">
- <TypeDescriptors>
- <TypeDescriptor TypeName="BDC.Supplier,SuppliersServiceWCF" Name="Item">
- <TypeDescriptors>
  <TypeDescriptor TypeName="System.String, mscorlib, Version=2.0.0.0
➥, Culture=neutral, PublicKeyToken=b77a5c561934e089" Name="Address" />
  <TypeDescriptor TypeName="System.String, mscorlib, Version=2.0.0.0,
➥ Culture=neutral, PublicKeyToken=b77a5c561934e089" Name="City" />
  <TypeDescriptor TypeName="System.String, mscorlib, Version=2.0.0.0,
➥Culture=neutral, PublicKeyToken=b77a5c561934e089" Name="Country" />
  <TypeDescriptor TypeName="System.String, mscorlib, Version=2.0.0.0,
➥Culture=neutral, PublicKeyToken=b77a5c561934e089"
➥Name="EmailAddress" />
  <TypeDescriptor TypeName="System.String, mscorlib, Version=2.0.0.0,
➥Culture=neutral, PublicKeyToken=b77a5c561934e089" Name="FaxNumber" />
  <TypeDescriptor TypeName="System.String, mscorlib, Version=2.0.0.0,
➥ Culture=neutral, PublicKeyToken=b77a5c561934e089"
➥IdentifierName="SupplierID" Name="ID" />
  <TypeDescriptor TypeName="System.String, mscorlib, Version=2.0.0.0,
➥Culture=neutral, PublicKeyToken=b77a5c561934e089"
➥Name="MobileNumber" />
  <TypeDescriptor TypeName="System.String, mscorlib, Version=2.0.0.0,
➥ Culture=neutral, PublicKeyToken=b77a5c561934e089"
➥Name="PhoneNumber" />
  <TypeDescriptor TypeName="System.String, mscorlib, Version=2.0.0.0,
➥Culture=neutral, PublicKeyToken=b77a5c561934e089" Name="PostalCode" />
  <TypeDescriptor TypeName="System.String, mscorlib, Version=2.0.0.0,
➥ Culture=neutral, PublicKeyToken=b77a5c561934e089" Name="Region" />
  <TypeDescriptor TypeName="System.String, mscorlib, Version=2.0.0.0,
➥Culture=neutral, PublicKeyToken=b77a5c561934e089" Name="Street" />
  <TypeDescriptor TypeName="System.String, mscorlib, Version=2.0.0.0,
➥Culture=neutral, PublicKeyToken=b77a5c561934e089"
➥Name="SupplierName" />
  <TypeDescriptor TypeName="System.String, mscorlib, Version=2.0.0.0,
➥Culture=neutral, PublicKeyToken=b77a5c561934e089" Name="WebAddress" />
  </TypeDescriptors>
  </TypeDescriptor>
  </TypeDescriptors>
  </TypeDescriptor>
  </Parameter>
  </Parameters>
- <MethodInstances>          <-- Finder method
  <MethodInstance Type="Finder" ReturnParameterName="Return"
➥ReturnTypeDescriptorName="Return" ReturnTypeDescriptorLevel="0"
```

```
➥Name="SuppliersFinder" />
  <MethodInstance Type="IdEnumerator" ReturnParameterName="Return"
➥ReturnTypeDescriptorName="Return" ReturnTypeDescriptorLevel="0"
➥Name="SuppliersEnumerator" />                    Specific
  </MethodInstances>                               finder method
  </Method>
```

The snippet shown in listing A.3 focuses on the specific finder method, which is used to return a single row.

**Listing A.3   Definition for the entity, its specific finder, and filter methods**

```
- <Method Name="GetSupplier">
- <FilterDescriptors>
  <FilterDescriptor Type="Wildcard" Name="SupplierIDFilter" />
  </FilterDescriptors>
- <Parameters>
- <Parameter Direction="In" Name="SupplierID">
  <TypeDescriptor TypeName="System.String, mscorlib, Version=2.0.0.0,
➥Culture=neutral, PublicKeyToken=b77a5c561934e089"
➥IdentifierName="SupplierID" AssociatedFilter="SupplierIDFilter"
➥ Name="SupplierID" />
  </Parameter>
+ <Parameter Direction="Return" Name="Return">
- <TypeDescriptor TypeName="BDC.Supplier,SuppliersServiceWCF"
➥Name="Return">
- <TypeDescriptors>
  <TypeDescriptor TypeName="System.String, mscorlib, Version=2.0.0.0,
➥Culture=neutral, PublicKeyToken=b77a5c561934e089" Name="Address" />
  <TypeDescriptor TypeName="System.String, mscorlib, Version=2.0.0.0,
➥Culture=neutral, PublicKeyToken=b77a5c561934e089" Name="City" />
  <TypeDescriptor TypeName="System.String, mscorlib, Version=2.0.0.0,
➥Culture=neutral, PublicKeyToken=b77a5c561934e089" Name="Country" />
  <TypeDescriptor TypeName="System.String, mscorlib, Version=2.0.0.0,
➥Culture=neutral, PublicKeyToken=b77a5c561934e089"
➥Name="EmailAddress" />
  <TypeDescriptor TypeName="System.String, mscorlib, Version=2.0.0.0,
➥ Culture=neutral, PublicKeyToken=b77a5c561934e089" Name="FaxNumber" />
  <TypeDescriptor TypeName="System.String, mscorlib, Version=2.0.0.0,
➥Culture=neutral, PublicKeyToken=b77a5c561934e089"
➥IdentifierName="SupplierID" Name="ID" />
  <TypeDescriptor TypeName="System.String, mscorlib, Version=2.0.0.0,
➥Culture=neutral, PublicKeyToken=b77a5c561934e089"
➥Name="MobileNumber" />
  <TypeDescriptor TypeName="System.String, mscorlib, Version=2.0.0.0,
➥Culture=neutral, PublicKeyToken=b77a5c561934e089" Name="PhoneNumber" />
  <TypeDescriptor TypeName="System.String, mscorlib, Version=2.0.0.0,
➥Culture=neutral, PublicKeyToken=b77a5c561934e089" Name="PostalCode" />
  <TypeDescriptor TypeName="System.String, mscorlib, Version=2.0.0.0,
➥Culture=neutral, PublicKeyToken=b77a5c561934e089" Name="Region" />
```

```
  <TypeDescriptor TypeName="System.String, mscorlib, Version=2.0.0.0,
➡Culture=neutral, PublicKeyToken=b77a5c561934e089" Name="Street" />
  <TypeDescriptor TypeName="System.String, mscorlib, Version=2.0.0.0,
➡Culture=neutral, PublicKeyToken=b77a5c561934e089"
➡Name="SupplierName" />
  <TypeDescriptor TypeName="System.String, mscorlib, Version=2.0.0.0,
➡Culture=neutral, PublicKeyToken=b77a5c561934e089" Name="WebAddress" />
  </TypeDescriptors>
  </TypeDescriptor>
  </Parameter>
  </Parameters>
- <MethodInstances>
  <MethodInstance Type="SpecificFinder" ReturnParameterName="Return"
➡ReturnTypeDescriptorName="Return" ReturnTypeDescriptorLevel="0"
➡Name="SupplierFinder" />
  </MethodInstances>
  </Method>
```

Note that, in listing A.4, there are tags for parameters that specify a direction and then a given `TypeDescriptor` for the type. This is how the BDC knows which way the information flows for the given method, and also what the type of the data is.

**Listing A.4   The in and return parameters and the TypeDescriptors for them**

```
- <Parameters>
- <Parameter Direction="In" Name="SupplierID">
  <TypeDescriptor TypeName="System.String, mscorlib, Version=2.0.0.0,
➡Culture=neutral, PublicKeyToken=b77a5c561934e089"
➡IdentifierName="SupplierID" AssociatedFilter="SupplierIDFilter"
➡Name="SupplierID" />
  </Parameter>
- <Parameter Direction="Return" Name="Return">
- <TypeDescriptor TypeName="BDC.Supplier,SuppliersServiceWCF"
➡Name="Return">
- <TypeDescriptors>
  <TypeDescriptor TypeName="System.String, mscorlib, Version=2.0.0.0,
➡Culture=neutral, PublicKeyToken=b77a5c561934e089" Name="Address" />
  <TypeDescriptor TypeName="System.String, mscorlib, Version=2.0.0.0,
➡Culture=neutral, PublicKeyToken=b77a5c561934e089" Name="City" />
  <TypeDescriptor TypeName="System.String, mscorlib, Version=2.0.0.0,
➡Culture=neutral, PublicKeyToken=b77a5c561934e089" Name="Country" />
  <TypeDescriptor TypeName="System.String, mscorlib, Version=2.0.0.0,
➡Culture=neutral, PublicKeyToken=b77a5c561934e089"
➡Name="EmailAddress" />
  <TypeDescriptor TypeName="System.String, mscorlib, Version=2.0.0.0,
➡Culture=neutral, PublicKeyToken=b77a5c561934e089" Name="FaxNumber" />
  <TypeDescriptor TypeName="System.String, mscorlib, Version=2.0.0.0,
➡Culture=neutral, PublicKeyToken=b77a5c561934e089"
➡IdentifierName="SupplierID" Name="ID" />
  <TypeDescriptor TypeName="System.String, mscorlib, Version=2.0.0.0,
```

```
➥Culture=neutral, PublicKeyToken=b77a5c561934e089"
➥Name="MobileNumber" />
 <TypeDescriptor TypeName="System.String, mscorlib, Version=2.0.0.0,
➥Culture=neutral, PublicKeyToken=b77a5c561934e089" Name="PhoneNumber" />
 <TypeDescriptor TypeName="System.String, mscorlib, Version=2.0.0.0,
➥Culture=neutral, PublicKeyToken=b77a5c561934e089" Name="PostalCode" />
 <TypeDescriptor TypeName="System.String, mscorlib, Version=2.0.0.0,
➥Culture=neutral, PublicKeyToken=b77a5c561934e089" Name="Region" />
 <TypeDescriptor TypeName="System.String, mscorlib, Version=2.0.0.0,
➥Culture=neutral, PublicKeyToken=b77a5c561934e089" Name="Street" />
 <TypeDescriptor TypeName="System.String, mscorlib, Version=2.0.0.0,
➥Culture=neutral, PublicKeyToken=b77a5c561934e089"
➥Name="SupplierName" />
 <TypeDescriptor TypeName="System.String, mscorlib, Version=2.0.0.0,
➥Culture=neutral, PublicKeyToken=b77a5c561934e089" Name="WebAddress" />
 </TypeDescriptors>
 </TypeDescriptor>
 </Parameter>
 </Parameters>
```

Looking at these snippets, or looking at the complete file, can make it seem like a daunting task. But tools are available to help generate the ADF by simply pointing the application to the proper URL for the WSDL. BDC Meta Man and a third-party company called Sitrion can help you configure your connections to SAP.

Taking the next step down our backward path, we come to the web service that's providing the BDC with the means to access the data. This could be a web service created using Web Dynpro, SAP NetWeaver Developer Studio, or our preferred toolset, Visual Studio .NET. In fact, VS.NET becomes more of a preference if you're looking at apps that interact with SAP, but really don't need to live in SAP. Furthermore, if you want to implement a service that can be exposed via any number of protocols, VS.NET using Windows Communication Foundation is the way to go. Furthermore, using the Microsoft toolkit opens up using the WCF LOB Adapter Pack to connect to SAP and define WCF-based services that expose the BAPI (Business Application Programming Interface), RFC (Request for Comments), and IDoc (intermediate document) interfaces—thus generating all of the proxy and metadata code you'd need to make the desired calls. What's more, tools that are built using the WCF LOB Adapter Pack make developing the service less of a coding experience and more of a visual drag-and-drop building block experience. Using one of these tools, you could not only combine more than one call to the system to make the service a point of composition for work to be done, but also orchestrate that work with Windows Workflow Foundation.

Stepping back from our excitement over the available tools, in the example illustrated here, the WCF Adapter Pack was used to directly connect to SAP, and that WCF-based service was exposed via SOAP (Simple Object Access Protocol) over HTTP, thus giving it the traditional web service interface that's needed by the BDC. Tracing through the code, the GetSupplier method is exposed as the service endpoint to retrieve supplier information. That method subsequently makes a call to a method of a static class Services. Listing A.5 returns a supplier ID used for the specific finder.

**Listing A.5   The GetSupplier method**

```
public Supplier GetSupplier(string SupplierID)
{
    try
    {
        return Services.GetSupplier(SupplierID);
    }
    catch (Exception)
    {
        throw;
    }
}
```

The Services object method GetSupplier implements the call to the proxy objects that reach back into SAP to the data via BAPI_VENDOR_GETDETAIL. The method returns a Supplier object, as in listing A.6.

**Listing A.6   The public static supplier method**

```
public static Supplier GetSupplier(string SupplierID)
{
    Supplier supplier = new Supplier();
```

Thus, referring back to the TypeDescriptor in the ADF, the definition for the return value described by the type descriptor matches the definition for the Supplier type. In the next snippet, the rfcClient proxy object that was generated by the WCF adapter creates the proxy using EC127SAPServiceBinding_Rfc. The binding defines the endpoint for the SAP instance:

```
        using (SAPProxies.Supplier.RfcClient rfcClient = new
➥SAPProxies.Supplier.RfcClient("EC127SAPServicesBinding_Rfc"))
        {
```

This binding name refers back to the configuration in the web.config file that's under the system.serviceModel element. From the web.config shown in listing A.7, we can see all of the information needed to connect to the SAP instance.

**Listing A.7   web.config settings to support SAP**

```
<system.serviceModel>
     <sapBinding>
        <binding name="EC127SAPServicesBinding" closeTimeout="00:01:00"
           openTimeout="00:01:00" receiveTimeout="00:10:00"
sendTimeout="00:01:00"
           enableBizTalkCompatibilityMode="true" receiveIdocFormat="Typed"
             enableSafeTyping="true"
generateFlatFileCompatibleIdocSchema="true"
           maxConnectionsPerSystem="50" enableConnectionPooling="true"
           idleConnectionTimeout="00:15:00"
flatFileSegmentIndicator="SegmentDefinition"
           enablePerformanceCounters="false" autoConfirmSentIdocs="false"
           enableBusinessObjects="false" acceptCredentialsInUri="false"
           padReceivedIdocWithSpaces="false" sncLibrary=""
sncPartnerName="" />
     </sapBinding>
   </bindings>
   <client>
     <endpoint address="sap://CLIENT=800;LANG=EN;@a/ecredsap5v/00?
RfcSdkTrace=False&amp;AbapDebug=False"
        binding="sapBinding" bindingConfiguration="EC127SAPServicesBinding"
        contract="Rfc" name="EC127SAPServicesBinding_Rfc" />
   </client>
```

WCF will be able to use this information to establish a connection with SAP. In listing A.8, the credentials are set, parameter objects are instantiated and assigned values as required by the BAPI, and finally the call is made to BAPI_VENDOR_GETDETAIL.

**Listing A.8   Credentials, parameter objects, and call to BAPI_VENDOR_GETDETAIL**

```
            using (SAPProxies.Supplier.RfcClient rfcClient = new
SAPProxies.Supplier.RfcClient("EC127SAPServicesBinding_Rfc"))
          {
            rfcClient.ClientCredentials.UserName.UserName =
CredentialsProviderManager.Provider.UserName;
            rfcClient.ClientCredentials.UserName.Password
CredentialsProviderManager.Provider.Password;

        rfcClient.Open();

          BAPIVENDOR_04 sapVendor = new BAPIVENDOR_04();
          BAPIVENDOR_05 sapCompany = new BAPIVENDOR_05();
          BAPIVENDOR_06[] sapSupplierBanks = new BAPIVENDOR_06[0];
        BAPIRET1 sapBAPIRet1 = new BAPIRET1();

          sapCompany = rfcClient.BAPI_VENDOR_GETDETAIL(
            "",
```

```
     SupplierID,
     ref sapSupplierBanks,
     out sapVendor,
     out sapBAPIRet1
);
```

The balance of the code in this example (not shown here) assigns the values from the out parameter `sapVendor` and the ref object `sapSupplierBanks` into the Supplier object instance that will be returned to the caller. The adapter takes care of the proxy object and data type generation. This leaves calling the BAPI and marshalling the data from the call return to the type returned from the service call. Thus, if calls needed to be orchestrated across multiple BAPIs and/or RFCs, it would likely happen at this level within the implementation. Discussing this topic any deeper starts to get into the depths of not only service development but also service composition and SAP development. It's probably best to save this for a different venue! Figure A.9 shows a simplified summarized view.

Additionally, figure A.10 shows a list of items that must be in place in order to get data exposed to all of SharePoint through the BDC.

With this, the backward walk is complete.

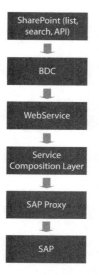

**Figure A.9   A high-level view of a BDC/SAP configuration**

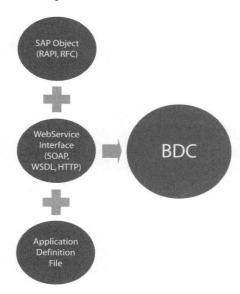

**Figure A.10   A high-level view of BDC/SAP and the supporting objects**

## A.3    *Summary*

Within this appendix, you've seen the benefits of connecting to SAP via the Business Data Catalog. We've also explored how to configure the application definition file and `web.config` file to allow us to connect to this complicated data source. As mentioned in chapter 2, a lot of time can be spent writing application definition files. Through the use of third-party tools such as Sitrions and BDC Meta Man, all of the hard work can be done for you.

In the next appendix, we'll explore what's different when connecting to Oracle as a data source.

# Connecting to Oracle with BDC

Connecting to Oracle is similar to connecting to SQL, as we fully explained in chapter 2. There are just a few differences that we need to mention. Within the application definition file, you'll need to set authentication. Of course, you can use Single Sign-On, which was explained in chapter 3. But this is required only if you want to map your Active Directory credentials to the Oracle database credentials.

## B.1 Configuring Single Sign-On

Setting up SSO for Oracle is the same as setting up SSO for SQL. If you're connecting without SSO, you need to set the authentication type to `PassThrough`, even though PassThrough isn't used and the username and password are stored within the ADF as clear text. (See figure B.1.)

Third-party products such as BDC Meta Man can write the application definition file for you, allowing you to quickly get up and running with the Business Data Catalog for an Oracle data source. One requirement is to have the Oracle client installed on the web front-end server that's connecting to the database.

```
<?xml version="1.0" ?>
- <LobSystem xmlns:xsi="http://www.w3.org/2001/XMLSchema-instance"
   xmlns:schemaLocation="http://schemas.microsoft.com/office/2006/03/BusinessDataCatalog BDCMetadata.XSD"
   Type="Database" Version="1.0.0.0" Name="OracleLOBSystem"
   xmlns="http://schemas.microsoft.com/office/2006/03/BusinessDataCatalog">
 - <Properties>
     <Property Name="WildcardCharacter" Type="System.String">%</Property>
   </Properties>
 - <LobSystemInstances>
   - <LobSystemInstance Name="OracleInstance">
     - <Properties>
         <Property Name="DatabaseAccessProvider" Type="System.String">Oracle</Property>
         <Property Name="AuthenticationMode" Type="System.String">PassThrough</Property>
         <Property Name="RdbConnection Data Source" Type="System.String">localhost</Property>
         <Property Name="RdbConnection Pooling" Type="System.String">false</Property>
         <Property Name="RdbConnection User Id" Type="System.String">hr</Property>
         <Property Name="RdbConnection Password" Type="System.String">          </Property>
         <Property Name="RdbConnection Integrated Security" Type="System.String" />
         <Property Name="WildcardCharacter" Type="System.String">%</Property>
     </Properties>
   </LobSystemInstance>
 </LobSystemInstances>
- <Entities>
  - <Entity EstimatedInstanceCount="0" Name="DEPARTMENTS">
    - <Identifiers>
        <Identifier TypeName="System.Decimal" Name=""DEPARTMENT_ID"" />
      </Identifiers>
    - <Methods>
      - <Method Name="GetDEPARTMENTS">
        - <Properties>
            <Property Name="RdbCommandText" Type="System.String">Select
              "DEPARTMENT_ID","DEPARTMENT_NAME","MANAGER_ID","LOCATION_ID" From DEPARTMENTS</Property>
            <Property Name="RdbCommandType" Type="System.Data.CommandType">Text</Property>
```

**Figure B.1   The application definition file configured to connect to Oracle**

## B.2   *Installing the Oracle client*

In addition to the preceding, you'll need to have the Oracle client installed on
the web front-end server that's connecting to Oracle. Another problem with Oracle and BDC is that Oracle stored procedures aren't supported. Therefore, in
order to connect to Oracle stored procedures, you'll need to wrap them with a
web service. Creating web services is explained in appendix C.

# *Connecting to data sources with web services*

Using web services allows you to connect to just about any data source, as you can create the connection from within your web methods and expose the data. This is great for data sources that don't have a direct way of connecting to them, and perhaps rely on ODBC. Also, web services can help you get around certain issues, such as BDC not offering any support for Oracle stored procedures.

In this appendix, we'll explore how to author your own WCF web services to provide the data in a format that works well with the Business Data Catalog. It's sometimes assumed that, because an application exposes data via web services, you can consume those web services with the Business Data Catalog. Often that's not the case, as we've seen with SAP. The web services really need to provide the data in a format that's acceptable and works well with BDC.

Of course, you don't have to write your web service as a WCF, but this is generally becoming useful, as you can pass your data securely using WCF, and you can use multiple end points, giving you additional options for protocols and transports. If you're unfamiliar with WCF, there's a useful article available on the MSDN: http://msdn.microsoft.com/en-us/library/ms731082.aspx.

## C.1    *Creating web methods*

Web services that you create should have three methods for each entity that you want to connect to. These correspond to:

1    Finder method
2    Specific finder method
3    ID enumerator

The method shouldn't return a data set or XML but a list of objects. This helps BDC understand the data type of each property. Before you create your web methods, you need to create a class to serve as a data contract that describes the entity you're connecting to, as shown in listing C.1.

Also in listing C.1, you can see an example web service that connects to a Customer table in Northwind. It then creates a data set, but reads the data into a Customer object, which is then returned. The GetCustomersFinder method exposes all of the rows, as with a finder method in your ADF.

---

**Listing C.1    The GetCustomersFinder web method, which returns all data**

```
public List<Customers> GetCustomersFinder()          Connects to data
  {                                                    source and
  List<Customers> customersList = new List<Customers>();   creates DataSet

  string sqlQuery = "Select * From dbo.[Customers] ";

  using (SqlConnection sqlConnection = new SqlConnection(connectionString))
    {
  sqlConnection.Open();

  SqlCommand comm = new SqlCommand(sqlQuery, sqlConnection);

  DataSet dataSet = new DataSet();

  SqlDataAdapter adapter = new SqlDataAdapter(comm);
  adapter.Fill(dataSet, "dbo.[Customers]");

  foreach (DataRow dr in dataSet.Tables[0].Rows)
    {
  Customers customers = new Customers();

  customers.CustomerID = dr["CustomerID"] is DBNull ? string.Empty :
➡ (String)dr["CustomerID"];
  customers.CompanyName = dr["CompanyName"] is DBNull ? string.Empty :
➡ (String)dr["CompanyName"];
  customers.ContactName = dr["ContactName"] is DBNull ? string.Empty :
➡ (String)dr["ContactName"];
  customers.ContactTitle = dr["ContactTitle"] is DBNull ? string.Empty :
➡ (String)dr["ContactTitle"];
```

```
customers.Address = dr["Address"] is DBNull ? string.Empty :
➥(String)dr["Address"];
customers.City = dr["City"] is DBNull ? string.Empty : (String)dr["City"];
customers.Region = dr["Region"] is DBNull ? string.Empty :
➥(String)dr["Region"];
customers.PostalCode = dr["PostalCode"] is DBNull ? string.Empty :
➥(String)dr["PostalCode"];
customers.Country = dr["Country"] is DBNull ? string.Empty :
➥(String)dr["Country"];
customers.Phone = dr["Phone"] is DBNull ? string.Empty :
➥(String)dr["Phone"];
customers.Fax = dr["Fax"] is DBNull ? string.Empty : (String)dr["Fax"];

    customersList.Add(customers);          ◁─┐ DataSet populates Customer
    }                                         │ object as appropriate
    }


    return customersList;
    }
```

After you've created your finder, we'll need a specific finder so that a single row
can be returned. This is used in places such as a Business Data column. The web
method takes a parameter of `CustomerID`, which happens to be the unique identifier for the Customers entity, as shown in listing C.2.

**Listing C.2  The `GetCustomersSpecificFinder` method returning a single record**

```
public Customers GetCustomersSpecificFinder(String customerid)
    {
    Customers customer= new Customers();
                                                          ┐ Specific finder
    string sqlQuery = "Select * From dbo.[Customers] Where │ method requires
➥    ([CustomerID]=@CustomerID)";                      ◁─┘ an Identifier

    using (SqlConnection sqlConnection = new SqlConnection(connectionString))
    {
    sqlConnection.Open();

    SqlCommand comm = new SqlCommand(sqlQuery, sqlConnection);
    comm.Parameters.AddWithValue("@CustomerID", customerid);
    DataSet dataSet = new DataSet();

    SqlDataAdapter adapter = new SqlDataAdapter(comm);
    adapter.Fill(dataSet, "dbo.[Customers]");

    if(dataSet.Tables[0].Rows.Count > 0)
    {
    DataRow dr = dataSet.Tables[0].Rows[0];
    customers.CustomerID = dr["CustomerID"] is DBNull ? string.Empty :
➥(String)dr["CustomerID"];
customers.CompanyName = dr["CompanyName"] is DBNull ? string.Empty :
➥(String)dr["CompanyName"];
```

```
customers.ContactName = dr["ContactName"] is DBNull ? string.Empty :
➥(String)dr["ContactName"];
customers.ContactTitle = dr["ContactTitle"] is DBNull ? string.Empty :
➥(String)dr["ContactTitle"];
customers.Address = dr["Address"] is DBNull ? string.Empty :
➥(String)dr["Address"];
customers.City = dr["City"] is DBNull ? string.Empty : (String)dr["City"];
customers.Region = dr["Region"] is DBNull ? string.Empty :
➥(String)dr["Region"];
customers.PostalCode = dr["PostalCode"] is DBNull ? string.Empty :
➥(String)dr["PostalCode"];
customers.Country = dr["Country"] is DBNull ? string.Empty :
➥(String)dr["Country"];
customers.Phone = dr["Phone"] is DBNull ? string.Empty :
➥(String)dr["Phone"];
customers.Fax = dr["Fax"] is DBNull ? string.Empty : (String)dr["Fax"];

  }
  }

 return customer
  }
```

Finally, each entity should also have an `IDEnumerator` so that the data can be indexed and used in the MOSS Search. Listing C.3 shows a web method that simply returns all of the identifiers.

**Listing C.3 `GetCustomersIDEnumerator()` method that returns IDs of the entity**

```
public List<String> GetCustomersIdEnumerator()
  {
  List<String> ids = new List<String>();

  string sqlQuery = "Select CustomerID from dbo.[Customers]";

  using (SqlConnection sqlConnection = new SqlConnection(connectionString))
  {
  sqlConnection.Open();

  SqlCommand comm = new SqlCommand(sqlQuery, sqlConnection);

  DataSet dataSet = new DataSet();

  SqlDataAdapter adapter = new SqlDataAdapter(comm);
  adapter.Fill(dataSet, "dbo.[Customers]");

  foreach (DataRow dr in dataSet.Tables[0].Rows)
  {
  ids.Add(dr["CustomerID"] is DBNull ? string.Empty :
➥(String)dr["CustomerID"]);
  }
  }

  return ids;
  }
```

The Customer class, shown in listing C.4, is simple and basically returns a property for each column within the entity. The data type is specified for each column. The class is then used as the return type for each of the previous methods.

**Listing C.4   The Customer class**

```
[ServiceContract (Namespace = "devguide")]
public interface INorthwindWCFService
{

     [OperationContract]
     List<Customers> GetCustomersFinder();

     [OperationContract]
     Customers GetCustomersSpecificFinder(String customerid);

     [OperationContract]
     List<String> GetCustomersIdEnumerator();

}

[DataContract]
public class Customers
{

     private String _CustomerID;

     [DataMember]
     public String CustomerID
     {
     get { return _CustomerID; }
     set
     {
     _CustomerID = value;
     }
     }


     private String _CompanyName;

     [DataMember]
     public String CompanyName
     {
     get { return _CompanyName; }
     set
     {
     _CompanyName = value;
     }
     }


     private String _ContactName;

     [DataMember]
     public String ContactName
```

```
{
get { return _ContactName; }
set
{
_ContactName = value;
}
}

private String _ContactTitle;

[DataMember]
public String ContactTitle
{
get { return _ContactTitle; }
set
{
_ContactTitle = value;
}
}

private String _Address;

[DataMember]
public String Address
{
get { return _Address; }
set
{
_Address = value;
}
}

private String _City;

[DataMember]
public String City
{
get { return _City; }
set
{
_City = value;
}
}

private String _Region;

[DataMember]
public String Region
{
get { return _Region; }
set
{
```

```
 _Region = value;
 }
 }

private String _PostalCode;

 [DataMember]
 public String PostalCode
 {
 get { return _PostalCode; }
 set
 {
 _PostalCode = value;
 }
 }

private String _Country;

 [DataMember]
 public String Country
 {
 get { return _Country; }
 set
 {
 _Country = value;
 }
 }

private String _Phone;

 [DataMember]
 public String Phone
 {
 get { return _Phone; }
 set
 {
 _Phone = value;
 }
 }

private String _Fax;

 [DataMember]
 public String Fax
 {
 get { return _Fax; }
 set
 {
 _Fax = value;
 }
 }

}
```

Now that we've created the web service, we can test it and then create the application definition file.

## C.2    *Testing the web service*

The screenshot in figure C.1 displays the web service methods available, and you can see the finder, specific finder, and IDEnumerator methods available with the data returned.

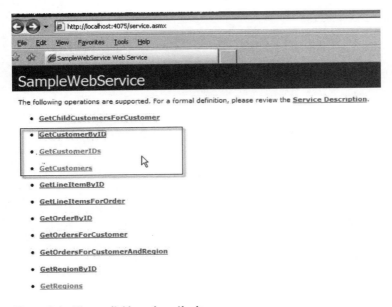

**Figure C.1    The available web methods**

In figure C.2, you can see the results of the `IDEnumerator`, which returns the IDs of the Customers entity.

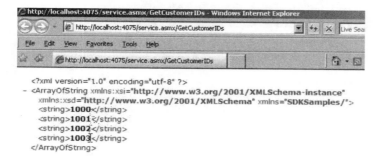

```
<?xml version="1.0" encoding="utf-8" ?>
- <ArrayOfString xmlns:xsi="http://www.w3.org/2001/XMLSchema-instance"
    xmlns:xsd="http://www.w3.org/2001/XMLSchema" xmlns="SDKSamples/">
    <string>1000</string>
    <string>1001</string>
    <string>1002</string>
    <string>1003</string>
  </ArrayOfString>
```

**Figure C.2   The results of the `GetCustomerIDs` method, which is used for indexing the data**

The specific finder method is also displayed in figure C.3, and demonstrates how you can pass an ID to the method to return a single row.

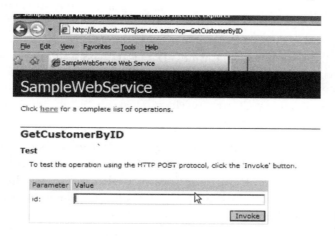

**Figure C.3   The specific finder web method**

The results of the specific finder method look like figure C.4, where a single record is returned. This is useful when looking for a particular customer, like in the Business Data field type.

**Figure C.4  The results of the specific finder method**

**NOTE**    Microsoft has stated that the Business Data Catalog doesn't support WCF. But following the example shown here, using WCF is achievable. Lightning Tools also has a product called BDC Web Man, which makes it simple to generate the WCF web services. This can be downloaded from http://www.lightningtools.com.

Once the web services are created, the last thing you need to do is create your application definition file. The easiest way to do this is to use either BDC Meta Man or the Microsoft Application Definition Creator tool. You can see the difference between the two in our earlier examples of ADFs in chapter 2 of this book. Most of the structure is the same as an application definition file for an RDMS (Relational Database Management System). The main difference is in the LOB-SystemInstance properties. The type of the ADF is set to WebService, and then the WebServiceProxyNamespace, Wildcardcharacter, and WsdlFetchUrl properties are set to point to the web service, as shown in figure C.5.

```
<?xml version="1.0" ?>
- <LobSystem xmlns:xsi="http://www.w3.org/2001/XMLSchema-instance"
    xmlns:schemaLocation="http://schemas.microsoft.com/office/2006/03/BusinessDataCatalog BDCMetadata.XSD"
    Type="WebService" Version="1.0.0.0" Name="SampleWebService"
    xmlns="http://schemas.microsoft.com/office/2006/03/BusinessDataCatalog">
  - <Properties>
      <Property Name="WebServiceProxyNamespace" Type="System.String">SampleWebServiceProxy</Property>
      <Property Name="WildcardCharacter" Type="System.String">$</Property>
      <Property Name="WsdlFetchUrl" Type="System.String">http://localhost:4075/service.asmx?wsdl</Property>
    </Properties>
  - <LobSystemInstances>
    - <LobSystemInstance Name="SampleWebServiceInstance">
      - <Properties>
          <Property Name="LobSystemName" Type="System.String">SampleWebService</Property>
        </Properties>
      </LobSystemInstance>
    </LobSystemInstances>
  - <Entities>
    - <Entity EstimatedInstanceCount="0" Name="Customers">
      - <Properties>
          <Property Name="Title" Type="System.String">Name</Property>
        </Properties>
      - <Identifiers>
          <Identifier TypeName="System.String" Name="CustomerID" />
        </Identifiers>
      - <Methods>
        - <Method Name="GetCustomers">
          - <FilterDescriptors>
              <FilterDescriptor Type="Wildcard" Name="name" />
              <FilterDescriptor Type="Limit" Name="Limit" />
            </FilterDescriptors>
          - <Parameters>
```

**Figure C.5   An application definition file configured to connect to a web service**

We have now generated an application definition file to connect to a web service and have explored each of the required settings, such as the WsdlFetchUrl. Using a web service to connect to your data source is often a requirement—for instance, when you are not allowed to query a database directly.

## C.3   Summary

In this appendix, we learned the benefits of using a web service to connect to our data source, and also explored how to create a WCF web service to create our finder, specific finder, and IDEnumerator. Once this has been achieved, you can connect using the application definition file via BDC Meta Man.

# *index*

# MORE TITLES FROM MANNING

*SQL Server 2008*
*Administration in Action*
by Rod Colledge

> ISBN: 1-933988-72-X
> 464 pages
> $44.99
> August 2009

*ASP.NET MVC in Action*
by Jeffrey Palermo, Jimmy Bogard,
  and Ben Scheirman

> ISBN: 1-933988-62-2
> 400 pages
> $44.99
> September 2009

*For ordering information go to www.manning.com*

*The Art of Unit Testing*
by Roy Osherove

ISBN: 1-933988-27-4
320 pages
$39.99
May 2009

*C# in Depth*
by Jon Skeet

ISBN: 1-933988-36-3
424 pages
$44.99
April 2008

*For ordering information go to www.manning.com*

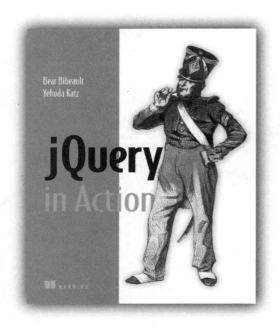

*JQuery in Action*
by Bear Bibeault and Yehuda Katz

ISBN: 1-933988-35-5
376 pages
$39.99
February 2008

*Becoming Agile*
by Greg Smith and Ahmed Sidky

ISBN: 1-933988-25-8
408 pages
$44.99
May 2009

*For ordering information go to www.manning.com*